ROCKY TIMES

YASUYUKI FUCHITA
RICHARD J. HERRING
ROBERT E. LITAN
Editors

ROCKY TIMES

*New Perspectives on
Financial Stability*

NOMURA INSTITUTE OF CAPITAL MARKETS RESEARCH
Tokyo

BROOKINGS INSTITUTION PRESS
Washington, D.C.

Rocky Times: New Perspectives on Managing Financial Stability
may be ordered from: Brookings Institution Press, 1775 Massachusetts Avenue, N.W.
Washington, D.C. 20036
Telephone: 1-800/537-5487 or 410/516-6956
E-mail: hfscustserv@press.jhu.edu; www.brookings.edu

Library of Congress Cataloging-in-Publication data
Rocky times : new perspectives on financial stability / Yasuyuki Fuchita, Richard J. Herring,
and Robert E. Litan, editors.
    pp   cm
Includes bibliographical references and index.
ISBN 978-0-8157-2250-2 (pbk. : alk. paper)
1. Monetary policy—Japan. 2. Monetary policy—United States. 3. Global Financial
Crisis, 2008–2009. I. Fuchita, Yasuyuki, 1958– II. Herring, Richard. III. Litan, Robert E.,
1950–
HG1275.R595 2012
339.5′30952–dc23   2012034641

9 8 7 6 5 4 3 2 1

Printed on acid-free paper

Typeset in Adobe Garamond

Composition by Circle Graphics
Columbia, Maryland

Printed by R. R. Donnelley
Harrisonburg, Virginia

Contents

Preface

I N 2004 THE Brookings Institution partnered with the Nomura Institute of Capital Markets Research to present timely and cutting-edge research on selected topics relating to financial market structure and policy that would be of interest to policymakers, scholars, and market practitioners in the United States, Japan, and elsewhere. Initially led by Brookings senior fellow Robert E. Litan and Yasuyuki Fuchita, senior managing director of the Nomura Institute, the collaboration was broadened in 2008 by the addition of Richard J. Herring of the Financial Institutions Center at the Wharton School of the University of Pennsylvania. This collaboration has convened a conference each year since then.

This volume, the seventh in what is now the Brookings-Nomura-Wharton series, is based on "New Perspectives on Financial Stability," a conference held on October 14, 2011, at the Brookings Institution in Washington, D.C. The conference brought together scholars, policymakers, and practitioners to discuss drafts of papers that have become chapters in this volume. The authors and editors are grateful to the participants for a lively debate and many constructive suggestions.

As discussed in the Introduction, the papers covered a wide range of topics, but they had a common theme: the elements missing from post-crisis financial reform that should be high on policymakers' agendas in the future. All of the chapters represent the views of the authors and not necessarily those of the staff, officers, or trustees of the Brookings Institution, the Nomura Institute of Capital Markets Research, or the Wharton Financial Institutions Center.

The editors thank Michael Mannweiler for his excellent assistance in coordinating the conference that led to this volume and Eileen Hughes for careful editing. Both the conference and this publication were funded by the Nomura Foundation.

YASUYUKI FUCHITA
RICHARD J. HERRING
ROBERT E. LITAN

1

Introduction

R ECOVERY REMAINS WEAK from the Great Recession, arguably the worst
financial crisis since the Great Depression, which quickly spread from its
origins in the United States to much of the rest of the world. Over-leveraged
consumers have been hesitant to spend, while over-leveraged banks have been
too weak to lend. It will take time, perhaps a very long time, for economies that
entered the crisis in such precarious financial condition to heal and for
strong, sustained growth to take hold.

In the United States, the Financial Crisis Inquiry Commission, the official
body charged with investigating the causes of the crisis, highlighted numerous
factors that together led to excessive subprime mortgage lending and leverage
among many of the financial institutions that bought securities backed by subprime loans. Even before the commission issued its report, in December 2010,
the U.S. Congress had enacted the Dodd-Frank Wall Street Reform and Consumer Protection Act of 2010, which the president signed into law immediately
in July of that year. Supporters of the legislation argued that its multiple provisions were necessary to prevent future financial crises as well as the bailouts of
unsecured creditors of a number of the largest financial institutions, which were
engineered principally in 2008 by policymakers in an effort to head off the feared
collapse of the U.S. financial system in the wake of the crisis.

Controversy still swirls, however, over the wisdom and effectiveness of the Dodd-
Frank law and similar reform measures adopted by other developed countries. In

particular, questions surround the ability of governments to better manage the stability of their financial institutions and sectors going forward, both to prevent future crises and to contain the damage when it occurs.

The chapters in this volume are based on papers by financial experts in the United States and Japan that were presented at the annual Brookings-Nomura Institute-Wharton School conference. The authors of these chapters, which focus on how to restore and protect financial stability, come to their tasks from several different perspectives and voice different, and sometimes conflicting, views. But readers should not find that surprising. Debate over the causes and appropriate cures for the financial crisis began as the crisis itself was unfolding and continues to this day. The debates over the future direction of financial regulatory policy are healthy, because they help expose both the strengths and weaknesses of various prescriptions. We trust that readers will agree after reading the contributions to this volume.

Chapter 2 is about Japan, which is still attempting, more than two decades later, to recover from its own deep financial crisis of the late 1980s and early 1990s. Given the weakness of the economic recovery from the most recent crisis, many have been looking to the Japanese experience for lessons. The subsequent four chapters discuss various features of the U.S. response to its crisis, with special emphasis on ideas or concepts that did not make it into the Dodd-Frank legislation but that policymakers may want to consider as they implement the regulations or revise the landmark legislation itself.

This introduction provides an overview of some of the key themes that are elaborated in the chapters that follow. Before turning to these summaries, however, we begin with a very brief summary of the Dodd-Frank legislation itself so that readers unfamiliar with the law have a basic idea of how U.S. policymakers responded to the crisis.

It is impossible to do full justice in this very brief introduction to the Dodd-Frank legislation, which contained more than 2,000 pages of legislative language and instructions to various U.S. financial regulatory bodies to issue more than 500 rules, conduct 81 studies, and present 93 reports to implement the statute. At this writing, some of the rulemakings have been completed, but many have not. Nor have all of the numerous reports about specific aspects of the crisis and responses mandated by Dodd-Frank been completed. Nonetheless, the broad outlines of the bill can be briefly summarized and usefully described as having three main features.

First, the bill requires banks and "systemically important" nonbank financial institutions to have substantially higher capital and liquidity cushions than they maintained before the crisis. The Basel Committee, which had been setting capital standards for banks since 1989, began work to increase bank capital standards shortly after the crisis began. Because the United States is a member of the committee, this particular feature would likely have been adopted without the legislation, although the United States delayed implementation of the second version of the Basel Accord until the crisis hit. But Dodd-Frank went further, creating the new multi-agency Financial Stability Oversight Council (FSOC) to define systemically important nonbank financial institutions and to include them in the new regulatory regime. Moreover, the legislation has charged the FSOC with the difficult—some would say impossible—task of monitoring the financial system in the future for signs of systemic risk and adopting measures to head it off, such as new reporting requirements for a wide range of financial institutions, even higher capital or liquidity standards, and reduced loan-to-value ratios for all kinds of lending.

Second, various provisions of the bill are designed to promote more careful lending of all kinds, not just mortgage lending. They include new "skin in the game" provisions that require mortgage originators and/or those who package mortgages into securities to have some minimum equity stake in them should the mortgages turn sour (regulators have since specified 5 percent, but the requirement is applicable only to mortgages with a loan-to-value ratio greater than 80 percent); various new rules aimed at improving the quality of credit ratings while removing the legal requirement that such ratings be used by various federal authorities in the future (except in setting bank capital requirements, when credit ratings remain an important part of the process); constraints on compensation for bank employees and executives to discourage short-term profit seeking at the cost of excessive short-run risks; and creation of the new, controversial Consumer Financial Products Bureau to consolidate and strengthen federal consumer protection rules governing consumer credit.

Third, the act contains several measures aimed at curbing and ideally eliminating one of the most controversial aspects of the financial crisis: the bailout of creditors of large financial institutions, what has colloquially been called the "too big to fail" (TBTF) problem. There is a new resolution procedure for failing nonbanks, much like the one that the Federal Deposit Insurance Corporation (FDIC) has traditionally administered for banks, but with one crucial difference: in principle, no unsecured creditors of failed nonbanks are to be made whole. Skeptics still wonder whether the special liquidity support mechanism for creditors of failing nonbanks, funded by other, healthy, large financial institutions, will be used somehow to bail out those creditors and thus perpetuate the moral hazard now associated with the expected bailout of technically uninsured depositors of banks. One safeguard against that outcome is a revision to section 13(3) of the Federal

Reserve Act, which prohibits lending programs aimed at propping up failing financial firms while requiring that the security for future emergency loans be sufficient to protect taxpayers from losses. We will not know whether these provisions really will end TBTF without contributing to systemic concerns in the midst of a future crisis until a crisis actually occurs.

Another important set of TBTF-related reforms are those stemming from the mandated reforms to the over-the-counter (OTC) derivatives markets, in particular central clearing of standardized OTC contracts and regulated margin requirements for customized derivatives, which in theory should eliminate the need to bailout derivative counterparties, as happened in the case of AIG. At this writing, in the fall of 2012, not all of the required rules to implement these reforms were yet in place; even when they are, it will take some time to see whether they work.

The one conspicuous omission from Dodd-Frank was the failure to reform the two large government-sponsored enterprises (GSEs), Fannie Mae and Freddie Mac, whose substantial purchases of subprime mortgages and related securities contributed significantly to the excesses in that market that helped trigger the financial crisis. While this volume does not cover this important topic because there is already a substantial literature on the subject, its omission from the U.S. legislative response to the crisis is noteworthy. It is an important aspect of the crisis that is simply not addressed and continues to distort financial markets.

The legislation and accompanying regulation also failed to address other aspects of the U.S. financial system that contributed to the crisis as well. These topics will be addressed in subsequent chapters. But chapter 2, by Yasuyuki Fuchita and Kei Kodachi of the Nomura Institute of Capital Markets Research, appropriately begins the discussion by looking back on the Japanese experience, but only after addressing one particular aspect of the post-crisis response to the financial crisis: the anti-bailout provisions of Dodd-Frank in resolving future failing financial firms. Unlike many supporters of these provisions in the United States, Fuchita and Kodachi suggest that, if truly enforced, these provisions will make it more difficult to resolve the debts of large multinational financial firms without damaging spillover to the rest of the financial system. For that reason— and in the interest of ensuring systemic stability—Japan has not followed the United States and other developed economies in attempting to prohibit all future bailouts of creditors of large financial firms. Indeed, the authors argue that even in the United States there is skepticism that the anti-bailout stance will hold in a future crisis, at least with respect to systemically important banks, noting that credit rating agencies "uplift" their ratings of these banks because they believe that policymakers would support such institutions in a future crisis. The authors also quote a number of current U.S. public officials who express doubts that the resolution (or "living will") plans required by Dodd-Frank that rely on putting various financial activities in "silos" to ease resolution can actually work without losing significant economies of scope.

After expressing their doubts about the effectiveness of new anti-bailout resolution regimes going forward, Fuchita and Kodachi turn back to examine the resolution regime adopted in Japan after its financial crisis. Stripped to its essence, that regime has fully protected bank depositors in an effort to maintain confidence in the financial system, through mergers, loss sharing by local governments, and direct national government support. Failed securities firms and their creditors have been treated differently, much as they would be under a U.S.-style bankruptcy system, with creditors suffering losses. The first major test case was the failure of Sanyo Securities in 1997, a second-tier but still relatively sizable brokerage firm. Yet the novelty of creditor losses in the Sanyo case caused sufficient damage to confidence in the banking system that it led to a funding crisis and eventual failure of one of Japan's top twenty banks, Hokkaido Takushoku Bank. The turmoil in the financial markets then spread to Yamaichi Securities, one of the four largest Japanese securities firms at the time, which ultimately failed. And following that, markets lost faith in a major regional Japanese bank, Tokuyo City Bank.

The authors draw a simple conclusion from this sequence of events: that in an environment of general financial weakness, the failure of even one relatively minor financial actor (Sanyo) can damage the confidence of money market participants enough that they withdraw funding from—and thereby trigger the collapse of—other larger financial actors, even in different financial sectors. They further develop this theme when they argue that even the seemingly orderly resolution of a failing firm (Yamaichi) did not necessarily end the crisis.

By 1998, the Japanese financial authorities had switched strategies and injected capital directly into twenty-one of the nation's largest banks. We will never know, but perhaps that decision (along with the urging of Britain's prime minister, Gordon Brown) helped motivate the sudden switch by U.S. policymakers in 2008 to do the same thing in the midst of the U.S. crisis, using funds provided under the controversial Troubled Asset Relief Program (TARP) to buy bank capital rather than distressed securities from the banks. In any event, Japan institutionalized the capital injection strategy, in exceptional circumstances, when its Deposit Insurance Act was revised in 2000. By examining a number of specific cases and through more general reasoning, the authors strongly defend this approach. They express some concern over the viability and wisdom of the post-crisis cutbacks in U.S. emergency lending and loan guarantees for large failing financial firms in the future.

Fuchita and Kodachi are not the only authors in this volume to express reservations about bankruptcy-like resolutions for financial firms. In chapter 3, Gavin Bingham, formerly at the Bank for International Settlements, voices different concerns, but by discussing the following conundrum, vividly on display during the European banking/sovereign debt crisis: how actions by states to alleviate distress among financial institutions can cast doubts on the viability of the government's debt, especially when the financial sector is large relative to the size of the overall economy, and how doubts about the ability of sovereigns to aid their troubled financial institutions can in turn aggravate the fragility of those institutions.

Bingham begins by discussing the importance of bankruptcy regimes for firms: how they promote market discipline and thus efficiency, allowing market forces to cull out the weak so that the strong are not penalized. At the same time, bankruptcy systems should be designed so that they do not trigger contagion, a caution especially appropriate in the financial context.

There are no accepted international bankruptcy rules for sovereigns, however, and efforts over the years to establish them have foundered for various reasons. Nonetheless, there is a long history of sovereign debt restructuring, which Bingham briefly surveys. Typically, such restructuring imposes some losses on creditors, with senior status accorded to post-resolution funding (analogous to debtor-in-possession financing in private sector bankruptcies).

Likewise, there is no effective mechanism, despite the efforts to establish one since the 2007–08 financial crisis, for effectively resolving the debts of TBTF institutions. Bingham reviews the alternatives and finds them all wanting in different respects. He devotes the rest of his chapter to showing the similarities and differences in the resolution challenges relating to both sovereigns and TBTF institutions. These issues relate to the problems of contagion and the so-called time inconsistency problem, namely, the fact that bailouts provided in the short run do not provide appropriate incentives to avoid excessive risk taking (either by sovereigns or TBTF institutions) in the longer run. Other common problems relate to deciding the priority of claimants; the difficulty of "staying" creditors, avoiding "asset grabs," and enforcing claims even when they are awarded; and the complexity of the resolution (a problem mostly unique to TBTF institutions).

Bingham concludes his chapter by outlining a number of principles that he argues can best guide the resolution of troubled sovereigns and TBTF institutions. While no perfect answers exist, Bingham believes that the best possible solutions lie in what he calls "soft law," which of necessity must evolve over time and take shape as different crises are dealt with.

One of the unique aspects of the 2007–08 financial crisis was the role played by the so-called shadow banking system: the range of nonbank financial institutions that issued subprime mortgages and securities (mortgage lenders and securities firms) and the institutions that bought them (hedge funds, structured investment vehicles attached to banks, money market funds, insurance companies, pension funds, and the like). In chapter 4, Morgan Ricks, of Harvard Law School, takes an in-depth look at the contribution of these institutions to the crisis and offers some interesting out-of-the-box recommendations for regulating them in the future based on his analysis.

Ricks begins with a simple, broad definition of "shadow banking": maturity transformation that takes place outside the depository banking system. A central premise of his overall thesis is that the activity of maturity transformation creates a prima facie case for some kind of regulatory oversight or intervention. The simple reason: short-term funders of longer-term assets can "run" (or refuse to roll over their obligations) once they lose confidence that they will be repaid. Deposit insurance and lender-of-last-resort lending by the central bank can prevent that from happening in the banking system, but neither of those tools is available for shadow banks. What then should be done to stabilize the shadow banking system?

In Ricks's view, the new "orderly liquidation authority" provided for failing nonbanks under Dodd-Frank will not solve the stability problem since short-term creditors who fear that they will be forced to take a loss will run at the first chance. Ricks argues that some other tool is needed to prevent shadow banks from creating or aggravating financial crises and that that tool is a licensing system that limits the types of firms that are allowed to fund themselves with short-term debt. Such firms would have to adhere to portfolio restrictions and capital requirements, much like banks. Perhaps most controversially, Ricks proposes that government explicitly commit to insuring the short-term money claims issued by shadow banks, while requiring these institutions to pay risk-based fees for the insurance.

As a practical matter, Ricks's proposal would effectively treat bank-like institutions, such as finance companies, as banks, while forcing securities firms, hedge funds, and other financial institutions now relying heavily on short-term funding to "term out" or substantially lengthen the maturity of their borrowings—and even to raise more equity capital. Ricks acknowledges that his regime would substantially raise the cost of doing business for shadow banks, perhaps ending some business models (such as the current money market mutual fund business, which he suggests would be unlikely to generate sufficient returns to cover the higher funding costs).

Ricks's approach to the financial instability problem is completely different from the approaches discussed in the rest of this volume. It eschews the need for capital injections for failing firms, as advocated in the Japanese context by Fuchita and Kodachi. But in advocating a new regime of strict regulation of financial firms with short-term funding models, it has elements of a market-based approach as well: forcing firms that do not want to be regulated as banks or their functional equivalent to rely totally on more stable, long-term sources of funding and thus enforcing market discipline.

The authors of chapter 5, Charles Calomiris of Columbia University and Richard Herring of the University of Pennsylvania, offer yet another approach for both stabilizing the financial system and providing incentives for financial institutions to act carefully so that they do not cause financial crises. Their focus is banks, and their approach suggests a novel way to operationalize the notion of "contingent capital," debt that converts to equity upon some trigger of bank weakness.

One of the earliest and most prominent responses to the financial crisis was the decision by bank regulators in developed economies—operating under the auspices of the Basel Committee—to significantly increase bank capital requirements in an effort both to provide greater cushions against the kinds of losses that led to the crisis and to give shareholders more "skin in the game" so that they have an incentive to discourage bank management from taking the kinds of risks that result in losses. The authors criticize the earlier Basel standards for improperly measuring risk and thus ironically contributing to the crisis itself. But they also criticize bank regulators for failing to compel banks that suffered losses to recapitalize in a timely fashion so as to avoid the funding crisis that damaged, in some cases fatally, many of the largest ones in the fall of 2008.

The solution to both of these shortcomings, they say, is to require banks to issue and maintain some significant amount of "contingent capital" (CoCos). CoCos, when converted to equity, *automatically* add a new layer of capital to weak institutions. And because CoCos dilute the equity positions of the current owners when they are converted to equity, the owners have strong incentives to pressure managers (most of whom also typically have some significant fraction of their wealth tied up in bank shares) to avoid taking excessive risks.

The trick is to design CoCos so that the conversion trigger is truly automatic and not subject to the discretion of managers or regulators, who have a history of engaging in forbearance when seeing bank troubles, but also not so sudden and arbitrary that it discourages potential investors from purchasing the convertible debt in the first place. The authors come up with an intriguing way to meet both challenges.

First, they suggest that CoCos represent a large fraction of overall required capital. Otherwise, they cannot provide the necessary additional capital cushion to keep a troubled bank from actually failing, even after conversion. Second, the CoCo conversion trigger should be based on the *market value* of a company's stock, to avoid the forbearance problem. And to avoid potentially misleading volatility in daily stock prices, they suggest that the market value be measured over a ninety-day moving average, so that a temporary drop in a bank's stock price cannot prematurely cause conversion. Third, all CoCos outstanding should convert at the trigger, so that all holders of the instrument are treated identically. Fourth, the conversion ratio should significantly dilute the equity of preexisting equity holders so that they have incentives to avoid that outcome.

The authors conclude their chapter by showing how their CoCo proposal might have worked during the 2007–08 financial crisis and how it might have avoided many of the banking system problems, at least, that occurred. Their analysis establishes a lower bound for the effectiveness of CoCos because it omits the important impact of incentives on shareholders and managers to take corrective actions before a crisis arises.

A final lesson from the financial crisis that many policymakers and analysts have drawn is the need for both policymakers and regulators to engage in what has been called "macroprudential" regulation and supervision. This is to be distinguished from the historic focus on the safety and soundness of individual financial institutions. How should macroprudential regulation actually work? Will it work going forward? Those are among the many questions that Doug Elliott of the Brookings Institution tackles in chapter 6, the concluding chapter in this volume.

On the question of who should run macroprudential policy, after weighing the pros and cons of each alternative—a single authority, multiple bodies, or a committee—Elliott comes down on the side of a single authority. He considers the arguments in favor of and against having the central bank assume this role, and although he does not reach a definitive conclusion, he suggests that if the single authority is not the central bank, it should be an entirely new entity.

Whichever organization carries out macroprudential policy, it should have numerous tools at its disposal, including the setting of countercyclical capital and liquidity requirements, dynamic loan loss provisioning, leverage limits on asset purchases, loan-to-value and loan-to-income guidelines or requirements for home mortgages, caps on aggregate lending, and even credit controls. Other devices, almost surely outside the authority's scope, would include changes in tax policy. If the authority is not the central bank, then its actions must be closely synchronized with monetary policy. Indeed, Elliott devotes an entire section of his chapter to how macroprudential policy and monetary policy should be coordinated, which at a minimum will require exchange of information between the monetary authority and the macroprudential regulator (assuming that they are not one and the same) on the state of the financial system and of systemically important financial institutions in particular.

Perhaps the most difficult challenge for any macroprudential body is when and how to take action. In particular, any such authority runs the risk of acting too early and thereby thwarting an expansion prematurely, but there is also the risk of acting too late, after a bubble or systemic risk has expanded enough to jeopardize the stability of the financial system. Elliott runs through the various issues entailed in striking this balance, pointing out that it is not possible to dispense with some subjective judgments in any event.

In the remaining sections of his chapter, Elliott addresses such difficult issues as how macroprudential policy should be coordinated with regulation of the safety and soundness of individual financial institutions and with similar policies being pursued by other countries (especially to avoid or minimize regulatory arbitrage); how to ensure proper accountability for macroprudential policy decisions; the major risks that the authority would confront; and how best to communicate the decisions that it reaches.

The debate over the appropriate course for future financial regulatory policy has not ended with the financial crisis and the immediate responses to it. Heated debates continue in both the United States and other countries. In a fundamental sense, the process of reform has just begun, because the initial responses were incomplete in many of the respects highlighted in the chapters in this book. This book is designed to raise the level of public debate about the future course of reform and to provide suggestions for effective policy modifications that will ensure a more stable and efficient financial system.

YASUYUKI FUCHITA
KEI KODACHI

2

Managing Systemwide Financial Crises: Some Lessons from Japan since 1990

BECAUSE NO INTERNATIONAL resolution regime for large and complex cross-border financial firms has been established, doubts are often expressed over whether the orderly liquidation stipulated in Title II of the Dodd-Frank Act can be achieved as intended. This chapter emphasizes that pursuing orderly liquidation without using taxpayer money itself acts as a barrier to reaching global agreement on such a regime.

Some argue that financial firms need to modify their lines of business and organizational structure to give them higher resolvability. We doubt, however, that supervisory authorities can actually force financial firms to make major changes to their business and their organizational structure during normal times or in the beginning stages of a crisis; even if they could, we doubt that such changes would be appropriate.

We stress here that even if such problems are solved, there is a case when Title II is infeasible. When there is a systemwide financial crisis—that is, when many financial institutions all suffer major losses at once because of an event such as the bursting of a bubble—an attempt to liquidate individual financial institutions in an orderly manner without using taxpayer money may actually propagate disorder throughout the financial system.

We outline the lessons learned from previous systemwide financial crises, using the financial crisis that began in Japan in the mid-1990s as our reference point. These lessons show that although the systemwide stress tests stipulated in the Dodd-Frank Act are an effective means of gaining the big picture of a crisis, prior to running the tests provision must be made for backstops, including injections of public capital. Moreover, when backstops and the provision of emergency liquidity are required to maintain system stability, we think it is a mistake to treat nonbank systemically important financial institutions (SIFIs) less favorably than banks when SIFIs are subject to similar enhanced supervision.

The latest global financial crisis proved that pursuing microprudence at individual financial institutions does not necessarily lead to prudence within the financial system as a whole. That realization has led to the introduction of a macroprudential approach. Nor does pursuing orderly resolution at individual financial institutions necessarily lead to the orderly resolution of the financial system as a whole. A macro approach is needed not only in prudential regulation but also in the area of crisis management policy.

Feasibility of New Resolution Regimes for Financial Firms

Under the Dodd-Frank Act, the United States has implemented a framework for the resolution of financial institutions that precludes the possibility of taxpayer-funded bailouts. To make this approach work, it aims to improve financial institution resolvability by using recovery and resolution plans (living wills). Under the leadership of the Financial Stability Board, a similar framework is being introduced at the global level. Harmonizing the bankruptcy laws of individual countries will not be easy, however, and poses a challenge moving forward. Furthermore, orderly resolution will likely be difficult in the event of a systemwide financial crisis, even if the resolvability of individual financial institutions is improved.

Reform in Financial Crisis Management: Progress So Far

Three years have passed since the Lehman bankruptcy sent shockwaves through global financial markets. During this time, the G-20, the Basel Committee, and the Financial Stability Board (FSB) have been considering future global frameworks for both preventing financial crises and managing them once they occur. The major preventive measures are Basel III and the regulation of global systemically important financial institutions (G-SIFIs), but measures aimed at preventing the recurrence of financial crises are being introduced in a broad range of areas, including securitization, over-the-counter (OTC) derivatives, hedge funds, credit ratings, and compensation. Individual countries are also establishing domestic rules largely consistent with the global regulatory efforts.

In contrast, measures to deal with crises once they occur are still a work in progress, as explained in the report by the Basel Committee's Cross-Border Resolution Group (CBRG) in July 2011.[1] The CBRG was organized to study how to cope with the failure of cross-border financial firms, a problem that emerged with the Lehman bankruptcy, and it issued ten recommendations in March 2010.[2] In its latest report, however, it identified as a problem the many countries that have made little headway in establishing domestic rules prior to the creation of a cross-border framework.

The CBRG noted, for example, that although financial firms require a special resolution regime (SRR) that is different from the usual regime for resolving bankruptcies, many countries have yet to establish an SRR. An SRR gives the competent authorities powers such as those to suspend the early termination of agreements and to transfer assets quickly to a bridge company.

Such powers are necessary because when a financial firm is in crisis, the value of its assets declines rapidly, and its large number of transaction partners causes the crisis to spread. An important goal of a normal resolution regime is the fair and orderly resolution of creditor claims, but an SRR also requires financial firms to meet public interest objectives, namely, maintaining financial stability and protecting retail account holders. In many countries, however, there is no SRR for nonbanks, even if there is one for banks. There is also a problem in that among those countries that do have an SRR, the threshold conditions for their use may differ.

Although temporary funding is needed in the resolution process to prevent chaos and ensure that the financial firm in crisis is able to continue providing critical functions and honoring contracts, in many countries there is no clear provision for such funding. Many countries have deposit insurance funds set aside for depository institutions, but most jurisdictions do not have resolution funds and seem instead to still rely on ad hoc arrangements by the government or central bank to fund broader resolution efforts that are not narrowly confined to protecting depositors.

The fact that many countries do not have adequate national resolution toolkits makes it that much more difficult to achieve orderly resolution across borders. Furthermore, according to the CBRG report, there has been no progress toward the development of a framework for cross-border enforcement of resolution actions, such as cross-border mutual recognition and enforcement of resolution powers by home and host jurisdictions.

1. Basel Committee on Banking Supervision, "Resolution Policies and Frameworks: Progress So Far" (July 2011).
2. Basel Committee on Banking Supervision, "Report and Recommendations of the Cross-Border Bank Resolution Group" (March 2010).

Because there are no prospects of achieving agreement on a cross-border crisis management framework in the near future, the Financial Stability Board has proposed a plan that puts the priority on establishing a framework for dealing with crises of global systemically important financial institutions. This entails preparing a recovery and resolution plan (RRP) under the direction of each G-SIFI's home national authorities, improving resolvability, and establishing a cross-border crisis management group comprising the competent authorities from each G-SIFI's home country and primary host countries in order to share information on and prepare for potential crises, deal with crises that have occurred, and review RRPs.[3]

Difficulties in Creating a Cross-Border Resolution Framework Agreement

Although these efforts are admirable, they may make it even more difficult to achieve agreement among countries on cross-border bankruptcy resolution for financial firms, the importance of which should have been driven home by the global financial crisis. The difficulty arises from the increased popularity since the financial crisis of the idea that public bailouts of financial firms should be ruled out.

Governments in Europe and the United States were compelled to use public funds to rescue financial firms during the recent financial crisis. The use of public funds to rescue private firms created a major backlash from voters, making it politically expedient to push financial regulatory reform in the direction of not allowing a repeat of taxpayer-financed bailouts. Avoiding public bailouts also has economic significance: financial firms' expectation of a bailout may create a moral hazard that leads to excessive risk taking, which in turn may lead to the next crisis. Too-big-to-fail (TBTF) and too-interconnected-to-fail financial firms have been especially large beneficiaries of the low cost of capital resulting from the potential for a bailout; as a result, they have become even bigger and more interconnected, thereby increasing the potential damage to the economy in the event of their failure.

At the G-20 Toronto Summit in June 2010, leaders agreed on this statement: "We are committed to design and implement a system where we have the powers and tools to restructure or resolve all types of financial institutions in crisis, without taxpayers ultimately bearing the burden."

U.S. law clearly prohibits the bailout of financial firms using taxpayer funds. The Dodd-Frank Wall Street Reform and Consumer Protection Act, passed in July 2010, regulates the orderly liquidation of financial companies. Section 214 (a) states: "All financial companies put into receivership under this title shall be

---

3. Financial Stability Board, "Effective Resolution of Systemically Important Financial Firms: Recommendations and Timelines," consultative document (July 19, 2011).

liquidated. No taxpayer funds shall be used to prevent the liquidation of any financial company under this title." Section 214(b) states: "All funds expended in the liquidation of a financial company under this title shall be recovered from the disposition of assets of such financial company, or shall be the responsibility of the financial sector, through assessments." And section 214(c) states: "Taxpayers shall bear no losses from the exercise of any authority under this title." In addition, section 212(b) states that "no governmental entity may take any action to circumvent the purposes of this title."

Section 13(c)(4)(G) of the Federal Deposit Insurance Act had allowed, in the event of systemic risk, for capital injections, debt guarantees, and other supports for insured depository institutions that go beyond the principle of least-cost resolution. In the latest financial crisis, systemic risk determinations were made in providing assistance to Wachovia and Citigroup and in establishing the Temporary Liquidity Guarantee Program, which guaranteed certain debt issued through October 31, 2009, and certain uninsured deposits of participating institutions through December 31, 2010.

Section 1106(b) of Dodd-Frank modifies that section of the Federal Deposit Insurance Act, however, to require that assistance in the event of systemic risk be provided "for the purpose of winding up the insured depository institution for which the Corporation has been appointed receiver," thus disallowing "open bank assistance" transactions.

Under Dodd-Frank, the FDIC is allowed to create a widely available program to guarantee obligations of solvent insured depository institutions or solvent depository institution holding companies in order to avoid or mitigate potential adverse effects on the U.S. financial system or economy, but that may not include the provision of equity in any form (sections 1104 and 1105).

Dodd-Frank also revised section 13(3) of the Federal Reserve Act regarding Emergency Lending from the Federal Reserve Bank, a program that was used in the latest financial crisis, including in JPMorgan Chase's acquisition of Bear Stearns in March 2008. Section 13(3), which was added in 1932 as part of the Emergency Relief and Construction Act, allowed for loans from the Federal Reserve Bank (FRB) to individuals, partnerships, or corporations "in unusual and exigent circumstances," but section 1101 of Dodd-Frank requires that the loans be part of a "program or facility with broad-based eligibility for the purpose of providing liquidity to the financial system, and not to aid a failing financial company" and also requires that "the security for emergency loans be sufficient to protect taxpayers from losses and that any such program be terminated in a timely and orderly fashion." In addition, it states that "the Board shall establish procedures to prohibit borrowing from programs and facilities by borrowers that are insolvent" and requires that the program and facility report to Congress and receive the prior approval of the secretary of the treasury. Previously, the FRB had more flexibility in fulfilling its function as lender of last resort to individual companies, but it is now much more limited in this regard.

Of course, if a global financial firm headquartered in its home country is at risk of bankruptcy, whether the home country implements emergency fiscal and financial measures to constrain the turmoil will make a big difference in the ultimate size of the losses suffered by the counterparties and creditors of both the head office and overseas operations. That is clear when one considers the differences between the international impact from the Lehman bankruptcy and the impacts of the crises precipitated by Bear Stearns, Fannie Mae, Freddie Mac, and AIG.

If each country contains the crisis at home, differences among the countries in how they resolve cross-border bankruptcy will not pose a major problem. Because bankruptcy would not occur in the event of a bailout, there would be no need to worry about problems with cross-border bankruptcy resolution in that case either. However, the increase in the number of countries that are not allowing public bailouts has greatly increased the seriousness of problems with cross-border resolutions and simultaneously made it that much more difficult to agree on a solution.

Japan's Systemic Risk Exception

At least one of the G-20 countries, Japan, has chosen not to disallow public bailouts of financial firms. Under the system established by Japan following its financial crises in the 1990s, when systemic risk is a concern, it is possible to provide open bank assistance to solvent financial firms—that is, inject them with public funds without wiping out shareholders—in order to prevent a crisis from developing into a bankruptcy and causing substantial systemic impacts. If the institution is insolvent, it is possible to nationalize it temporarily while providing protection to some creditors other than insured deposit holders. In all cases, the Bank of Japan (BOJ) is able to provide the necessary liquidity through special loans. Japan participated in the debate at the CBRG and FSB over cross-border bank resolution and among the G-20 over adoption of the FSB recommendations, but it is not currently considering eliminating the system described above.

The differences extend to important components of policy tools, even in regard to the technical workings of bankruptcy resolution regimes. Although the G-20 agreement proposes resolution without the use of taxpayers' money, there are countries, like Japan, that clearly leave open the possibility of using tax revenues. Public support is not completely barred under rules in the European Union or the United Kingdom, either. The differences across countries in their stance on crucial components of resolution regimes also suggest that forging an agreement will not be easy.

Adoption of a Homogeneous Approach to Crisis Management after the Lehman Bankruptcy

The fact that it is taking time to build a unified approach to cross-border resolution and that it has actually become more difficult to forge an agreement is exactly the opposite of the situation that existed when the last financial crisis erupted and each country took almost the same actions.

In the G-7 Finance Ministers and Central Bank Governors Plan of Action, announced on October 10, 2008, shortly after the failure of Lehman Brothers, there was agreement to "take decisive action and use all available tools to support systemically important financial firms and prevent their failure." The idea of ending the too big to fail approach was nowhere to be found in that document.

In addition, each country was following the same macro policies: increasing government spending and easing monetary policy while injecting capital into, guaranteeing the loans of, and providing liquidity to the banks and a wide range of financial firms, including nonbanks. In the United States, special programs were established to channel funding from the Treasury Department and the central bank to specific markets and products, including money market funds, commercial paper, and asset-backed securities.

The measures introduced by the United States to deal with new financial crises and the cross-border resolution framework currently targeted by the G-20 rule out public support, but the fact that such measures proved necessary in the last financial crisis raises doubts over the feasibility of this new approach. Japan has learned that ruling out bailouts is not realistic.

In Japan in 1996, public funds totaling ¥685 billion (US$6.3 billion, using the exchange rate at that time) were injected to resolve the bankruptcies of home mortgage lenders (*jusen*) in order to limit the losses suffered by the agricultural financial firms that had equity in them. That caused a public backlash, however, that made it impossible for Japan to flexibly implement measures to facilitate recapitalization or the purchase of nonperforming loans (NPLs) that year or the next. Even while the economic bubble was imploding further, NPLs were growing even at the major banks, and the financial system was becoming less stable. As a result, the crisis only worsened, until it got to the point that an injection of public funds 100 times larger than the one that caused the uproar in 1996 was needed. Japan learned that injecting public funds into a financial firm leads to a taxpayer revolt. It also learned that it is unwise to shut down this policy option because of such opposition, because that inevitably winds up increasing the taxpayers' burden.

What sets Japan apart is that not only does it use public funds to achieve an orderly resolution of insolvent financial firms but it also has a mechanism for preventively injecting public funds into solvent financial firms that are weak and at risk of destabilizing the financial system. This is in alignment with the October 1998 statement of the G-7 Finance Ministers and Central Bank Governors that was directed at Japan.[4]

The fact that governments in Europe and the United States rescued a variety of financial firms during the last financial crisis seems to be consistent with the lesson that Japan learned: that such rescues are at times unavoidable. The weight of opinion in Japan holds that ruling out rescues as a policy option, while an understandable response, is not a good idea.

Skepticism over Dodd-Frank's Title II

In our opinion, skepticism about ruling out rescues is not unique to observers in Japan; it is shared by many others. For example, MIT professor Simon Johnson comments: "In some official minds, Dodd-Frank has made it impossible for 'too big to fail' banks to exist—meaning that if any such bank got into trouble, it would be shut down without any significant costs being incurred by taxpayers. Most independent analysts and many people active in financial markets regard this proposition as unproven at best and, most likely, simply incorrect."[5] Johnson argues that for that reason, banks should be split up so that they are no longer "too big," but given the lack of support for and poor prospects of realizing such a plan, it is natural to expect that bailing out financial firms as well as some of their creditors may be unavoidable.

For example, the credit rating agencies "uplift" their ratings of the major U.S. banks based on their assumption of systemic support, and this practice has been amplified by the fact that support was actually provided during the financial crisis. This rating enhancement has not completely disappeared, even though the enactment of Dodd-Frank proclaimed the end of TBTF.

Before the revision of their ratings in September 2011, Standard & Poor's (S&P) reported that potential government support enhanced the ratings of the long-term debts of Bank of America Corporation and Citibank by two notches each; Moody's reported an uplift of four notches for Bank of America and three notches for Citibank. In June 2011, Moody's announced that it would revise its policy for uplift in the event of a financial crisis and review the potential of a downgrade for Bank of America, Citibank, and Wells Fargo, but it was referring

---

4. Statement of the G-7 Finance Ministers and Central Bank Governors on October 3, 1988, in Washington, D.C.: "We stress the importance that we attach to the swift and effective action to strengthen the financial system, including the prompt enactment of measures to support viable banks with public assistance in sufficient amounts to be provided swiftly with appropriate conditions."

5. Simon Johnson, "Three Questions for the Financial Stability Oversight Council," The Baseline Scenario, September 3, 2011.

to an adjustment of the unusual uplift applied as a result of the public assistance rendered at the height of the financial crisis; the uplift reflecting a pre-crisis level of government support would remain. In addition, it would not be revising the uplift of those financial firms for which the uplift during the financial crisis was not unusual. Moody's senior management noted in regard to this that, despite the passage of the Dodd-Frank Act, "Moody's continues to believe that such a group could not be resolved without risking a disorderly disruption of the marketplace and the broader economy."[6]

Moody's downgraded all three of the banks in September 2011, dropping its long-term debt rating by two notches for Bank of America and by one notch for Wells Fargo. It left its long-term debt rating for Citigroup the same but lowered its short-term debt rating to P2 from P1. Commenting on its downgrade of Bank of America, Moody's noted that it "continues to see the probability of support for highly interconnected, systemically important institutions as very high, although that probability is lower than it was during the financial crisis." It added that "the final form of several critical components of Dodd-Frank intended to reduce such interconnectedness, such as resolution plans or changes to the over-the-counter derivatives market, are still pending. There is also no global process yet in place whereby regulators could resolve a global financial company such as Bank of America in an orderly fashion. As a result, Moody's believes that it would be very difficult for the U.S. government to utilize the orderly liquidation authority to resolve a systemically important bank without a disruption of the marketplace and the broader economy."

S&P has written that "we believe that under certain circumstances and with selected systemically important financial firms, future extraordinary government support is still possible."[7] Congressman Barney Frank, co-author of the Dodd-Frank Act, criticized this S&P report as misleading in regard to Title II of the act because it omitted the fact that Dodd-Frank repealed section 13(3) of the Federal Reserve Act. He commented, "Any fair reading of the American public and the appetite of Congress suggests that there is absolutely no support for more bank bailouts."[8]

This may be the current mood, but there is a possibility that those now arguing against a bailout during the next crisis may quickly change their tune to demanding a bailout, as occurred in Japan from 1997. The public can change its mind fairly quickly, as can politicians in reflecting the public's mood.

6. Moody's, "Global Credit Research" (June 2, 2011).
7. Standard & Poor's, "The U.S. Government Says Support for Banks Will Be Different 'Next Time'—But Will It?" July 12, 2011.
8. Rep. Barney Frank, open letter to Deven Sharma, president, Standard & Poor's, July 14, 2011.

Former FDIC chairwoman Sheila Bair admitted that there are doubts over the new resolution framework.[9] She noted that "many large banks and nonbank SIFIs maintain thousands of subsidiaries and manage their activities within business lines that cross many different organizational structures and regulatory jurisdictions. This can make it very difficult to implement an orderly resolution of one part of the company without triggering a costly collapse of the entire company."

Bair proposed a solution similar to, albeit not as radical as, that proposed by Simon Johnson. She said that the FDIC and the Federal Reserve Bank "must be willing to insist on organizational changes that better align business lines and legal entities well before a crisis occurs. Unless these structures are rationalized and simplified in advance, there is a real danger that their complexity could make a SIFI resolution far more costly and more difficult than it needs to be."

That brings with it new reasons to be skeptical. Namely, is it really possible for the FDIC and the Fed to change the global structure of SIFIs in a way that makes them easily resolvable just by making them submit a resolution plan? Can they reach consensus on the most appropriate size and organizational structure for achieving true financial stability? Is this an example of bureaucratic overreach, the exercise of excessive authority and discretionary power? And finally, can the new global financial firms that result properly support the economic activity of their customers?

In this regard, FRB governor Daniel K. Tarullo's recent speech is worth noting (Tarullo 2011). He said, "At least some advocates of orderly liquidation regimes seem to favor resolution plans that silo activities as much as possible. However, in the presence of significant economies of scope, this approach might result in loss of efficient forms of organization. In these circumstances, resolution plans that seek to preserve the scope economies even as a firm is dismembered might result in better liquidation outcomes. In addition, siloing activities in the context of a resolution plan could affect day-to-day operations during normal times and might reduce efficiency by preventing firms from realizing economies of scope, resulting in increased costs of financial services for households and businesses."

As long as such doubts and concerns remain, it will be difficult for people to believe that future failures of financial firms will be orderly and thus impossible for them to have confidence that there will be no bailouts. We have the same doubts and concerns at the global level, including in regard to the FSB's proposal to improve the resolvability of SIFIs via the implementation of RRPs and resolvability assessments.

9. Remarks by FDIC chairwoman Sheila C. Bair, "We Must Resolve to End Too Big to Fail," at the 47th Annual Conference on Bank Structure and Competition, sponsored by the Federal Reserve Bank of Chicago, May 5, 2011.

The Rationale and Potential Defects of the New U.S. Resolution Regime

Given taxpayers' opposition to bailing out large financial firms and the problems of moral hazard, it is understandable that the United States and other countries want to end TBTF. The problem is whether an orderly bankruptcy process is possible if they do. Insisting on no government rescues and giving priority to preventing moral hazard are meaningless unless the larger goal of avoiding an expansion of the systemic crisis can be achieved. It is important not to forget, as shown by the Lehman bankruptcy, that such a crisis is very costly and places a huge burden on the overall global economy.

An FDIC report released in April 2011 argued that under Dodd-Frank, Lehman would not have sparked systemic turmoil but would have been liquidated in an orderly fashion.[10] It is true that the United States is now equipped with the following policy measures, which were unavailable at the time:

—Nonbank financial companies supervised by the Fed and large bank holding companies are required to prepare and submit resolution plans meant to enable them to be rapidly liquidated in an orderly manner under Title 11 of U.S. Code. The Fed and FDIC review the plans and may notify and impose measures to correct deficiencies. This makes both the Fed and the FDIC well prepared for material financial distress or failure.

—A special resolution regime has been introduced for bank holding companies and nonbanks designated as covered financial companies whereby the FDIC can be a receiver.

—As a receiver of a covered financial company, the FDIC has a number of special powers, the most critical of which are the following four:

It is an immediate source of liquidity for an orderly liquidation, which allows continuation of essential functions and maintains asset values.

It has the ability to issue advance dividends and make prompt distributions to creditors based on expected recoveries.

It has the ability to continue key, systemically important operations, including through the formation of one or more bridge financial companies.

It has the ability to transfer all qualified financial contracts with a given counterparty to another entity (such as a bridge financial company) to avoid their immediate termination and liquidation in order to preserve value and promote stability.

10. FDIC, "The Orderly Liquidation of Lehman Brothers Holdings Inc. under the Dodd-Frank Act," *FDIC Quarterly*, vol. 5, no. 2 (2011).

These improvements are reasonable and should be seen as positive factors that have substantially reduced the potential of bankruptcy resolution to lead to major turmoil. The FSB's cross-border resolution proposal includes the introduction of a special resolution regime, RRPs, temporary funding, and bridge companies, putting the U.S. framework at the forefront of the global trend.

The report by the FDIC speculates about what would have happened if the authority given the FDIC by Dodd-Frank had been available after the Bear Stearns crisis in March 2008 and thereby in time for the Lehman Brothers failure in September 2008. The FDIC estimates that if it had started looking at resolution during the six months between the two crises and stationed personnel inside Lehman Brothers to gather and analyze detailed information on its operations while looking for a potential buyer, it probably would have been able to continue Lehman's business, honor its agreements, and find a buyer in a timely manner. And by ensuring that the shareholders and unsecured creditors bore losses, the losses of creditors would have been only minimal.

Nevertheless, the crisis did not wait even six months from the initial signs before it developed overnight into a grave situation, and a buyer might not be found that quickly. Losses would already have become huge by the time the authorities intervened, creating a situation in which a large number of counterparties would experience losses unless there was an injection of public funds. There was probably no guarantee that counterparties' losses would not cause the crisis to spread.

The United States may have been better off because it had the FDIC, an institution with considerable power. In other countries, it may be difficult to achieve the sort of rapid intervention by a resolution authority that the FDIC is capable of. There is a risk that in other countries, it would have been hard to justify, just because of the Bear Stearns crisis, the intervention of regulators and use of the authority to mandate an early capital increase for Lehman Brothers, which had an A rating, a tier 1 capital ratio of 10.7 percent, and a total capital ratio of 16.1 percent as of end-March 2008.

There are reasons to question whether even U.S. regulators would have been able to intervene suitably and in a timely manner. Problems with regulatory forbearance have long been pointed out, even in the United States. In contrast, although a mechanism for prompt corrective action (PCA) has been implemented, the capital ratios that serve as the trigger for such action are lagging indicators.

Section 166 of Dodd-Frank stipulates early remediation requirements for SIFIs and allows for the introduction of forward-looking indicators as a basis for action. It is also possible, as already noted, to correct potential risks using a resolution plan. In addition, section 172 of Dodd-Frank allows for the FDIC to conduct special examinations of SIFIs for the purpose of orderly liquidation.

Even given that authority, however, there is no objective numerical trigger, as there is with prompt corrective action, and the questions of when to take action and what action to take are left to the discretion of the regulators. That may mean that the problem of regulatory forbearance is unavoidable.[11]

Possibility of Coping with a Systemwide Financial Crisis

Even under an improved set of rules, it may be difficult to achieve the orderly resolution of an international financial firm as large and complex as Lehman Brothers. Likewise, it would not be easy to turn a large and complex financial firm into a smaller, simpler one. Accordingly, as pointed out by the rating agencies, public bailouts are likely to be necessary to prevent turmoil.

It is important to focus not only on the nature of financial firms—their large size and complexity—but also on the nature of crises. Particularly in the case of financial crises that are not triggered by particular companies but that are systemwide—occurring within an environment of macroeconomic and financial instability conducive to the outbreak of multiple systemic risk events, as was the shock generated by Lehman Brothers—it would likely become that much more difficult to implement Title II.

Normally, systemic risk refers to risks triggered by externalities of the financial industry, whereby a crisis rooted in particular financial firms spreads to other financial firms. This is different from the term "systemwide financial crisis" used here, which refers to a crisis that arises when a significant part of the financial industry becomes unsound as a result of most firms' shared exposure to a serious economic contraction resulting, for example, from the collapse of a bubble. In such a crisis some event triggering a broad increase in uncertainty among market participants leads to a run on deposits and the freezing up of market transactions, making it difficult for financial firms to get funding, as well as to the panic selling of assets, to the point that there is fear that large numbers of financial firms will go bankrupt. In addition, such a serious contraction of the overall economy is associated with huge damage to the balance sheets not only of financial firms but also of households, corporations, and the government. Recovery from such a contraction takes time, during which the financial system overall remains in an unstable state and systemic risk events continue to occur in waves over an extended period.

It is not only large and interconnected financial firms that are capable of triggering this sort of financial crisis. Accordingly, even if it were possible to turn such firms into smaller, simpler ones, it would not prevent such a crisis. That is

11. See Edwards (2011).

because a systemwide financial crisis is defined as one that occurs when a large number of financial firms—irrespective of their interconnectedness or their size—suffer significant losses, greatly reducing the confidence that depositors and investors have in financial firms in general and making it impossible for the overall financial system to function. This is what happened in the 1930s during the Great Depression, in the 1990s during the collapse of Japan's bubble economy, and during the latest global financial crisis, making it appropriate to make a distinction between those periods of crises and more limited systemic risk events.[12]

The appropriate analogy is not an orderly row of dominoes in which if one falls, adjacent ones also fall, but rather to a table scattered with many dominoes that itself becomes unstable, so that it is impossible to tell which dominoes are going to fall as a result of a shock to the table. Furthermore, the table is exposed not just to a single shock but to repeated shocks over an extended period. Prudential regulation seeks to make each domino less likely to fall. Orderly resolution seeks to improve resolvability by implementing appropriate measures in normal times, such as by designing a system to ensure that if a domino does fall, it does not take the other dominoes with it, and setting up an early detection and intervention system so that signs that a domino is about to fall will trigger its quick removal from the table. Nevertheless, although these measures may be effective in preventing a typical domino-like succession of failures, none are effective if it is the table itself that has become very unstable.[13]

---

12. The fact that this crisis is often referred to as the Great Recession suggests that it was not as deep as the Great Depression of the 1930s. Reinhart and Rogoff (2009), however, refers to the 1930s crisis as the "Great Contraction" and to the latest crisis as the "Second Great Contraction."

13. Brunnermeier and others (2009) refers to a financial crisis in which losses at one bank lead to losses at other banks as the domino model of contagion. The authors argue that the focus should not be on the chain reaction of losses but on the problem caused by banks becoming concerned over the losses at other banks and reducing their transactions and increasing their haircuts as a way to maintain their own microprudence. Such behavior leads to the drying up of market liquidity by way of the worsening of interbank liquidity and the fire sale of assets. The domino model mentioned in this chapter refers to the type of crisis that originates in one financial firm and spreads throughout the entire system through a chain reaction of losses and contraction of liquidity. This stands in contrast to a systemwide financial crisis, which occurs when a crisis of the overall economy, rather than a crisis emanating from a single financial firm, results in a large number of financial firms suffering losses. In this case, contagion among financial firms brought by a contraction of liquidity is a key element in the deepening of a systemwide financial crisis, but a systemwide financial crisis can include cases in which no contagion spreads among financial firms; instead, retail depositors simply initiate a bank run at a large number of banks. Brunnermeier and others argue that preventing financial crises caused by a reduction of liquidity requires not only microprudential but also macroprudential regulation. In this chapter, as detailed later, we argue that instead of a micro approach based on achieving the orderly liquidation of individual financial firms, there is a need for a macro approach, not only to prevent financial crises but also to deal with a financial crisis that has already begun in order to prevent it from worsening into a systemwide crisis.

In fact, there is a real possibility that early intervention, such as the FDIC making serious preparations for the resolution of the bankruptcy of a financial firm, will be the catalyst that destabilizes the table. News of such an FDIC action would be difficult to keep secret and would probably be leaked immediately. The FDIC argues that "while it is possible in this situation or in other situations that the FDIC's on-site presence could create signaling concerns, this argues for the FDIC having a continuous on-site presence for resolution planning during good times"; however, fooling the market is no easy task. Previously, the possibility of a systemic risk exception, which allowed the FDIC to bail out failed banks and their creditors, made it conceivable that the market would not be overcome by panic, but Dodd-Frank rules out that possibility and makes losses on equity and subordinated debt certain, creating the risk that panic will set in early in a crisis and cause the market to stop functioning. Under those circumstances, the FDIC would be hard pressed to find a buyer, given that market participants would probably have lost trust in each other.

Gordon and Muller (2010) points out that the FDIC's new resolution authority "works best in the case of financial firms that fail because of idiosyncratic reasons and whose failure produces only isolated consequences. Resolution authority will be inadequate to address serious financial sector distress if single firm failure spreads systemically because of counterparty exposure or similarity risk." The authors argue that "this resolution straitjacket is a prescription for a future disaster." They make another important point in noting that "the international impact would be much aggravated by multiple close-in-time receiverships."

We think that in a systemwide crisis, it may be impossible in some cases to avoid providing individual financial firms, be they banks or nonbanks, with central bank credit or capital injections. That is because a rapid freezing of markets makes access to funding suddenly difficult for a large number of financial firms, including those that are perfectly sound, and that could eventually cause them to become insolvent in succession.

Although Dodd-Frank allows for a facility to supply liquidity to solvent financial firms, at the height of a crisis it becomes difficult to determine which institutions are solvent and which are not. That difficulty would probably force a situation in which liquidity must be supplied through the facility to financial firms without knowing whether they are solvent. That is true also because one of the causes of insufficient liquidity is counterparties' mutual lack of trust in each other's solvency. It is difficult to solve the problem of insufficient liquidity without dealing with insolvency and with situations in which there is a risk of solvent financial firms becoming insolvent.

In a systemwide crisis, even supplying liquidity or capital injections to individual financial firms, both of which are prohibited under Dodd-Frank, may be insufficient to ease overall market uncertainty. That is not just speculation; it is what was actually experienced during the latest crisis and in Japan's financial crises in the 1990s and the 1930s.

On the basis of the lessons learned then, the resolution regime under Dodd-Frank in the United States and the framework proposed by the FSB represent major progress but remain incomplete. Even after the latest crisis, Japan has no intention of changing its resolution regime, which it built based on its experiences in the 1990s and which allows for bailouts using public funds. Rather, the experiences in the latest crisis further validated Japan's existing regime. In this context, we look back at Japan's crisis in the 1990s to explore in greater detail the lessons learned from that experience with systemwide crisis.

Japan's Systemwide Financial Crisis

Japan underwent a systemwide financial crisis in the 1990s. The lesson Japan drew from that experience is that abolishing the option of bank recapitalization with public fund injections amplifies the crisis. Japan's experience also suggests that allowing the failure of nonbanks seemingly too small to be systemically important can also lead to a systemwide crisis.

The Nature of Japan's 1990s Financial Crisis

The bubble that was inflating in Japan in the late 1980s burst in 1990 and led to a period of financial system instability that lasted for over a decade. Japan's bubble was financed by the growth of loans backed by land and stocks that had increased in price. The most visible recipients of the loans were golf courses, resorts, and commercial real estate developments. It was not only banks and financial co-ops that made the loans but also affiliated housing lenders, insurance companies, and the financial subsidiaries of brokerage firms. Consequently, nearly every subsector of the financial industry suffered major losses when the bubble collapsed. In that sense, the financial system was in a systemwide crisis during that period.

The systemwide crisis brought on by the collapse of a major bubble and other common macro factors spread across a wide range of sectors and created large realized and potential losses. Because of the enormity of scale, the tendency was to opt for the time-consuming approach of putting together a combination of micro- and macroeconomic policies instead of realizing the potential losses quickly and expediting recovery. Because this long-term process was accompanied by deleveraging on a wide scale, it was difficult to stimulate the economy.

Each time during this period that domestic or overseas factors worsened more than expected, the financial system's instability resurfaced and led to the failure of more financial firms. Another defining feature of Japan's systemwide crisis is that it was experienced over a period lasting more than a decade.

In the early 1990s, shortly after the bubble burst, a succession of business crises and failures took place among small and mid-size financial firms. They were initially resolved through "rescue mergers," but with conditions becoming challenging at other financial firms, it became steadily more difficult to find financial firms to do the rescuing.[14] Although deposit insurance existed, the public already had confidence in the safety of bank deposits, making it difficult to opt to inflict losses on deposits that exceeded the maximum insured amount, which in turn made it difficult to resolve failures with a rescue merger. In 1995, the Bank of Japan and private sector financial firms chose to jointly establish and capitalize a bridge bank and use a resolution approach in which local governments also bore some of the losses. However, the decision to use public funds in the resolution of financial firms caused a major political furor that came to a head when public funds were injected into seven housing mortgage lenders (*jusen*).

Because Japan's postwar financial firms were focused primarily on meeting the demand for funds from corporations and proved insufficient to provide home loan services, the *jusen* were established to fill that need. During the bubble, the *jusen* also expanded their lending to include real estate projects besides housing, and that led to losses after the bubble collapsed. A crisis emerged in 1995 when 48 percent of their loan portfolios became unrecoverable, and their losses rose to the equivalent of the total GDP of the Philippines at the time. Nevertheless, there was major resistance to allowing the financial co-ops, partners in the *jusen,* to bear the losses because the smaller financial firms were already struggling and the financial co-ops served as financial intermediaries for the politically powerful agricultural sector. That resulted in the injection of public funds, and the parties to the joint venture wound up suffering only minor losses. As already noted, that decision evoked a major political backlash, eliminating for a while the option of rescuing financial firms with public funds.

In 1996, Japan entered a recession that some attribute in part to a hike in the consumption tax rate, to fiscal retrenchment policies advanced by the Hashimoto administration then in power, and to an increase in the portion of health care costs borne by taxpayers. The 1997 Asian monetary crisis also had a big impact,

---

14. For more on Japan's financial crisis and the policy response, see Nishimura (2011).

and it wound up causing a financial crisis, which included the bankruptcy of some large financial firms, from 1997 to 1998. After that crisis, Japan instituted a bankruptcy resolution regime that allowed the injection of public funds and came to recognize the need for the orderly resolution of nonbanks.

During the recession triggered by the collapse of the dotcom bubble in 2000, there also were rising international concerns over Japan's overhang of non-performing loans. Japan implemented a comprehensive special audit in the fall of 2002 and injected public funds into large banks that were solvent but weak in May 2003. Around that time, helped in part by a robust economic recovery in the United States (that wound up leading to the subprime loan crisis), Japan's decade-plus systemwide crisis came to an end. We focus next on the period from 1997, when the crisis became more serious, and on Japan's response.

Systemic Risk Brought on by Small Default Amounts

The first casualty of Japan's financial crisis of 1997–98 was the failure of Sanyo Securities in November 1997. Sanyo Securities, whose business had deteriorated owing primarily to the write-off of NPLs held by an affiliated firm, filed for bankruptcy protection under the Corporate Reorganization Act on November 3, and its bankruptcy was resolved through a court-ordered liquidation. That resulted in the first default ever in Japan's money market, which caused the market to lose confidence, and the situation developed into a serious financial crisis. Sanyo Securities had assets in custody of approximately ¥2.7 trillion ($25 billion), giving it the rank of a second-tier brokerage firm in Japan, and it was not big enough to be deemed "too big to fail." In addition, the deterioration of Sanyo Securities's business was already in the news and widely known; therefore, it was not really an example of "sudden death." Nevertheless, the money market defaults that occurred as a result of the brokerage firm's failure caused financial market disruptions that Japan had never before experienced and wound up triggering a financial crisis.

While receiving assistance from the Ministry of Finance and the Bank of Japan, Sanyo Securities tried to rebuild its business through a rescue merger with another brokerage firm; however, its efforts failed. With the financial position of Sanyo Securities worsening, the firm's equity capital ratio was expected to drop below Japan's 120 percent minimum regulatory requirement. Consequently, regulators abandoned their plans to orchestrate a rescue merger with another brokerage firm and changed course, opting for a court-ordered liquidation of the firm. On learning of the regulators' change in plans, Sanyo Securities became Japan's first listed securities company to file for bankruptcy in a district court under the Corporate Reorganization Act.

Because Japan's brokerage firms are nondepository institutions and thus are not covered by the Deposit Insurance Act, they cannot use the special resolution regime prescribed in the act for depository institutions (including banks). Furthermore, Japan has established no SRR framework for brokerage firms and other nonbank financial firms to avoid systemic risk and ensure their orderly resolution. Consequently, Sanyo Securities elected to resolve its bankruptcy through a court-ordered liquidation under the Corporate Reorganization Act, which is similar to Chapter 11 bankruptcy in the United States.

We think it chose the Corporate Reorganization Act because, first, it was thought that resolving Sanyo Securities under the act would have only a limited impact on the financial system because brokerage firms, unlike banks, do not provide payment services and, second, Japan was in the process at the time of changing the way that it regulated the financial sector, moving away from the "convoy system" (*goso sendan*)[15] and toward one based on market mechanisms, and court-ordered liquidation placed greater emphasis on market discipline.[16]

While filing for protection under the Corporate Reorganization Act with the Tokyo District Court, Sanyo Securities also filed for a protective order prohibiting the repayment of debt, the disposition of property, and new borrowing in order to fund the smooth return of client assets. That protective order was immediately granted by the court. Because of the order, the company became unable to repay ¥1 billion ($7.8 million) in unsecured call loans obtained from *shinkin* banks (credit associations) in the interbank market and ¥8.3 billion ($65 million) in funds borrowed from an agricultural cooperative in the repo markets, resulting in the first-ever default in Japan's money market.

The Sanyo Securities default did not involve a large amount; therefore, it did not directly cause large losses in the financial sector. As the first-ever default in Japan's money market, however, it reduced market confidence, making market participants less willing to provide credit, and thereby developed into a serious crisis. The default in the money market radically reduced the provision of credit to market participants and shrank liquidity throughout the financial system. In other words, the default triggered a severe market liquidity crisis.

With the Sanyo Securities default having destroyed market confidence and tightened liquidity in the money market, Hokkaido Takushoku Bank—which

---

15. The convoy system refers to the form of government administration previously used in Japan. In the context of a military strategy, a convoy of ships adjusts its speed to that of the slowest ship in the convoy, thereby allowing unified control of the entire group. In the business context, designated industries in Japan are kept under control by bureaucrats, who exercise their authority to provide permits and approvals so as to ensure the survival of the weakest and least competitive.

16. Karube and Nishino (1999).

was one of the twenty largest banks at the time and was in the process of rebuilding its business, which had been hurt by NPLs—became unable to secure funding in the interbank market. Unable to maintain the level of reserve deposits at the Bank of Japan required under the Bank of Japan Act because of difficulty in obtaining funding from the markets, Hokkaido Takushoku Bank experienced a liquidity-induced bankruptcy, announced on November 17. Sanyo Securities' small default wound up leading to the failure of a major bank.

The turmoil in financial markets spread to Yamaichi Securities, one of the big four brokerage firms. Yamaichi, which was in the process of restructuring, had sought help from its main bank, Fuji Bank (now Mizuho Financial Group), but Fuji Bank refused, and Yamaichi's capital became insufficient. The brokerage firm subsequently sought an equity investment from Credit Suisse and then tried to negotiate the sale of its business to Merrill Lynch, but both efforts failed, eliminating any possibility for Yamaichi to restructure in the private sector. Overcome by the financial market turmoil triggered by the Sanyo Securities default, Yamaichi was considered likely to fail by market participants, found it difficult to get funding, and ultimately became unable to meet its funding targets. As a result, on November 24 Yamaichi announced its voluntary closure pursuant to the Securities and Exchange Act in force at the time (which has since been superseded by the Financial Instruments and Exchange Act).

Stock prices dropped sharply on news of Yamaichi's failure, while currency markets experienced heavy selling of the yen. Although the BOJ supplied the market with ample liquidity, short-term yields rose and long-term yields declined as a result of a flight to safety. Market participants lost trust in each other, and with rumors flying about other financial firms going bankrupt, market turmoil reached its peak. On November 26, the regional bank Tokuyo City Bank declared bankruptcy, the fourth such failure since the beginning of November. The minor default by Sanyo Securities thus triggered bankruptcies at a major bank, a major brokerage firm, and a regional bank and led to an unprecedented financial crisis.

The Lehman Brothers Chapter 11 filing on September 15, 2008, dried up market liquidity worldwide and triggered a financial crisis on a global scale. Because Lehman Brothers was both too big to fail and too interconnected to fail, its failure pushed the entire world into crisis. In contrast, the default resulting from the Sanyo Securities failure in November 1997 was about ¥9.3 billion ($72.8 million), an extremely small amount relative to the size of Japan's money market. The mere fact of a default, however, greatly reduced the supply of credit to market participants and destroyed market confidence, thereby drying up liquidity and triggering a financial crisis. When the potential exists for major losses by financial firms as a whole and for market participants to lose trust in each other, it is possible that a crisis can result from even a small default or even just the possibility of a restructuring or haircut on a claim.

Orderly Resolution of a Large Nonbank

As already noted, the financial market turmoil triggered by the Sanyo Securities failure shut off funding to Yamaichi Securities, which then announced a voluntary closure on November 24, 1997. Because Yamaichi was not a depository institution, like Sanyo it did not have access to the SRR provided for under the Deposit Insurance Act.

Yamaichi had client assets of ¥22 trillion ($172 billion) and operated internationally as a brokerage firm, with overseas offices in various parts of the world, including the United States, the United Kingdom, the Netherlands, Germany, Switzerland, Hong Kong, and Singapore. While Sanyo had only 200,000 client accounts, Yamaichi had 2.8 million. Although Yamaichi was smaller than Lehman Brothers and was not as interconnected, it apparently was still too big and too interconnected to achieve an orderly resolution with financial markets in turmoil.

Although Sanyo chose resolution under the Corporate Reorganization Act, Yamaichi opted for voluntary closure, for several reasons. First, its more than ¥200 billion in unlawful off-balance-sheet debt made it difficult to reorganize under the Corporate Reorganization Act and, second, there was concern that a court-ordered liquidation of Yamaichi would force it to cease operations and make an orderly wind-down difficult. Another aspect of Yamaichi's resolution process was that although the BOJ had provided emergency liquidity as lender of last resort to Yamaichi (even though it was a nonbank) in order to head off financial market turmoil, there was a possibility of losses if the BOJ provided liquidity to a company being resolved under the Corporate Reorganization Act.

The biggest difference between the bankruptcy resolutions of Yamaichi and Sanyo was that Sanyo temporarily suspended operations while Yamaichi continued operating. Because Sanyo closed down under the bankruptcy laws, it suspended operations, including its debt payments, under a protective order from the court and defaulted in the money market. In contrast, Yamaichi resolved its bankruptcy through voluntary closure, a liquidation process that includes the continuation of operations and the settlement of various types of financial agreements.

The financial crisis had become substantially more serious at the time because of Sanyo's failure. If Yamaichi had chosen court-ordered liquidation under those conditions, it would have immediately ceased operations and failed to adhere to various financial agreements, possibly causing even greater turmoil in the markets. Because of Yamaichi's size and interconnectedness, court-ordered liquidation was expected to result in a major default in both domestic and over-seas markets, and there was concern that if that led to a chain reaction of financial firm failures, it would not only deepen the crisis in Japan's financial system but also cause the financial crisis to spread to overseas markets.

In fact, a statement by the governor of the BOJ on the day that Yamaichi announced its voluntary closure noted that "when we consider the fact that the firm conducts a wide range of business in domestic and overseas markets and that it has a large number of customers, we believe it extremely important for the stability of the Japanese and overseas financial markets to bring about a smooth closure of the firm."

In order to fund the liquidation process following Yamichi's voluntary closure, the BOJ provided "special loans (*tokuyu*)" to Yamaichi totaling over ¥1.2 trillion at the peak, and that appears to have made an orderly wind-down possible. The loan was an unsecured and unlimited emergency loan under the Bank of Japan Act. The BOJ decided, with permission of the finance minister, that it was neces-sary to provide special loans to brokerage firms, acting as lender of last resort.[17] In Japan, not only depository institutions but also brokerage firms are eligible to hold current account deposits at the central bank (the BOJ).

There was concern that Yamaichi was insolvent because one of the causes of its failure was off-the-books debt of ¥264.8 billion. However, even including that unrecorded debt, it was solvent, having shareholders' equity at the time of ¥100 billion, and the BOJ, as a temporary measure, provided Yamaichi with the funds needed for the liquidation process pursuant to Article 25 of the Bank of Japan Act then in force (Article 38 under the current version of the act).

The statement by the BOJ governor mentioned above went on to say that "the Bank of Japan, as the nation's central bank, in order to fulfill its respon-sibility of maintaining stability of the financial system, has decided to take the extraordinary measure of providing necessary liquidity pursuant to Article 25 of the Bank of Japan Act, in cooperation with the main bank of the firm so that it may return customer assets, orderly settle outstanding transactions, and with-draw from overseas activities." Because the BOJ provided liquidity as a lender of last resort, Yamaichi's voluntary closure did not put any further stress on the financial system, and an orderly resolution was possible.

---

17. This is similar to section 13(3) loans by the Federal Reserve Bank (before the amendments by the Dodd-Frank Act). But 13(3) loans are made to nonfinancial corporations, individuals, and partner-ships, whereas special loans from the BOJ are meant only for the banks and brokerage firms with which it transacts. In addition, section 13(3) loans require collateral, whereas special loans from the BOJ can be unsecured.

It was during the liquidation stage of its voluntary disclosure that Yamaichi became insolvent. Yamaichi had planned to cancel ¥43 billion of subordinated loans that it had borrowed from fourteen insurance companies to eliminate its excess of debt over assets, but the insurance companies filed suit. They wound up settling on a 50 percent reduction in the amount of the subordinated loans. In addition, the BOJ ultimately wound up taking a loss of approximately ¥100 billion on the special loans that it extended to Yamaichi.

Although Yamaichi Securities did not propagate the financial crisis globally and was generally liquidated in an orderly manner, that did not serve to stop the financial crisis that was already in train. The fact that a major brokerage firm suffered large losses and closed its business, even though it continued operations meanwhile and avoided causing any turmoil from the sudden cancellations of transactions, inevitably caused a major shock to the system.

As already noted, news of Yamaichi's bankruptcy further worsened the market conditions, which had already been hurt by the failure of Sanyo Securities, and that bankruptcy was followed two days later by the failure of a regional bank. Depositors were queued for a bank run in eight different locations nationwide, and the major banks also saw a record-high outflow of deposits. Both bank and brokerage firm stocks dropped sharply, the supply of funds to money markets shrank, and short-term yields rose despite BOJ's provision of substantial liquidity to the market. The premium demanded by overseas financial firms of Japanese banks (the "Japan premium") rose to 1.1 percentage points.

The regional bank did not fail because of its transactions with Yamaichi; it failed because market participants were reminded of the seriousness of the systemwide financial crisis that was already in progress, resulting in a substantial reduction in the overall amount of financial transactions.

The minister of finance and the governor of the BOJ held emergency meetings and announced that they would do everything in their power to maintain financial system stability, while the Securities and Exchange Surveillance Commission clamped down on speculators aiming to profit from market rumors. Those measures, which eased the turmoil, were followed by critical policy shifts aimed at further stabilizing the financial system. One was the injection of public funds into financial firms. In the November 1997 financial crisis, no public funds were used because of lingering regret over the resolution of the *jusen,* and special loans from the BOJ carried most of the weight. Nevertheless, both the International Monetary Fund and the United States were strongly in favor of the use of public funds. Because the Asian monetary crisis was still going on, there was concern that letting the situation in Japan continue as it was would trigger a global depression. That led to the drafting of legislation authorizing the injection of public funds at the end of 1997. In addition, the Ministry of Finance announced that it would provide guarantees for the full amount of deposits and bank debentures, including those not covered by deposit insurance, until March 2001. Macroeconomic policies were also mobilized, with Prime Minister Hashimoto altering course on his fiscal reforms and announcing a major tax cut.

However, even those measures were not enough to get the financial crisis under control.

Temporary Nationalization of Insolvent Banks

In March 1998, twenty-one major banks were given capital injections of public funds totaling ¥1.8 trillion ($13.4 billion), and the market was temporarily stabilized. That amount was spread throughout the banks, however, and the total capital injection was insufficient relative to the amount of the banks' nonperforming loans, primarily because the banks were hesitant to apply for public funds. In addition, the injected capital was primarily tier 2 capital (subordinated bonds and loans), and therefore had insufficient loss-absorbing capacity.

Although prompt corrective action was implemented in April 1998, concerns over the stability of the financial system in Japan were widespread from November 1997. Believing that publicizing unfavorable facts would make things more difficult for the financial sector, regulators became less inclined to assess and disclose business conditions at individual financial firms. Financial firms were also pressed to maintain their capital ratios, but because conditions made it difficult to increase capital, they tended to refrain from making loans. That created concerns that the overall economy would suffer a credit crunch.

Because it was discovered that the affiliated nonbanks had large amounts of NPLs, in mid-1998 the market started targeting a major bank, the Long-Term Credit Bank of Japan (LTCB), as a problem bank that had not received a sufficient capital injection. Once again, Japan's financial system was destabilized. The LTCB and the government tried to arrange a merger with Sumitomo Trust and Banking (STB), but negotiations broke down when STB indicated concern over LTCB's nonperforming loans, making it evident that there was no longer a private sector solution.

The summer to fall of 1998 was also a period of political instability. The ruling party lost the upper house in July 1998, and that change was followed by a change in prime minister, from Ryutaro Hashimoto to Keizo Obuchi. The now-energized opposition party advocated a hard landing through the resolution of the bankruptcies of troubled financial firms. In contrast, the ruling party emphasized the need to respond prior to the point of bankruptcy.

In October 1998, two temporary laws were passed permitting emergency measures to stabilize the financial system: the Financial Revitalization Act, which incorporated the opposition party's proposals nearly word for word and in principle called for the "special public administration" (temporary nationalization) of insolvent banks, and the Early Strengthening Act, which reflected the ruling party's proposal and called for injecting public capital into solvent banks.

An additional provision in the Financial Revitalization Act, however, allowed for the nationalization of a bank that was not yet insolvent but whose failure was at risk of causing serious harm to the financial function through a chain reaction of failures and of having a grave impact on international financial markets. It was under that provision that LTCB was resolved. As we see later, however, LTCB was treated as insolvent.

An approach that emphasizes the resolution of problem financial firms is referred to as the RTC approach, referencing the approach used by the Resolution Trust Corporation, which was established in 1989 to resolve the bankruptcies of U.S. savings and loan companies. Another approach that emphasizes measures, including capital injections, that are more oriented toward preventing bankruptcy rather than resolving bankruptcy is referred to as the RFC approach, referencing the approach used by the Reconstruction Finance Corporation,[18] which was established to rescue banks during the Great Depression in the 1930s. The former, the so-called hard landing approach, is nevertheless designed not to be triggered by an event of default in order not to destabilize the financial system.

In the case of the LTCB, an inspection by the Financial Supervisory Agency— the predecessor of the Financial Services Agency (FSA), which took over supervisory authority from the Ministry of Finance—found that the bank's liabilities exceeded its assets by ¥2.6 trillion. On passage of the Financial Revitalization Act, on October 23, 1998, it invoked the act and announced that authorities would begin bankruptcy resolution by temporarily nationalizing the bank. Because the LTCB was insolvent, the government wiped out shareholders by taking over the common shares at a value of ¥0 while protecting subordinated and other credit claims. The resolution was structured so that the remaining losses would be covered by the Deposit Insurance Corporation of Japan (DICJ).

One reason why the temporary nationalization approach was used is that the LTCB, with total assets of ¥26 trillion ($223 billion), was too big. It also had outstanding derivative positions totaling ¥50 trillion ($430 billion) on a notional

18. More precisely, the Emergency Banking Act passed in March 1933 authorizes the RFC to purchase the capital stock of banks, railways, and other institutions.

principal basis. The counterparties to its derivative portfolio, consisting primarily of interest rate swaps and currency swaps, were major financial firms both in and outside Japan, and there was concern that LTCB's failure would have a great impact on domestic and overseas markets. If the initiation of temporary nationalization under the Financial Revitalization Act were deemed an event of default under the International Swaps and Derivatives Association (ISDA) master agreement, counterparties would initiate closeout clauses, create turmoil in financial markets, and make an orderly resolution difficult. Consequently, the authorities were very careful in confirming whether temporary nationalization constituted an ISDA event of default prior to nationalizing LTCB.[19]

The Nippon Credit Bank (NCB), another large bank, like the LTCB, had trouble obtaining funding because of a credit downgrade, and that prompted the Ministry of Finance to lead a consortium of private sector financial firms to infuse capital into the bank in 1997. Nevertheless, the Financial Supervisory Agency conducted an inspection, found that NCB's liabilities exceeded its assets by ¥3 trillion, and announced on December 13, 1998, that it would temporarily nationalize the bank. NCB's shares were also forcefully taken at a value of ¥0, completely wiping out shareholders.

Both LTCB and NCB, after having the problem assets on their balance sheets disposed of while they were temporarily nationalized, were sold to the private sector and stayed in business. LTCB became Shinsei Bank in March 2000, and NCB became Aozora Bank in September 2000.

Blanket Capital Infusion into Multiple Solvent Banks

In the fall of 1998, solvent major banks were recipients of open bank assistance. As already noted, insolvent banks like LTCB and NCB were resolved under the Financial Revitalization Act, while solvent banks were given capital injections under the Early Strengthening Act. The Financial Reconstruction Commission (FRC) announced the following policy guidelines.

—Financial firms are asked to ensure the soundness and reliability of their financial positions through rigorous assessment of asset quality and reserve provisions at the financial firms and through timely and appropriate disclosures. They will also be required to carry out appropriate write-offs and provisioning so as to complete bad debt cleanup as quickly as possible.

19. Nakaso (2001) says that the translation of the Japanese term used in the Financial Reconstruction Act is "special public administration," but because that term was listed as an event of default in the ISDA master agreement, the term "temporary nationalization" was used, with the understanding of the ISDA.

—Financial firms are encouraged to seek capital injections of sufficient size, so that they can proceed with the disposal of bad debts, provide smooth flows of credit, and cope with risks that may be encountered in the future.

—Financial firms that fail to make efforts to rebuild their business, rationalize their management, and realign their institutions will not be provided with capital injections, while those that do endeavor to undertake such efforts will be given priority in terms of the size and terms of capital injections. That will improve the competitiveness and profitability of individual financial firms so that the government will be able to recover invested funds by selling preferred shares and other capital instruments in the markets.

—Failed institutions, those which are judged to be unable to achieve sound management, will not be allowed to continue to exist in the market.

On receiving applications for capital injections from various banks, the FRC made an assessment based on the results of an inspection of the banks by the Financial Supervisory Agency (and an examination by the BOJ), and in March 1999 it injected capital totaling ¥7.5 trillion ($62.5 billion)—of which ¥6.2 trillion ($51.6 billion) was tier 1 capital—into fifteen major banks that it deemed to be solvent. Heeding the lessons learned from the capital injection of the year before, the agency saw that injection of capital was composed primarily of tier 1 preferred stock, which has a relatively high loss-absorption capacity.

When a systemwide financial crisis occurs, it is not enough to focus the policy response only on individual banks' solvency problems; what is needed is a policy response for the financial system as a whole. During the latest financial crisis, the U.S. government used the Troubled Asset Relief Program (TARP) to inject public capital into nineteen bank holding companies to keep the financial system from destabilizing following the failure of Lehman Brothers. Likewise, because Japan's financial crisis of 1997–98 was a systemwide crisis, capital was injected into a large number of banks in order to stabilize Japan's financial system.

Special Inspections and Use of the Systemic Risk Exception for Major Solvent Banks

The Deposit Insurance Act was revised in 2000 on the basis of lessons learned during the 1997–98 financial crisis, and both temporary nationalization and capital injections using public funds, which until then were temporary extraordinary measures, were introduced as permanent exceptional measures. Specifically, under the Deposit Insurance Act, insured deposit holders of a failed bank were protected, while shareholders, creditors, and uninsured deposit holders were required to bear losses under deposit payoffs and purchase and assumption (P&A) transactions. When no successor is found, the DICJ establishes a bridge bank as the bank special resolution regime.[20]

Under Article 102 of the Deposit Insurance Act, when there is deemed to be a risk of an extremely serious obstacle to maintaining the stability of the financial system, the Council for Financial Crises Response—chaired by the prime minister and including the minister for financial services, the minister of finance, and the BOJ governor—may grant a systemic risk exception, allowing solvent banks to be rescued with capital injections and insolvent banks to be temporarily nationalized. The 2000 revisions to the Deposit Insurance Act allowed for an additional levy to be collected from financial firms, separate and apart from the deposit insurance premium, to avoid burdening taxpayers in the event of a public capital injection or temporary nationalization in response to a financial crisis.

Japan's financial system became unstable again when it was hit by the collapse of the dotcom bubble before the NPL disposition process had been completed. The Koizumi administration, which entered office in April 2001, aimed for aggressive structural reform of the economy, and speeding up the disposition of NPLs was high on its agenda. This hard-landing approach became especially evident in September 2002, when Heizo Takenaka took over as minister for financial services. Specifically, in October 2002 the government, attempting to implement a radical solution to the NPL problem in order to restore confidence in Japan's financial system and financial administration, announced the Financial Revival Program, which set a target of a 50 percent reduction in the NPL ratios of the major banks over a two-year period. Under the program, the FSA conducted special inspections focused on examining credit risk, requiring the major banks to rapidly complete their disposal of bad loans. That led to widening concerns in the market that the major banks would be resolved based on the RTC approach, and bank shares led the stock market lower.

It was within this context that the capital ratio of one of the major banks subject to the FSA's special inspection, Resona Holdings (formerly Daiwa Bank and Asahi Bank), fell below the regulatory minimum, reflecting the cost of disposing of NPLs discovered in the inspection.[21] The government responded by conven-

---

20. In Japan, the Deposit Insurance Corporation of Japan, which operates the deposit insurance program, is the resolution authority for the banking sector.

21. It was learned that Resona Bank's capital ratio at the end of March 2003 had dropped to approximately 2 percent, below the minimum 4 percent required for domestic banks.

ing a meeting of the Council for Financial Crises Response on May 17, 2003, which decided to inject approximately ¥2 trillion ($16.8 billion) of capital into Resona with a combination of common shares and preferred shares.[22] Because the council deemed Resona solvent, in order to maintain financial system stability it decided to invoke the systemic risk exception under the Deposit Insurance Act, allowing for a capital injection using public funds without wiping out shareholders.

In explaining its decision to apply the systemic risk exception, the Council for Financial Crises Response declared "currently, we do not perceive the bank is experiencing an exodus of deposits or difficulty in getting market funding, but we recognize that if it is put in such a situation, there is a risk of an extremely serious obstacle to maintaining the stability of the financial system, as per the Deposit Insurance Act." In other words, it made the decision to apply the exceptional measure of a capital injection in order to prevent a financial crisis that had yet to occur. To prevent the moral hazard created by using public funds to support solvency under the Deposit Insurance Act, the recipient institution is required to streamline its business and clarify the responsibility of both management and shareholders; Resona was also required to bring in new management and to formulate and execute a business improvement plan.

The rescue of Resona with a public capital injection led to an exit from the system instability that began in the 1990s and to the eventual restoration of stability. We view that as evidence that when a financial system becomes unstable, establishing mechanisms to support the solvency, without wiping out shareholders, of at least those financial firms that are deemed solvent—the approach that the G-7 recommended to Japan in 1998—is an effective way to stabilize the financial system.

With a roughly ¥2 trillion public recapitalization backstop, Resona brought in a new management team, put its assets through a strict due diligence process, and after receiving a ¥2 trillion tier 1 capital injection, quickly disposed of ¥1.3 trillion of nonperforming loans. That enabled Resona to restore its business to health. Its business improvement plan also contributed to recovering sound management. The plan included not paying the retirement benefits of retiring senior management officers; cutting executive compensation by 40 percent; cutting employees' annual income by 30 percent; cutting the workforce from 20,000 to 16,000 employees; and paying no dividend on common shares.

---

22. Capital was strengthened with approximately ¥300 billion in common shares and approximately ¥1.6 trillion in preferred shares. The amount of new common shares was kept small to avoid exceeding the limits set in the delisting criteria.

As of March 2011, the government had recovered ¥1.2 trillion of the ¥2 trillion in public funds that it invested in Resona. With the remaining ¥700 billion currently generating valuation gains, the expectation is that the taxpayers will not be left with any bills to pay.

Managing Systemwide Financial Crises

The situation in Europe suggests that the systemwide financial crisis is still in train. Although a resolution regime for financial institutions predicated on no bailouts has been in the works at the global level, in several instances the recapitalization of financial institutions using public funds has become unavoidable. The new resolution frameworks are an important step forward, but the risk that they cannot cope with a systemwide crisis must be acknowledged.

Will the Next Time Be Different?

Summarized below are the lessons learned from the systemwide financial crises experienced by Japan, specifically the ongoing instability of the financial system brought about by large realized and unrealized losses spread widely throughout the financial sector and triggered by the bursting of Japan's economic bubble and other macroeconomic factors.

—Because market participants across the board suffered serious losses in an atmosphere of strongly rooted mutual distrust between counterparties, the possibility existed that even an ostensibly small catalyst could lead to the freezing up of the overall market and a succession of financial firm failures.

—Under those conditions, the adverse impact on the overall system from the insolvency of a single financial firm is greater than it would be if there were no systemwide financial crisis, and a solvent financial firm could become insolvent. That could lead to a vicious cycle in which a contraction of credit weakens the macro economy and amplifies the losses on financial firms' balance sheets.

—It is not just bank failures that exert negative shocks on the market but also the distress of a wide range of market participants, including nonbanks.

—In a systemwide financial crisis, a large number of players suffer losses, harbor substantial uncertainty over the future, and become risk averse, making it difficult to find a private sector player willing to acquire an ailing institution for purely economic reasons.

—Within such an environment, to prevent a bankruptcy crisis from spreading to a wide range of participants, including global counterparties, it is to some extent effective to rescue some creditors and provide temporary funding in the process of resolving insolvent financial firms (including nonbanks). Not only that, it is also important to leave open the possibility of preventative public capital injections and the provision of liquidity from the central bank for those solvent financial firms that may be at risk of becoming insolvent if conditions fail to improve.

—There is a need to conduct rigorous inspections or stress tests of a wide range of market participants and then gauge their degree of solvency in order to decide on and implement either a rescue or a smooth bankruptcy resolution. Confirming the soundness of participants using such inspections or tests reduces to some extent the mutual distrust among market participants and is essential if the market is to function properly.

—Nevertheless, although such rescue measures are necessary to ease the shock, a systemwide financial crisis is not a problem of losses on the balance sheet of individual financial firms; it is a problem of losses on balance sheets in aggregate. Accordingly, the crisis will not completely end until there is progress in reducing the debt overhang of the corporate, household, and public sectors, as well as the amount of nonperforming loans at financial firms. Every time some event causes an economic contraction or deterioration in market sentiment during the interim, there is a possibility that yet another financial firm will fail. Although Japan's bubble burst in 1990, it did not have a financial crisis until the mid-1990s, and its major financial crises were in 1997, 1998, and 2003 (figure 2-1).

—A sense of urgency in introducing measures to restore soundness to government finances or the banking sector puts additional stress on the market and on financial firms and can actually make a crisis worse.

We framed the lessons above as lessons learned from Japan, but it goes without saying that they apply to other systemwide financial crises that have occurred, including the Great Contraction of the 1930s and the Great Recession (or Second Great Contraction) that began in 2007 (figure 2-2 and table 2-1). In the latter crisis, the percentage increase in share prices leading up to the peak of the bubble was not as large as it was in the late 1920s or in late 1980s Japan, nor was the subsequent decline as great, in part because governments were relatively quicker to apply fiscal and monetary stimulus and to inject public funds. As evident from the ongoing turmoil in Europe, however, the crises are similar in that they have lasted for a prolonged period. Another similarity is that the priority has been on restoring fiscal soundness, normalizing monetary policy, and introducing measures to bring banks back to health.

As shown in table 2-2, measures to deal with systemwide financial crises thus far have included deposit insurance, debt guarantees, public fund injections, the acquisition of and loss sharing in nonperforming loans, temporary nationalization whereby creditors are protected, and emergency lending from the central bank. Under Dodd-Frank, a number of these policy tools will be curtailed in

Figure 2-1. *Japan's Systemwide Financial Crisis*[a]

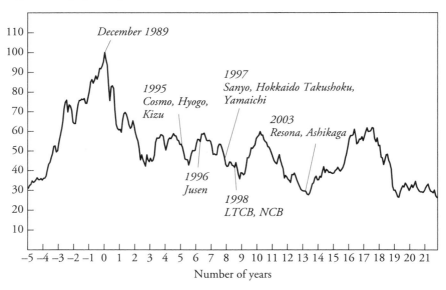

Sources: Tokyo Stock Exchange; Nomura Institute of Capital Markets Research.

a. Japan's Stock Index (TOPIX) for the years during and after the bubble period. The vertical axis shows the movement of TOPIX before and after the bubble burst (December 1989 = 100); the horizontal axis shows the number of years before and after the bubble burst (December 1989 = 0). Boxes show names of failed financial institutions and the year they failed.

Figure 2-2. *Great Depression and Great Recession*

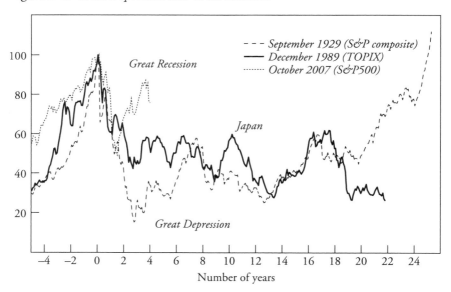

Source: Tokyo Stock Exchange (www.econ.yale.edu/~shiller/data.htm).

Table 2-1. *Cases of Systemwide Financial Crises*[a]

Period of crisis	1930s	1990s and early 2000s (Japan)	2007 to present
Stock index	S&P composite	TOPIX	S&P 500
Peak	31.30 (September 1929)	2859.57 (December 1989)	1539.66 (October 2007)
Five years to the peak	+238.4 percent	+221.7 percent	+80.2 percent
Bottom (the first)	4.77 (June 1932)	1023.68 (October 1998)	757.13 (March 2009)
Peak to the first bottom	−84.8 percent	−64.2 percent	−50.8 percent
New peak	September 1954	Not yet reached.	Not yet reached.
Prolonged periods of crisis	1930–1932: bank runs in several U.S. states; Credit–Anstalt Bank in Austria failed. February–March 1933: nationwide bank runs in the United States	1995, 1996: several bank runs; *jusen* problems emerged. 1997: Sanyo; Hokkaido-Takushoku; Yamaichi. 1998: Long-Term Credit Bank; Nippon Credit Bank. 2003: Resona; Ashikaga.	2007: Paribas shock; Northern Rock; SIVs. 2008: Bear Stearns; GSEs; Lehman; AIG. 2010, 2011: PIIGS and European banks.
Implementation of restrictive fiscal and monetary policies	Tight monetary policy continued after the crash of 1929. The Fed raised interest rate in 1931. Balanced budget principles were observed in the early 1930s and 1937.	Increase in consumption tax and medical costs. Introduction of the Sound Budget law in 1996. Bank of Japan terminated zero interest policy in August 2000.	ECB raised interest rates in July 2008, April 2011, and July 2011. Fiscal austerity policy is widely supported in the United States and Europe.

Source: Authors' compilation.

a. SIVs = special investment vehicles; GSEs = government-sponsored entities; PIIGS = Portugal, Ireland, Italy, Greece, and Spain; ECB = European Central Bank.

Table 2-2. *Will the Next Time Be Different?*[a]

Measure	1930s (United States)	1990s (Japan)	2007–09 (United States)	Under the Dodd-Frank Act
Deposit insurance	Federal Deposit Insurance Corporation created	Expanded	Expanded	Expanded
Obligation guarantee	None	Temporarily introduced (permanent guarantee of payment and settlement account)	Temporarily introduced	Limited to a program for solvent banks and bank holding companies
Capital injection	Started in March 1933	Implemented in 1996; restarted in March 1998	Started in October 2008	Prohibited
Purchase of bad assets and loss sharing	None	October 1998 – March 2005	PPIP in 2009	Permitted only for orderly resolution
Temporary nationalization (with protection of creditors)	None	October 1998: Long-Term Credit Bank December 1998: Nippon Credit Bank November 2003: Ashikaga	Fannie Mae, Freddie Mac	Prohibited
Emergency funding by the central bank	Introduced	Twenty-two cases implemented since 1995	TSLF; PDCF; AMLF; CPFF; MMIFF; TALF; Maiden Lane I–III	Limited to a facility for solvent borrowers

Source: Authors' compilation.
a. AMLF = Asset-Backed Commercial Paper Money Market Mutual Fund Liquidity Facility; CPFF = Commercial Paper Funding Facility; MMIFF = Money Market Investor Funding Facility; PDCF = Primary Dealer Credit Facility; PPIP = Public-Private Investment Program; TALF = Term Asset-Backed Securities Loan Facility; TSLF = Term Securities Lending Facility.

the next crisis—or even in the current crisis, which has yet to end. Public fund injections in particular are being prohibited, but how is that supposed to prove adequate moving forward?

Reinhart and Rogoff (2009) argues that a banking crisis is but one aspect of a financial crisis and that it can be related to a number of others, including a fiscal crisis (the default of domestically issued government bonds and sovereign bonds), a currency crisis, and hyperinflation. The authors note, for example, that one economic impact from a banking crisis is a dramatic expansion of public debt. On average, large banking crises during the post–World War II period have resulted in an 86 percent increase in the real stock of public debt. Consequently, a banking crisis becomes a public debt crisis, which in turn can lead to a currency crisis and hyperinflation. It is also important to consider whether attempts to minimize the impact of a banking crisis may risk exacerbating the other types of crises.

Conversely, in the Great Depression, the expansion of public debt was minor relative to the other crises because the government hesitated to use fiscal stimulus out of fear of a fiscal crisis; it thereby wound up prolonging and deepening the banking crisis.

Three Cautionary Notes Regarding the Current Systemwide Financial Crisis

The implementation of macroprudential supervision, the strengthening of microprudential regulations, and the implementation of measures improving resolvability are expected to reduce the probability of a systemwide financial crisis occurring in the future. We note three areas of caution in this regard, however. The first is that it is important not to forget that the current crisis is still ongoing. Particularly in the European Union, some countries, having experienced a banking crisis, are now also experiencing a sovereign crisis. Because the banks hold a large amount of sovereign bonds, that in turn is reigniting the banking crisis.

In July 2011, in order to deal with the rising stress on EU markets from concern over the Greek economy, European nations agreed to strengthen both the EFSF (European Financial Stability Facility) and the entity slated to be established in 2013 to make it permanent, the ESM (European Stability Mechanism). One of the changes is to allow the recapitalization of financial firms to be financed with loans to governments.

Such a public support scheme for banks goes against the grain of the FSB proposal as well as the proposed framework for the resolution of European financial firms finalized around the same time, and it also differs from Dodd-Frank. It could be interpreted as evidence that the EU, like Japan, recognized the need to institutionalize the bailout of financial firms.

Another event showing that the current crisis was not yet over and that the injection of public funds was essential to dealing with the crisis was the speech by IMF President Christine Lagarde at Jackson Hole, Wyoming, in August 2011, in which she emphasized the need to compel European banks to increase their capital and argued that public funds should be used if necessary.[23]

U.S. Treasury Secretary Tim Geithner said that "countries that forced more capital into their banking system early in the crisis are better placed to support the recovery. Those that did not should move more forcefully now."[24] Although he did not say that public funds should be used early on, that is probably the only means of providing public support to a private sector financial firm that is having trouble on its own.

A second note of caution is that, as happened in Japan, there is a risk that pushing financial firms to reduce their exposure to risk through soundness regulations and recovery and resolution plans can harm macro-prudence and prolong the exit from a crisis.[25] The experience in the 1930s and in Japan suggests that tightening fiscal policy can exacerbate the crisis.

Third, even if there is a reduced probability of financial firm failure or of the need to invoke too big to fail treatment in the event of a failure, as long as the probability is above zero there is a need to prepare for its occurrence. That suggests the need to design a system that can cope in the context of the lessons noted above. That is because we have already learned, both from Japan's financial crises and from the latest global financial crisis, that designing measures after a crisis has already erupted runs the risk of allowing the crisis to accelerate, given the difficulty in forging an agreement on legislation and the time it takes to do so.[26]

The Big Picture and Systemwide Inspections

It is important to have a big picture of the crisis at an early stage in order to distinguish between financial firms in serious trouble and those that are relatively sound. That makes it possible to intervene quickly with the former to ensure that the latter are not also subsumed in crisis and forced to initiate the resolution process. One way to get a big picture of the crisis is to conduct systemwide inspections or stress tests.

---

23. Lagarde (2011).

24. Geithner (2011).

25. Haldane (2011) was also concerned about the regulation's impact on macro-prudence.

26. Laeven and Valencia (2010) found that for the forty-two financial crises that occurred from 1970 until 2007, the first priority was on providing liquidity support and recapitalization, on average, took about 12 months because of the need for a political consensus and new legislation.

Sufficiently credible inspections or stress tests make clear which financial firms have problems, and once it is understood that financial firms with major problems are not simply forced into liquidation, the mutual lack of trust in the market can be eliminated and market transactions resumed. That should also stop the panic selling of financial firm stocks by shareholders and reduce the level of speculative short positions.

Whether to use inspections or stress tests and their specific content will vary depending on the environment and the factors that are the most likely to create uncertainty in the market. In Japan's financial crisis, the lack of consistency in how each bank assessed its nonperforming loans was a source of uncertainty, and thus rigorous inspections were conducted using uniform measures. During the recent financial crisis in the United States, there was concern over the impact on bank balance sheets from the decline in housing prices; hence, macro-level stress tests were effective.

From February until May 2009 in the United States, the Supervisory Capital Assessment Program (SCAP) was conducted on nineteen major financial firms, and that sparked a turnaround in the market. The systemization of a SCAP-type stress test under section 165(i) of Dodd-Frank represents important progress. There will be stress tests by the Federal Reserve Board and by the financial firms themselves; the former are conducted annually by the Fed—in coordination with the three appropriate primary financial regulatory agencies and the Federal Insurance Office—on nonbank financial companies supervised by the Fed and bank holding companies with consolidated assets totaling at least $50 billion (referred to as systemically important financial institutions below).

The financial firm stress tests are conducted every six months for SIFIs and once a year for all other financial companies that have total consolidated assets of more than $10 billion and are regulated by a primary federal financial regulatory agency. The tests require a report to the Fed and the primary federal financial regulatory agency. The administrators stipulate the methods, scenarios, and formulas to be used in the stress tests conducted by the financial firms. Summary results of the stress tests are published.

Backstops and Measures to Ensure Soundness of Financial Firms

Once the market is sufficiently sure that a financial crisis exists, policies must be crafted outlining how to deal with financial firms that have serious problems. Although those policies may be in agreement with the recovery and resolution plan, if many financial firms simultaneously implement an RRP, a decline in asset prices or other turmoil may occur. In some cases, the direct purchase of specific assets may be necessary. Furthermore, the recapitalization of financial firms with major problems may require the injection of public capital.

Conversely, blindly injecting public capital into firms without having the big picture of the crisis is not going to prevent the market from becoming spooked. During the latest crisis, there was an injection of funds through TARP in late 2008 and Citigroup was also provided with open bank assistance, but share prices continued to fall until early March 2009. It was not until stress tests were performed and it became clear that public funds would be used when necessary that the market stopped declining, and it was only after the results of the stress tests were announced in May 2009 that the market really began to climb.

In the United States, it is expected that the probability of a deepening crisis at a large number of financial firms is now less than before because stress tests will be conducted periodically. The problem, however, is that even if stress tests show that numerous financial firms have serious capital shortfalls, Dodd-Frank does not allow for capital injections.

William Dudley, president and CEO of the Federal Reserve Bank of New York, commented that one implication of SCAP in the United States is that there needs to be a credible capital backstop so that market participants can be sure that one way or another, banks will be able to raise the capital that they need in a stress environment.[27]

The European Central Bank, commenting on the European Commission's public consultation on the technical details of a possible EU framework for bank recovery and resolutions, noted that "in situations of market uncertainty, stress test results could be made public, provided that adequate backstop is granted, with the view to restoring market confidence."[28] Prior to the release of the 2011 EU stress test results, the Council of the European Union issued a statement on a backstop mechanism: "The Council confirmed that necessary remedial actions following results of the test will be taken. These measures privilege private sector solutions but also include a solid framework for the provision of government support in case of need, in line with state aid rules."[29] Thus, officials in both the United States and Europe acknowledge the need to backstop the stress tests and want to see the systemization of measures to respond to a systemwide crisis.

A backstop should probably include many of the different measures used following the Lehman collapse, including, in addition to direct asset purchases and

27. Dudley (2011).
28. European Central Bank, "European Commission's Public Consultation on the Technical Details of a Possible EU Framework for Bank Recovery and Resolution: ECB Contribution," May 2011.
29. Council of the European Union, "Council Statement on Backstop Mechanisms," July 12, 2011.

capital injections, emergency liquidity provision by the central bank and a comprehensive debt guarantee program.

In the United States, Dodd-Frank allows for emergency liquidity programs from the Fed and emergency guarantee programs from the FDIC. All of the programs are meant to provide liquidity support to solvent institutions, but as noted earlier, a liquidity shortfall is caused by market participants deciding not to provide funding out of concern over the future solvency of a counterparty. Consequently, it would probably be effective to provide in parallel some open bank assistance, like the preventative capital injections made in Japan.

The counterarguments to providing such a safety net, particularly the public capital injections, is that doing so is authorized only when there is deemed to be a systemwide financial crisis. That reduces the probability of a rescue and makes it harder to expect one ex ante, although it would alleviate financial problems. The fact that it is possible to place the final burden on the financial firm ex post should be effective in moderating that criticism. Needless to say, imposing a strict business improvement plan for bailed-out banks, as for Resona, is indispensable to reduce the moral hazard problem.

We have argued, on the basis of Japan's experience, that there will be circumstances when the difficulty of achieving orderly resolution under Dodd-Frank makes the use of public funds unavoidable in systemwide financial crises such as those seen in the past, but we also want to emphasize that it may not be appropriate to view bank bailouts using public funds as an intrinsically bad option that should be avoided whenever possible. Keister noted in his theoretical analysis (Keister 2010) that the anticipation of a bailout can have positive ex-ante effects while committing to a no-bailouts policy can actually create fragility in the financial system.

We have already noted the observation in Reinhart and Rogoff (2009) that one impact of a bank crisis on an economy is a dramatic increase in public debt, but the authors also noted that declines in taxes paid as a result of the economic contraction caused by the crisis have been greater than the increase in tax payments required to pay for the bank bailout. That suggests that the focus should not be on whether to use taxpayers' money to bail out a bank but on how to minimize the total burden on taxpayers, both present and future, resulting from the financial crisis. Avoiding the use of public money to purchase bank equity will wind up worsening the crisis and increasing the overall burden on taxpayers.

The lack of an injection of public funds can exacerbate the impact of a crisis through various channels; one will be through damage to a bank's lending function. As pointed out in Bernanke (1983), when a given bank fails, it becomes difficult for smaller firms that obtained loans from that bank through geographical and personal connections to find an alternative source of funding. For example, it took an especially long time for lending to smaller firms to recover following the series of bank failures in the 1930s.

We do not think it is realistic at the outset to completely prohibit the use of public funds, including when limited use is deemed to be effective and essential. An underlying principle of public policy is to look at both costs and benefits, and it is important to have a mechanism that makes use of specialized knowledge of current circumstances when deciding whether the benefits are sufficiently large. We doubt whether there is any form of economic activity today that receives absolutely no support from taxes, and we do not think it is wise to rigidly rule out from the outset the use of tax revenues in a particular industry.

A no-bail-out policy would make it impossible to meet the goal of establishing a cross-border resolution regime, as noted before. Accordingly, we think it may be necessary, at least for the time being, to proactively support on a global basis the concept of countries using a variety of tools to contain a crisis once it erupts in order to minimize cross-border contagion.

Regional and Global Backstops

Nevertheless, the size of the backstop thought to be necessary on the basis of the results of a systemwide stress test may exceed the affected country's resources. A mechanism for providing backstops at both the regional and the global levels is probably needed to keep a banking crisis from turning into a sovereign crisis.

Immediately after the Lehman failure, on the basis of Japan's proposal to the World Bank, the International Finance Corporation, together with the Japan Bank for International Cooperation (JBIC), established funds to recapitalize major local banks in small and medium-size developing countries by providing equity capital or subordinated loans to them to strengthen their capital bases, thereby helping to stabilize their countries' financial systems.[30] Banks do not have to be in trouble to receive capital. The main objective is to provide capital to banks so that they can continue to lend to businesses and individuals who otherwise would not have that money. The World Bank's website notes that "bank recapitalization is a key element in the World Bank Group's response to the global financial crisis."

The introduction of a mechanism to recapitalize banks through the EFSF as a response to the crisis now unfolding in Europe is evidence that a multilateral bank recapitalization facility is also needed for developed economies. In fact,

---

30. IFC Recapitalization (Equity) Fund and IFC Recapitalization (Subordinated Debt) Fund.

there may be a greater need in the developed economies, where major global financial firms do most of their business.

Accordingly, it is conceivable that an international bank recapitalization facility could be established as a final backstop to supplement the facilities in each country and regional facilities such as the EFSF. To deal with the additional moral hazard that results, qualifying for the use of the international recapitalization fund during a crisis could require that the country and the bank in question to adhere strictly to an FSB recommendation or to rules established by the Basel Committee or some other international standard-setting organization. In addition, at the time of recapitalization the FSB could establish conditions that the country and banks would have to meet. That would make it possible to minimize instances worldwide of a country's financial regulators or individual banks inappropriately limiting or attempting to avoid the rules set by the FSB or other international standard-setting organizations.

Economic Costs of a Nonbank's Failure

Nonbanks should not be excluded when decisions are made regarding the use of public funds as a backstop. We already noted that a bank failure has a major impact on the recovery of lending, particularly to smaller firms, but the failure of a nonbank could also have a serious negative impact on the real economy through several different channels. That has already been proven by the failure of Lehman Brothers, and below we consider further evidence of such an impact.

To start, the failure of a nonbank can create turmoil in money markets, possibly blocking short-term borrowing by corporations, commercial paper (CP) issuance, and trade credits. In the case of Lehman Brothers, the default of CP issued by Lehman caused money market funds to break the buck, suffer an exodus of funds, and sharply reduce their CP investments. As explained, the default by Sanyo Securities in the interbank and repo markets wound up triggering a subsequent financial crisis in Japan.

When the nonbank is a major investment bank, there is less of a risk that its failure will lead directly to a reduction in corporate lending than there is with a bank failure. However, turmoil can spread well beyond that in the money markets described above, including into securities markets and derivatives markets, and make it difficult for corporations to get medium-term to long-term funding through the markets. In that case, corporations that traditionally relied on markets, many of them large blue-chip companies, would shift their borrowing to banks. Although the banks would loan to large blue-chip companies, because banks also face funding uncertainty, their lending would wind up crowding out smaller firms from the bank loan market, creating the risk of negative impacts similar to those from a bank failure. When a nonbank specializing in lending to smaller firms fails, it could have a more direct impact on smaller firms' ability to get funding.

Shadow Banks and Central Bank Liquidity

We think it appropriate that Dodd-Frank's new rules on soundness and orderly resolution also cover nonbanks, given that in a systemwide financial crisis, financial firms other than banks also can trigger a deepening of the crisis. The problem, however, is that public capital injections are ruled out for both banks and nonbanks. Another problem is that nonbanks have considerably less favorable access to liquidity than do banks.

In a systemwide financial crisis, it is possible for a large number of financial firms, including nonbanks, to suddenly (virtually overnight) find it difficult to get short-term funding. Banks can potentially receive assistance from the Fed, but nonbanks must wait for the Fed to establish a liquidity program. As noted above, however, only solvent institutions are eligible for such programs.

Given how important it was for the Fed to supply liquidity to nonbanks during this latest financial crisis, the substantial curtailment of this source of liquidity resulting from the revision of section 13(3) of the Federal Reserve Act is a concern. When on March 14, 2008, the Fed announced that JPMorgan would merge with and thereby rescue Bear Stearns, which was in liquidity-induced bankruptcy, it also announced the introduction of the Primary Dealer Credit Facility (PDCF) pursuant to section 13(3).[31]

Another important difference in the treatment of banks and nonbanks in the United States during times of severe economic distress is that, in addition to deposit insurance, the FDIC provides its debt guarantee program to solvent insured depository institutions or solvent depository institution holding companies (including any affiliates thereof). Although that could be viewed as a social contract–based privilege given to banks that take deposits and offer settlement services, the fact that shadow banks play a larger role in financial intermediation than they used to also needs to be considered.

When short-term markets were under extreme stress following the Lehman failure, not only was there growth in the level of funding to nonbanks from the PDCF, the Term Securities Lending Facility (TSLF), and single-tranche market operations, Goldman Sachs and Morgan Stanley also converted to bank holding

---

31. Prior to implementation of the PDCF, the Fed offered primary dealers twenty-eight-day loans of Treasury securities under its Term Securities Lending Facility.

companies in September 2008, enabling them to borrow from the Fed's discount window, and they also used the Temporary Liquidity Guarantee Program (TLGP) introduced by the FDIC under the systemic risk exception and issued FDIC-guaranteed bonds in November 2008.[32]

The FDIC released a report arguing that Lehman could have been liquidated in an orderly manner under Dodd-Frank. It would be interesting, however, to see how Goldman Sachs and Morgan Stanley would have been dealt with if Dodd-Frank had been the law of the land at the time. Their use of section 13(3) loans would have been limited, and they would not have been able to use facilities like the TLGP because of their lack of affiliation with a bank. Maybe Title II would have been invoked, and, like Lehman, these two major investment banks and possibly Merrill Lynch as well would have undergone an orderly liquidation. Or again, as actually happened, these shadow banks may have received approval to convert into banking groups purely to obtain the privileges afforded only to banks and bank holding companies. The United States now regulates banks and Fed-supervised nonbanks more tightly, and provides a limited safety net only to banks and their affiliates. In certain respects the safety net for banks is stronger than it was; for example, the maximum coverage for deposit insurance has been permanently raised from $100,000 to $250,000.

Pozsar and others (2010) makes an important point, arguing that "given the still significant size of the shadow banking system and its inherent fragility due to exposure to runs by wholesale funding providers, it is imperative for policymakers to assess whether shadow banks should have access to official backstops permanently, or be regulated out of existence." If regulations are going to be tightened from a functional standpoint, it is probably worth considering providing shadow banks with a safety net commensurate with the social role that they perform.

Gordon and Muller (2010), noting that the resolution regime under Dodd-Frank responds only to idiosyncratic crises, proposed the creation of a Systemic Emergency Insurance Fund (SEIF) to provide a backstop in the event that the financial system cannot be stabilized under Dodd-Frank. The SEIF would also cover shadow banks. The authors argue that "with the growth of non-bank financial intermediaries in the shadow banking system, we need to broaden the FDIC concept" (Gordon and Muller 2010, p. 51). Ricks (2010) proposes a government insurance regime for all short-term liabilities of all maturity-transformation firms,

32. The first issue that TLGP was applied to was a $5 billion publicly subscribed bond issued by Goldman Sachs on November 25, 2008.

a functional approach that does not discriminate between banks and shadow banks.

In Japan, not only banks but also some brokerage firms (including foreign brokerage firms with operations in Japan) maintain accounts with the central bank and have access to the discount window. In addition, during the voluntary closure of Yamaichi Securities, the BOJ provided unsecured and nonguaranteed special loans while playing a critical role in achieving an orderly resolution.

Nonbanks in Japan can transact with the BOJ, and they also are subject to both off-site and on-site monitoring by the central bank. Monitoring provides an important complement to the FSA's oversight of banks and nonbanks. With its knowledge of activity in the BOJ current accounts of these banks and nonbanks, the BOJ is able to monitor systemwide liquidity positions and quickly provide the necessary liquidity through market operations and its complementary lending facility. Because this system was in place, Japan's financial markets never experienced a serious liquidity crisis during the Great Recession.[33] We think that it also should be possible to use such a supervisory approach at the global level, rather than depending excessively on mechanical liquidity rules driven by liquidity ratios.

What the New Financial Regulatory Framework Lacks

The financial regulatory framework has changed greatly as a result of the financial crisis. Thus far, efforts to strengthen regulations related to soundness, including Basel III and the SIFI surcharge, have dominated the conversation and seen the most reforms, but macroprudence and the introduction of an orderly resolution regime have not received the attention that they deserve. Paul Tucker, deputy governor for financial stability at the Bank of England, calls the last two measures the two revolutions in response to the financial crisis. In contrast, he refers to efforts to strengthen capital ratios and liquidity rules as nothing more than repairs of the existing regime.[34]

Figure 2-3 represents conditions ranging from normal on the left to an increasingly deeper financial crisis on the right and macro policies (above) and micro

33. BOJ, "Liquidity Risk Management in Financial Institutions Following the Global Financial Crisis," July 2, 2010 (www.boj.or.jp/en/announcements/release_2010/data/fss1007a.pdf); BOJ, "The Bank of Japan's Approach to Liquidity Risk Management in Financial Institutions," June 26, 2009 (www.boj.or.jp/en/announcements/release_2009/data/fss0906a.pdf).

34. "As you can see, the lessons of the crisis fall into two broad groups: Repairs and Revolutions. The changes in capital and liquidity regulation, however big, are essentially repairs. They improve on what was there before. There are revolutions on two fronts. Resolution regimes and macroprudential regimes" Tucker (2011, p. 6).

Figure 2-3. *Regulatory Framework*[a]

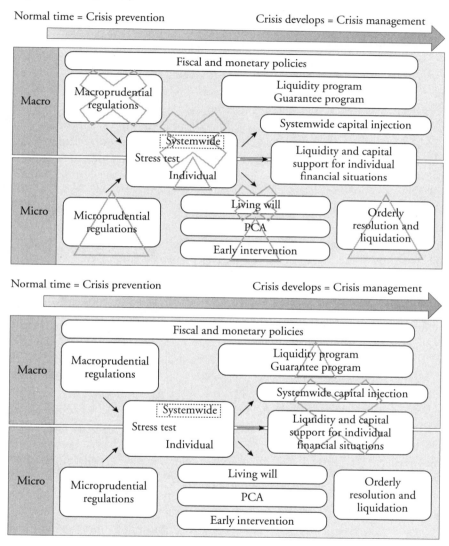

Source: Nomura Institute of Capital Markets Research.

a. "X" means unavailable; the triangle means insufficient. Regulatory action taken under normal conditions is considered crisis prevention; action taken during a crisis is considered crisis management.

policies (below) across these conditions. The top panel of the figure shows the situation in the United States prior to and during the financial crisis. The focus at that time was mainly on the soundness of individual banks, while insufficient attention was paid to nonbanks as well as to the economy as a whole. The treatment of individual financial firms during the financial crisis was also problematic, in that although there was a special resolution regime for financial firms covered by deposit insurance, bank holding companies and nonbanks could be resolved only by using the same bankruptcy laws applied to nonfinancial firms.

Meanwhile, the FDIC's rules for systemic risk exception allowed for a flexible policy, including open bank assistance. In addition, the Fed was able to respond quickly and offer emergency loans, including to nonbanks, on a flexible basis. In that sense, the policy tools needed to respond to a systemwide financial crisis existed to some extent. Policies to ensure transparency and prevent moral hazard were not very clear, however.

Prompt corrective action was a tool available for use during the deepening of the crisis. However, because PCA is based on a capital ratio trigger, in most cases it was initiated too late. The FDIC was able to intervene early if there were signs of a pending failure, but only in the case of financial firms covered by deposit insurance.

The new financial regulatory regime in the United States makes considerable improvements in all of these areas (bottom panel of figure 2-3). To start, it strengthened microprudential regulations while introducing macroprudential regulations for normal times. For responding to financial crisis, it introduced a new special resolution regime that includes bank holding companies and other nonbanks. It also improved the policy tools available during the transition from normal times to financial crisis. In addition to PCA, it introduced systemwide stress tests and RRPs. Depending on the results of the stress test, a revision to the RRPs may be encouraged. Government-administered stress tests based on macro scenarios like the SCAP are an important tool in macroprudential policy, while living wills play a key policy role in orderly resolutions. Living wills are designed to be revised on the basis of the results of the stress test results, and it is through this mechanism that macro- and microprudential policy regimes are linked with the orderly resolution policy regime. In addition, the FDIC's resolution authority was also extended to bank holding companies and nonbanks, making them also subject to early intervention.

This new regime is lacking in policy tools in the upper-right quadrant of figure 2-3 (bottom panel), specifically in measures to deal with a systemwide financial crisis. It was this part of the regime that provided the tools that proved essential when the current financial crisis erupted: broad-based capital injections from TARP, debt guarantees from the FDIC, and emergency loans from the Fed. There is cause to question whether a systemwide crisis could be overcome without these tools. Our main argument is that the emergency loan programs of the Fed and loan guarantees from the FDIC, both of which have been rolled back substantially in scale and flexibility, may not be sufficient.

We think that at the very least there should be a policy option that includes capital injections to provide a backstop when conducting systemwide stress tests. The current orderly resolution regime is overly focused on crises at individual financial firms. As with prudential regulations, there needs to be a crisis response from a macro perspective.

In Japan, although the existence of a policy option for the banks that includes capital injections is a good thing, there has yet to be a formal debate of the FSB's proposals to introduce RRPs and create an SRR for bank holding companies and nonbanks. In this respect, Japan also needs to draw a lesson from the global financial crisis.

References

Bernanke, Ben S. 1983. "Nonmonetary Effects of the Financial Crisis in the Propagation of the Great Depression." *American Economic Review* 73 (June): 257–76.

Brunnermeier, Makus K., and others. 2009. "The Fundamental Principles of Financial Regulation." Center for Economic Policy Research, Washington, D.C., July.

Dudley, William C. 2011. "U.S. Experience with Bank Stress Tests." Remarks at the Group of 30 Plenary Meeting, Bern, Switzerland, May 28.

Edwards, Jonathan M. 2011. "*FDICIA* v. *Dodd-Frank*: Unlearned Lessons about Regulatory Forbearance?" *Harvard Business Law Review* 1 (Spring 2011) (http://ssrn.com/abstract=1895728).

Geithner, Timothy. 2011. "What the World Must Do to Boost Growth." *Financial Times,* September 9.

Gordon, Jeffrey N., and Christopher Muller. 2010. "Confronting Financial Crisis: Dodd-Frank's Dangers and the Case for a Systemic Emergency Insurance Fund." Columbia Law and Economics Working Paper 374. Center for Law and Economic Studies, Columbia University School of Law (http://ssrn. com/abstract=1636456).

Haldane, Andrew G. 2011. "Risk Off." Speech delivered August 18 (www.bankofengland.co.uk/publications/speeches/2011/speech513.pdf).

Karube, K., and T. Nishino. 1999. *Kenshou Keizai Shissei* [Examination: Economic Policy Failure]. Iwanami Shoten.

Keister, Todd. 2010. "Bailouts and Financial Fragility." Federal Reserve Bank of New York, Staff Report 473 (September).

Laeven, Luc, and Fabian Valencia. 2010. "Resolution of Banking Crises: The Good, the Bad, and the Ugly." IMF Working Paper WP/10/146. International Monetary Fund (June).

Lagarde, Christine. 2011 "Global Risks Are Rising, but There Is a Path to Recovery." Remarks at Jackson Hole, August 27, 2011.

Nakaso, H. 2001. "The Financial Crisis in Japan during the 1990s: How the Bank of Japan Responded and the Lesson Learnt." BIS Papers 6. Basel, Switzerland: Bank for International Settlements.

Nishimura, Yoshimasa. 2011. *Kin'yuu Sisutemu Kaikaku Gojuunen no Kiseki* [Fifty Years of Financial System Reform]. Tokyo: Kinzai Institute for Financial Affairs.

Pozsar, Zoltan, and others. 2010. "Shadow Banking." Federal Reserve Bank of New York, Staff Reports 458 (July).

Reinhart, M. Carmen, and Kenneth S. Rogoff. 2009. *This Time Is Different.* Princeton University Press.

Ricks, Morgan. 2010. "Shadow Banking and Financial Regulation." Columbia Law and Economics Working Paper 370 (http://ssrn.com/abstract=1571290).

Tarullo, K. Daniel. 2011. "Industrial Organization and Systemic Risk: An Agenda for Further Research." Speech at the Conference on the Regulation of Systemic Risk, Federal Reserve Board, Washington, D.C., September 15.

Tucker, Paul. 2011. "Macro- and Microprudential Supervision." Speech at the British Bankers' Association Annual International Banking Conference, London, June 29.

GAVIN BINGHAM 3

The Bankruptcy of Bankruptcy

A LEGAL ENTITY, WHETHER a person or company, is bankrupt when it cannot make all payments due, on time and in full. A legal construct is bankrupt when it fails to achieve its political, social, or economic objectives. The thesis of this chapter is that bankruptcy as a legal device for resolving the financial condition of systemically important financial institutions (SIFIs) and insolvent states is bankrupt.[1] The international financial crisis that started in 2007 has demonstrated that there is no effective means for resolving the financial distress of SIFIs. As a result, the financial industry, which accounts for only about 5 to 6 percent of GDP, received something on the order of 25 percent of global GDP in government funds and pushed some sovereigns, such as Iceland and Ireland, to the brink of insolvency.[2] The debt crisis in Greece and other vulnerable member states in the euro area, following on from earlier sovereign crises in emerging market and developing countries, has demonstrated that there is at present no

I am grateful to both Eva Hüpkes and Andrew Large for very thoughtful comments. The views, however, are mine alone.

1. In the United Kingdom, bankruptcy procedures apply to individuals, not to companies, which are governed by insolvency procedures. In an increasing number of jurisdictions, financial institutions cannot be bankrupt, not because they are immune from being insolvent but because there are special resolution regimes.

2. See Herring (2011).

adequate mechanism for the orderly resolution of the financial distress of a sovereign debtor.

The absence of workable debt resolution for sovereigns and SIFIs is hardly surprising. After all, both nation-states and global financial institutions are largely beyond the pale of law. Sovereigns are by definition the source of law and therefore above it, except to the extent that peremptory international law (*jus cogens*) prevails and that they agree to give precedence to treaties and international conventions or find themselves subject to a restricted interpretation of sovereign immunity in the local courts where aggrieved parties seek legal redress.[3] SIFIs are so large and powerful—and the negative externalities associated with their failure so great—that the authorities are reluctant to use the meager set of tools that they have to resolve them. In addition, SIFIs are active in so many jurisdictions and are so legally complex that they can arbitrage away almost any binding legal constraint.

The absence of effective means to deal with the debt distress of sovereigns and SIFIs and the huge costs associated with sovereign and financial crises have spawned efforts to develop orderly debt resolution mechanisms for sovereigns and SIFIs. However, the efforts related to sovereigns have proceeded largely in isolation from those related to SIFIs, even though the two types of crises are closely bound together. Actions by states to alleviate distress in financial institutions can cast doubt on the sustainability of the sovereign's debt (viz Ireland and Iceland), especially in cases where the size of the financial sector is large relative to the size of the economy. Doubts about the ability of states to provide additional resources can make financial institutions more fragile (viz Greece). The last concerted effort to develop a sovereign debt resolution mechanism took place following the Asian debt crisis that began in 1997 and led to some modest changes in contract documentation, but at present there is no international effort to address this problem. By contrast, efforts are currently under way to develop an effective framework for the resolution of financial distress of SIFIs within the context of the G-20 and the Financial Stability Board (FSB).[4]

---

3. The doctrine of limited sovereign immunity was a product of the cold war. State-owned companies in communist countries claimed immunity from prosecution and enforcement in their commercial transactions, arguing that they were instrumentalities of the state. In 1976, the U.S. Congress addressed this issue by passing the Foreign Sovereign Immunities Act, which restricted sovereign immunities to the public policy actions (*jure imperii*) of foreign states and of their instrumentalities.

4. At the Cannes summit in November 2011, the G-20 endorsed the FSB Key Attributes of Effective Resolution Regimes, which set out the powers and tools needed to make the resolution of globally active financial institutions possible. See www.financialstabilityboard.org/publications/r_111104cc.pdf.

This chapter considers how these two largely disparate efforts can inform one another. It begins with a review of the economic and social rationale for insolvency procedures and then compares and contrasts the resolution frameworks that are applied to sovereigns and SIFIs. It then discusses the lessons that can be drawn and concludes by offering suggestions on how to go forward and setting out some principles and practices relevant for transnational resolution regimes.

The Rationale for Bankruptcy Procedures

Bankruptcy is a social, political, and legal device to deal with broken promises. Most promises are kept. The expectation that they will be kept is essential for the operation of a market-based economic system. Sometimes, however, debtors cannot perform on their contracts and must declare themselves insolvent. Bankruptcy arrangements are therefore a means of addressing a time inconsistency—the one that arises when the financial conditions that prevail at the time that the debt is due differ from the conditions that an individual believed would prevail when he or she made the contract.

While insolvency arrangements are meant to deal with time inconsistency, they create time inconsistency problems of their own. The very existence of bankruptcy procedures alerts both creditors and debtors to the possibility that debt will not be repaid on time and in full. In other words, they can, if not properly designed, give rise to moral hazard. A challenge in designing bankruptcy arrangements is striking a balance between the need to ensure that contracts will be paid on time and in full and the need to produce an outcome optimal for the debtor, creditor, and society at large when promises cannot be kept. If insolvency procedures fail to impose sufficient pain on the agent that defaults, they risk undermining the discipline needed for the operation of markets. In the absence of a credible threat of loss, debtors may default repeatedly. However, if insolvency procedures do not permit orderly resolution, they risk the loss of critical functions performed by the bankrupt firm or individual and a reduction in overall welfare.

Objectives Related to Individual Welfare

Maximize Recovery Value for the Debtor

Arguably the overriding original motivation for bankruptcy regimes was to permit creditors to collect when debtors could not or would not pay. This explains the draconian penalties that were imposed in the past (the "pound of flesh" demanded by the Merchant of Venice and the widespread use of debtors' prisons, such as the one where Charles Dickens's father was jailed). There was a distinct element of retribution in the system, but it served to keep moral hazard at bay.

Permit the Debtor to Retain the Tools of His or Her Trade

Historically debtors have enjoyed some protection under the law. The usury restrictions that were common well into the last century and that are still found in some jurisdictions were intended to prevent unprincipled exploitation of the borrower. In addition, modern insolvency legislation generally allows an agent that is declared bankrupt to retain some property both for humanitarian reasons and because of the recognition that the debtor will be able to resume economically useful activity more quickly if he is not deprived of the tools of his trade.

Objectives Related to the Public Good

Insolvency almost always affects third parties, and some of the provisions in insolvency legislation are designed to protect them. For example, restructuring procedures (for instance, Chapter 11), combined with arrangements for a debtor in possession of financing, permit a firm to continue to operate. That may not only help to maintain and perhaps even augment the value of the claims of the creditors but also permit the debtor to continue to provide jobs and provide access by customers and third parties to the goods and services produced by the distressed firm. Third-party effects are especially great in the case of both SIFIs and states.

Preserve Critical Functions

SIFIs often perform critical functions, either directly for ultimate customers or indirectly by providing services to other financial institutions.[5] A public policy objective of any insolvency regime should be to preserve the continued performance of those critical functions. In the case of financial institutions, there are different approaches to maintaining critical functions and insulating them from failure. The choice of the measure will depend on the nature of the business. Certain functions may be insulated ex ante from other risk-taking activities.[6] Alternatively, a special resolution framework could empower authorities to ensure the continued operation of the essential functions by transferring them to a newly established entity or third party while the remaining activities of the institution are wound up.

---

5. See Hüpkes (2005) for the rationale for designing insolvency arrangements for banks so that they preserve critical functions.

6. An example of this approach is the creation of the Continuous Linked Settlement (CLS) Bank, which insulates the clearing and settlement function for foreign exchange contracts from failure of individual market participants. The efforts under way to expand central counterparty (CCP) clearing into over-the-counter derivatives markets, including the credit default swap (CDS) market, and to move as much trading as possible to an organized exchange are another example.

Preserving the continuity of key funding markets is an especially important objective. Both the 2007–09 crisis and the current crisis in Europe illustrate how key funding markets can be impaired in a crisis, and regulation needs to be designed so that the threat to their continued depth and liquidity is minimal. The central bank of the relevant jurisdiction may need to act as lender of last resort and in some circumstances even as a substitute for financial markets, becoming a temporary financial conduit.

Promote Economic Efficiency

Properly designed insolvency regimes promote efficiency in the economic system. They provide incentives to repay debt in full and on time. They foster efficiency in the price mechanism by creating credible expectations about likely outcomes when debtors cannot or will not repay their debts. And, by providing a viable option to the socialization of losses, they reduce the risk of distortions in pricing and competition arising from bailouts. Finally, they serve as a kind of Darwinian mechanism to ensure that weak firms are culled, allowing more dynamic ones to emerge. This triage is essential for the effective operation of a dynamic market economy.

Avoid Negative Externalities

An insolvency regime should be designed so that it does not trigger contagion or otherwise lead to significant negative externalities. When authorities view the results of an insolvency process as socially unacceptable, they are more likely to opt for an ad hoc solution that relies on the use of public funds. That in turn creates greater time inconsistency and makes moral hazard worse.

Reconcile the Rights of the Individual and the Interests of Society (Address Collective Action Problems)

Individuals who insist that the original terms of a contract be honored perform a useful social function, even when it is difficult or impossible for the debtor to do so. They ensure that discipline is maintained and foster predictability in outcomes. Nonetheless, there are circumstances in which the rights of the individual and the interests of society at large are at odds. Unrelenting insistence on the observance of the original terms of a contract by a small minority of creditors can obstruct a debt restructuring that will be in the interest of the majority of creditors and make new or exchanged debt sustainable. A balance needs to be struck between these two competing objectives.

Statutory restructuring procedures generally provide for majority voting. Certain regimes also provide authorities with statutory powers to subordinate the interests of individual creditors to those of the collective if necessary to maximize value or minimize losses.[7]

Collective action clauses, exit consents, and other contractual provisions can be used to address the problem of holdouts. Settling on suitable supermajorities for use in contractual provisions that permit the entire stock of debt to be restructured permits debt to be restructured in an orderly manner without undermining the basic premise that debt must be paid on time and in full.

Observe Basic Legal Principles of Predictability, Due Process, and Fairness

Apart from being desirable in their own right, predictability, due process, and fairness foster efficient operation of the financial markets. The weight accorded to the different objectives determines the nature of the insolvency regime. Legal systems that provide for greater recognition of creditor rights in insolvency and stronger enforcement of those rights are "creditor friendly." Those that give the debtor greater power to continue or resume operations after resolution are "debtor friendly."[8] Legal systems that give precedence to the exercise or protection of the rights of the individual debtor or creditor are "individualistic." Those that give weight to third-party effects and public good considerations are "communitarian."

Current Resolution Regimes for Sovereigns

There are no agreed international rules or collective legal procedures to deal with sovereign debt distress that are similar in scope and nature to the insolvency regimes for individuals and corporations that exist under national laws. Efforts to create such a framework have foundered because of the unwillingness of countries to cede the prerogatives and protections that they have under the current piecemeal procedures.[9] One of the laments often heard with respect to the current debt crisis in Europe is that there is no mechanism to secure the orderly restructuring of the debt of Greece and other sovereigns. In its absence, great efforts are made to avoid default.

---

7. Dodd-Frank Wall Street Reform and Consumer Protection Act of 2010.

8. See La Porta and others (1998), which concludes that the applicable law is of significance for many creditor rights, with common law offering stronger creditor protection than civil law, and French civil law jurisdictions offering the lowest level of protection.

9. Efforts by the International Monetary Fund (IMF) to create a sovereign debt resolution mechanism in the wake of the Asian debt crisis came to naught in part because of the unwillingness of creditor countries to cede power and in part because of serious conflicts of interest embedded in the proposal. The IMF was supposed to serve as an arbiter, yet it was or could be a creditor to the sovereign.

There is, however, a long history of sovereign debt restructuring,[10] and the procedures that have been applied have resulted in a set of practices that, although imperfect, provide a means for addressing the debt distress of sovereigns. Implicit in these practices are a few common principles that guide resolution and would permit orderly restructuring.

The nature of the practices varies, depending on the nature of the debt. When the debt consists primarily of bilateral official claims, Paris Club procedures are used. When it consists primarily of multilateral official claims, practices under the Heavily Indebted Poor Countries (HIPC) Initiative are followed. When it consists largely of private credit in the form of bonds or loans, various forms of debt exchange are used. Disputes regarding sovereign debt tend to be resolved by national courts or in arbitration proceedings under bilateral investment treaties, subject to sovereign immunity. There is no collective proceeding that centralizes all claims and oversees all aspects of a case. In fact, there are not even arrangements for comity or mutual recognition. The UNCITRAL model law does not, for example, extend to sovereign defaults.[11]

The typical procedure for resolving debt distress of a sovereign is a negotiated debt exchange, with varying use of sticks and carrots. The principal stick is nonpayment in accordance with the original terms. In other words, even if the debt is restructured before default, the prospect of default conditions the outcome. Other sticks consist of some form of effective subordination of existing debt through the stripping out of collateral or guarantees. The principal sweetener is collateralization (sometimes provided by a third party) or effective priority relative to creditors who do not agree to the change. The common elements in the procedures used to deal with sovereign debt are the following:

—They recognize that the debt cannot be repaid in full and on time according to the original terms of the contract, but they do not entail the extremes of repudiation or complete forgiveness of all of the debt. In other words, they seek to make debt and debt service sustainable.

—They require some form of adjustment by the debtor, while permitting the debtor to continue operations, albeit on a reduced scale. In other words, they do not lead to liquidation but permit continued operation.

---

10. See Hague Conference Sovereign Insolvency Study Group (2010) and Sturzenegger and Zettelmeyer (2007). The first notes that sovereign defaults have been a pervasive historical feature, with more than 100 having occurred since 1980 and with almost all states having defaulted at least once in the past century. The second provides a more detailed account of the defaults by Russia, Ukraine, Pakistan, Ecuador, Argentina, Moldova, and Uruguay that occurred between 1998 and 2005.

11. See UN Commission on International Trade Law (2005 and 2010).

—They involve some loss for the creditor of the full amount that would have been repaid under the original terms.

—They provide for "super-senior status"—that is, a priority claim in any subsequent insolvency for investors that provide post-resolution funding.

—They deal with the question of equity and the allocation of losses across and within creditor classes through a wide range of contractual and conventional practices, including the following: collective action provisions (qualified majority voting, exit consents) in bonds that seek to ensure that similarly situated creditors are treated similarly—in other words, they seek to ensure that a small minority of holdouts will not scupper a restructuring that is acceptable to the vast majority; negative pledge clauses; pari passu clauses; comparability provisions in Paris Club deals; and the convention of according preference to multilateral lenders such as the International Monetary Fund (IMF), in analogy with the priority given to debtor-in-possession financing. In other words, they mimic the outcome of a judicial proceeding that would ensure that similarly situated creditors are treated similarly.

However, the procedures that are commonly applied do have significant shortcomings. In common with SIFI resolution procedures, they do not deal directly—or deal in only a limited way—with the issue of contagion. A second serious shortcoming is that they do not provide an adequate means to ensure that the behavior and structures that led to the original crisis will be altered in a manner that cures the underlying problem. These shortcomings are discussed below.

Current Resolution Regimes for "Too Big to Fail" Institutions

Just as in the case of sovereigns, there is no effective mechanism to resolve the debt of institutions that are variously termed "too big to fail" (TBTF), "large and complex financial institutions" (LCFIs), or "systemically important financial institutions" (SIFIs). The absence of such a mechanism has made it necessary to use massive amounts of taxpayers' money to bail out individual institutions and has introduced severe distortions in the operation of the market. The procedures commonly followed to resolve the debt distress of a SIFI differ in some important respects from those applied to sovereigns. There is generally no negotiated restructuring.

Typically, a SIFI resolution involves some form of quasi-nationalization or "assisted" merger. The initial action must be very rapid because the value of a financial institution funding itself with short-term liabilities can evaporate overnight, whereas the process of resolving a sovereign debt crisis is often protracted. Although the initial action is rapid in the case of a SIFI, the terms and conditions may be renegotiated, sometimes radically, as they were in the case of Bear Sterns. Quasi-nationalization helps deal with contagion as long as the scale of the problem is manageable. If it is of such a magnitude that the extension of a state guarantee threatens the sustainability of the country's debt, quasi-nationalization cannot do so. Ireland's experience illustrates this challenge.

Resolution procedures that rely on the use of public funds create an extreme asymmetry with respect to the gains and losses faced by a firm and its management. Moreover, to preserve the functions performed by the distressed financial firm, it is generally permitted to continue operating those parts of its business that are viable in much the same way that it did before the event. The current practice of assisted mergers makes matters worse in the long run. It increases the size of already large financial institutions and increases concentration in the financial industry. In other words, in addressing the TBTF problem in the short run, it makes it worse in the long run.

Because current procedures are inadequate, the international community is searching for alternatives. Drawing on earlier work—Basel Committee on Banking Supervision (2010), International Monetary Fund/World Bank (2009), and International Monetary Fund (2010)—the FSB developed guidelines for new procedures, entitled "Key Attributes of Effective Resolution Regimes for Financial Institutions."[12] According to the FSB, an objective of effective resolution regimes is to "make feasible the resolution of financial institutions without severe systemic disruption and without exposing taxpayers to loss, while protecting vital economic functions." Achieving that objective requires a resolution regime with several attributes that are set out by the FSB. Jurisdictions need to have designated resolution authorities with a broad range of powers to intervene and resolve the debt of a financial institution that is no longer viable, including the power to transfer business, to require creditor-financed recapitalization ("bail-in" within resolution), and to use other resolution tools that allocate losses to shareholders and unsecured and uninsured creditors in a manner that respects the hierarchy of claims.

The key attributes specify additional requirements for institutions that are systemic at the global level (G-SIFIs). For every G-SIFI there should be a recovery and resolution plan that sets out both measures that the financial institution

---

12. See Financial Stability Board (2011). This is, of course, not the first effort by the international community to address these issues. The G-22 (Willard Group) reports contain a set of principles for resolution; see Willard Group (G-22) Working Group on International Financial Crises (1998). The G-10 examined the legal underpinnings of workout arrangements (Group of Ten, 2002a), and a joint working group of the Basel Committee on Banking Supervision, the Financial Stability Forum, and the G-10 considered how to wind down large and complex institutions.

could implement to recover and, when that is not possible, measures to resolve the debt of the institution. These plans should be regularly reviewed and updated. Resolvability assessments should be undertaken to identify and remove obstacles to effective resolution that arise from a firm's structure, organization, or business practices. There should be a crisis management group for each G-SIFI that brings together home and key host authorities and is underpinned by institution-specific cross-border cooperation agreements and mandates in law for cooperation, information exchange, and coordination across borders.

This approach constitutes an important step forward on a long and arduous road. It is likely to reduce the need for public money once all of the FSB's recommendations are fully implemented. It remains to be seen whether it will fully address the time inconsistency problem or completely correct the distortions in incentives.

Common and Idiosyncratic Problems for Sovereign and SIFI Resolution Regimes

Although ways have emerged to resolve the debt problems of both sovereigns and SIFIs, they are not perfect. Some of the problems are common to the two regimes; others are confined to one or the other. Many of them have their origin in the fact that there is no cross-border collective procedure for either sovereigns or for SIFIs. Two of the most serious problems common to the two regimes are contagion and time inconsistency

Contagion

Contagion occurs for a number of reasons. They may be related to the restructuring procedures used, to the condition of the debtor, or to the behavior of creditors. The three are, of course, related. If, for example, the procedures to deal with closeout netting are inadequate, a restructuring could cause contagion because of actions by creditors. Similarly, a long and protracted process of resolution could cause liquidity problems that make creditors much more reluctant to roll over credits to other, similarly situated debtors. Contagion can also occur because of the belief that restructuring is no longer taboo.

A crisis can spread if a bailout of the financial system by a government leads to the recognition that sufficient funds are not available to support financial institutions on a similar scale in the future. Mergers of weak banks with strong institutions lead to greater concentration and result in institutions that are still bigger and still more expensive to bail out. More money is needed to save them at a time when governments have less capacity to borrow, owing in part to previous rescues. The Irish case illustrates that this is not just idle speculation. The creation of an effective framework for the resolution of SIFIs' financial problems should reduce contagion through this channel. It should also reduce the contagion that occurs because of the belief that default is no longer taboo. An orderly default does nothing more than regularize an irregular situation. Markets re-price debt continuously, and the prospect of less-than-full recovery is priced into debt that is traded. Restructuring procedures should therefore provide little new information that would affect the price.

The demonstrated ability to deal with a sovereign default in an orderly manner that permits the continued performance of critical functions, treats similarly situated creditors equitably, and deals effectively with third-party interests may help reduce contagion by reassuring creditors that there is in fact a viable mechanism to restructure sovereign debts in an orderly manner. However, it does not deal with the contagion that results from the reassessment by the market of the sustainability of the debt of other similarly situated sovereigns. Nor does it deal with the contagion resulting from a sudden reduction of risk appetite. Creating viable frameworks for dealing with SIFI and sovereign debt will help reduce contagion, but it cannot on its own eliminate it. Complementary actions are needed in other areas. Here the guiding principles should be to reduce or eliminate discontinuities in markets, clusters of exposures, and herd-like behavior.

Credit default swaps (CDSs) are a case in point. In themselves they are a useful instrument for managing risk. They permit a buyer of protection to insure himself against a contingency and spread risk if the sellers of protection are not linked to the buyer or exposed to the same types of risk as the buyer. If, however, master agreements all contain the same event-of-default provision, a significant discontinuity can emerge. Standardization of contracts helps make for homogeneity and ease of trading in the secondary market, but there is no reason for all CDSs to have identical triggers. Systemic risk regulators need to pay attention to whether such practices inadvertently make the financial system vulnerable to sudden implosion. Triggers could be set in terms of a sliding scale of discounts in the secondary market, not in terms of a somewhat theological concept of "event of default." Since prices in secondary markets are easily observable, such a practice would reduce or eliminate the need for judgment by the Determinations Committee of the International Swap Dealers' Association, which is in any case riddled with conflicts of interest since it is composed of representatives of institutions that are active in the CDS market and stand to lose or gain when the committee makes a determination.

There is a large body of opinion that says that a default by Greece on its government debt would trigger contagion. Prima facie, it is difficult to understand why an orderly restructuring of Greek debt that permitted one member of a currency union to convert an unsustainable debt burden into a sustainable one should trigger contagion in other members of the currency union. After all, the total fiscal debt of the currency area would decline and the prospect that fiscal resources of other members would have to be used in increasing amounts to sustain the payment by Greece of its current debt would diminish. To be sure, the debt restructuring would need to be designed so that the losses to systemically important financial institutions holding Greek debt would be manageable, but that is part and parcel of an orderly debt restructuring. All successful cases of sovereign debt restructuring contain such features. Orderly debt restructuring, such as offerings under the Brady plan, involves some form of guarantee that serves to ensure that the side effects are manageable. In short, an orderly debt restructuring must address the risk of contagion.

Time Consistency and Incentives

In the case of the current insolvency frameworks for both sovereign and SIFI debt resolution, there are severe time consistency and incentive problems. With sovereigns, the problem is how to ensure that governments act so that future crises do not arise after they have received financing. With SIFIs, the problem is that authorities may be reluctant to use their resolution tools out of concern about possible adverse systemic consequences of their actions. Another time inconsistency arises when authorities are reluctant to impose a radical restructuring once an institution is recapitalized or otherwise salvaged. That reluctance leads to significant distortions in the pricing of risk and makes future crises more likely.[13]

In a statutory resolution procedure, a resolution authority or an appointed receiver or administrator often assumes responsibility for the institution's management. In contrast, the affairs of insolvent states cannot be taken over and managed by a receiver or trustee. The proxy solution is to have the IMF or another official sector body impose some form of conditionality on the policies of the sovereign.

Current arrangements do not address these time consistency issues adequately. While debt contracts do contain covenants and while some sovereign debtors do issue debt instruments that permit a degree of recovery (GDP-linked bonds), the purpose of most covenants is not to change the behavior of the debtor. It is rather

---

13. For a discussion of the distortions arising from the difficulty of pricing the government guarantee, see Carbó-Valverde, Kane, and Rodríguez Fernández (2011). A practical illustration of the existence of such a guarantee can be found in the rating agencies' practice of taking into account the likelihood of a government bailout.

to secure the interests of the creditor vis-à-vis other creditors through negative pledge and pari passu clauses. Of course, most sovereign restructuring involves a commitment to change policies to ensure that the debtor will be able to meet the terms of the re-profiled debt, and most of the programs are monitored by a "neutral" third party, most commonly the IMF.

As helpful as these arrangements are, they face some inherent challenges. One is the inability of the current government to credibly commit future governments to maintain the agreed policies. A second is that there is a trade-off between effectiveness and impartiality in the process of securing adherence to adjustment policies. Conditionality is effective if the debtor is dependent on the renewal of short-term financing. If it is to work, the amount of such financing should not be notional. However, if the amounts of multilateral finance become large, the creditor becomes *parti pris* and is no longer able to make balanced judgments and to serve as an impartial arbiter or a trusted adviser. The creditor is no longer above the fray. A third difficulty is that investors are understandably forward-looking. While information on past behavior may provide relevant information, they will not withhold financing if they believe that the future will be different.

Public Good Considerations

Resolution affects third parties in the case of both SIFIs and states. SIFIs perform or may perform critical functions, either directly for ultimate customers or indirectly by providing services to other financial institutions. States provide essential public services. The frameworks for the orderly resolution of both SIFI and sovereign debt need to take account of third-party effects. They should be designed so that debt restructuring is not seen as a cataclysmic event but as one on a continuum of measures to deal with a debt problem.

In the case of both states and SIFIs, a full wind-down and liquidation is not feasible. In the case of states, such a process is not even available.[14] The emphasis must therefore be on a resolution that avoids the nonlinear and socially sub-optimal outcomes associated with liquidation and preserves the critical functions of the state or institution. In the case of a state, it should rehabilitate the public finances out of which the debt is to be paid and promote the necessary economic reforms. In the case of a SIFI, it must ensure that the critical functions of the failed institution will continue to be performed, whether or not the institution is

---

14. Chapter 9 of the U.S. Insolvency Code for municipalities applies a procedure to a political subdivision of a state. It has some similarities to the procedures used for corporations. Chapter 9 does not, however, permit the liquidation of the municipality and the sale of its assets, because to do so would violate state sovereignty and imperil the delivery of local public services.

broken up, wound down, or restructured. It must avoid a disorderly rush for the exit and destructive fire sales caused by the termination and liquidation of large volumes of financial contracts.

Hierarchies and Priorities

A feature common to all insolvency regimes is the use of hierarchies of claimants to determine the allocation of the estate. Frequently, absolute priorities are applied so that all claimants in a particular class are made whole before any of those in the next category can benefit. That provides for equality among members of the same class but introduces disparities among creditors in different classes and discontinuities that hamper the operation of the market. Much of the debt contracting that takes place under private law is shaped by what would happen if a firm is wound down under a public law insolvency procedure that treats different classes of creditor differently. SIFIs are subject to national laws that set out a statutory hierarchy of claims. However, the large number of jurisdictions relevant for the workout of a SIFI means that the applicable law and forum will determine which hierarchy applies and whether and how contractual agreements will alter the hierarchy.[15]

In the case of states, there is no mandatory hierarchy of creditors because there is no overarching framework. For states, there is an informal ladder of priorities based on consensus, notably that the payments to the main multilateral creditors (IMF, the World Bank) must be kept current and that ordinary trade, domestic, and similar creditors should be paid. Hence, banks, bondholders, and bilateral official creditors tend to rank lower in practice. Paris Club comparability-of-treatment procedures create a strong incentive for a sovereign with substantial bilateral official debt to negotiate similar terms with other creditors since failure

---

15. A good illustration is an English case related to the Lehman bankruptcy proceeding that illustrates how these differences can play out in a bankruptcy case. One London-based Lehman subsidiary, Lehman Brothers International Europe, had issued a series of notes under Saphir Finance Public Limited Company (Saphir), a special-purpose legal entity. Saphir was also counterparty to a series of swap agreements. Another Lehman subsidiary, Lehman Brothers Special Financing (LBSF), was the other counterparty for the series of notes in question. Normally, swap contracts are written to give the right to the collateral of the swap counterparty, in this case LBSF, priority over that of the note holder. However, a special clause in the contracts, sometimes called a "flip clause," specified that if LBSF, the swap counterparty, defaulted, priority would flip so that Perpetual, the note holder, would have rights to the collateral before LBSF. Following LBSF's bankruptcy filing in October 2008, the English courts ruled that the flip clause was valid and in effect. However, the U.S. Bankruptcy Court ruled that the flip clause was unenforceable because it violated U.S. bankruptcy law. On July 27, 2011, the English Supreme Court in its judgment in *Belmont Park Investments PTY Limited* v. *BNY Corporate Trustee Services Limited and Lehman Brothers Special Financing Inc.* upheld the enforceability of the flip clause.

to do so may cause it to forfeit the concessions that the bilateral official creditors are prepared to grant.

The taking of collateral, the recognition of setoff and netting, the incorporation of negative pledge and sharing clauses into contracts, and the use of various insurance and indemnification arrangements are all aimed at securing a creditor a better place in the pecking order in the event of insolvency. The final outcome in a workout is therefore a result of the interplay between public law provisions, private law contracting, and decisions by the administrator or the courts about the validity of the arrangements. In normal corporate insolvency, this interplay is shaped by competition between debtors and creditors and competition among different classes of creditors. Public policy considerations play a minor role. However, in the case of SIFIs and sovereigns, the externalities are so great that public policy should govern the extent and the way that recontracting affects insolvency outcomes.

Stays and Asset Grabs

In corporate insolvency law, a general stay is designed to allow time to achieve an orderly restructuring. It seeks to avoid the piecemeal seizure of assets by creditors in the interests of creditor equality and orderly resolution. In reorganization proceedings, there is also invariably a freeze on liquidation petitions since the aim is to rescue, not to liquidate, the entity. Most proceedings also stay payments and transfers by the debtor. The UNCITRAL model law on cross-border insolvency—which has been adopted by key jurisdictions such as the United States, the United Kingdom, and Japan—and other similar arrangements, such as the EU insolvency regulation, provide for the cross-border recognition of proceedings in corporate insolvency. This gives the stay a cross-border reach.

In the case of the threatened insolvency of sovereigns and SIFIs, there is no collective proceeding applying to the totality of the debtor. In the case of the sovereign, it is because of the absence of a framework for resolution that provides for a stay on action by creditors. Distressed debt funds—variously termed rogue creditors, vulture funds, or bottom fishers—make use of this fact to pursue their claims on sovereigns even when a vast majority of other creditors have agreed to a restructuring.

In the absence of a mechanism to impose a stay on litigation, the first imperative when insolvency looms for any claimant—or alter ego of the claimant, such as the government of his jurisdiction—is to "grab assets." That is because of the absence of clarity about the outcome of a workout and uncertainty about the ability to enforce a judgment.

In the case of SIFIs, it is likely that creditors will seek to terminate contracts, seize assets, and initiate local insolvency proceedings in the many jurisdictions where the institution has operations or assets. Authorities in host jurisdictions may also take action. In some cases they are even required to do so in order to protect local creditors of a firm headquartered in a foreign jurisdiction. Such actions give priority to local creditors' recovery and frustrate resolution measures aimed at maintaining the continuity of cross-border operations and supporting broader financial stability goals (such as the orderly and timely transfer of branch business and critical economic functions to a new entity). For SIFIs active in multiple jurisdictions, there is nothing analogous to the recognition procedures set out under the UNCITRAL model law on cross-border insolvency. In its report on cross-border bank resolution, the Basel Committee noted that one of the challenges in resolving the debts of a financial institution is the fact that the major constituent entities of a financial group are likely to be subject to separate proceedings in different jurisdictions with different resolution objectives, policies, and priorities.[16]

The UNCITRAL model law was designed to deal with corporate bankruptcies that are administered by judicial authorities. By contrast, the resolution of a financial institution is typically administered by a supervisory or resolution authority. A mechanism for cross-border resolution that emulates the UNCITRAL approach would require resolution authorities to have "recognition authority" that matches their respective resolution powers. Unless resolution authorities are given an explicit mandate and powers to cooperate and take action to support an agreed group resolution scheme and to bar individual creditor actions that would interfere with attempts to achieve a coordinated value-preserving resolution of the institution as a whole, there is little prospect of overcoming the value-destroying, fragmented nature of resolution proceedings for financial institutions.

Difficulty of Enforcement

Since both SIFIs and sovereigns are beyond the pale of a single legal system, it is difficult to enforce claims even when they are awarded. The reasons differ, but in both cases the difficulty complicates resolution. In the case of SIFIs, it arises because of the rapid erosion of value that occurs when an institution borrows short and lends long. Yet their global nature and legal complexity provide SIFIs with opportunities for forum shopping, and that means that litigation can drag on for years. By that time, there may be nothing to recover even if the resolution authority finds in favor of the creditor.

The difficulty of enforcement in the case of sovereigns arises from ambiguity about the nature and extent of their immunities. Prior to the last quarter of the

16. See Basel Committee on Banking Supervision (2010).

last century, sovereigns enjoyed almost complete immunity from legal action. In the intervening decades, many jurisdictions restricted sovereign immunity, either by statute or by case law, so that commercial acts no longer benefit from such protection. Moreover, most relevant credit contracts, notably bond issues and syndicated bank credits, contain comprehensive waivers of immunity from judgment and enforcement. Such contracts are often governed by a foreign law, are in a foreign currency, and are payable abroad. As a result, these claims are not alterable by unilateral action of the debtor state.[17] Courts abroad often do not recognize actions by the debtor state to diminish the validity of a creditor claim, in particular where the credit contract is governed by an external governing law so that a local decree of the debtor state cannot alter that law; it also may be because the claim is located abroad and is therefore outside the legislative territorial competence of the debtor state. Or, as a matter of public policy, states may not be permitted to interfere with foreign-held claims, regardless of location or governing law.

While the doctrine of restricted sovereign immunity has permitted creditors to bring cases to court and to win judgments, that has not necessarily meant that they can enforce their claims. A sovereign's principal asset is the discounted present value of its future tax receipts; such revenue streams are domestic and not subject to attachment. States have legislative sovereignty over assets that they hold and claims that they owe that are governed by their own law or are payable in local currency or otherwise located within their own territory. They can therefore impose moratoriums or use exchange controls to frustrate payment. Moreover, assets held abroad and used for noncommercial purposes are immune from attachment. Governments in creditor countries have also enacted legislation to protect their own payment systems from disruption resulting from attempts by disgruntled creditors to attach payments made by sovereign debtors to any party through these systems.[18] In short, even if a creditor obtains a judgment against a sovereign, he faces the dilemma of the Merchant of Venice—he has a claim that he cannot enforce.[19]

17. Greece constitutes an interesting exception. The great bulk of its sovereign debt was issued under domestic law; as a result, it could take action unilaterally to alter the terms and conditions of that debt. It has not done so, but it has signaled its willingness to subject the claims of swapped debt to the laws of other jurisdictions in exchange for some relief. That will make subsequent coercive exchanges more difficult, but not impossible.

18. Belgium changed legislation to safeguard the integrity of Euroclear following attempts by creditors to attach payments made through the system by delinquent sovereigns. See Wood (2007) for a discussion of the case that led to the change in Belgian law.

19. In the *Merchant of Venice,* the judge finds in favor of the merchant. He is entitled to his pound of flesh, but can, on pain of death, enforce his claim only if he does not shed a drop of blood.

Complexity

Complexity makes any debt restructuring difficult, but it is especially virulent in the case of SIFIs, which typically comprise hundreds or thousands of separate legal entities incorporated under the laws of multiple jurisdictions.[20] Sovereign debtors do not have anything like the legal complexity of SIFIs or the diversity of creditors typical of corporations, at least so far as restructuring is concerned.[21] The categories of debts to be restructured in the sovereign context are smaller than in corporate insolvency and confined primarily to debts to official lenders, bondholders, and commercial banks, plus distressed debt investors. Most sovereign debt is unsecured so that the legal procedures for exercising claims on collateral are not applicable. In the case of the sovereign, the question is ultimately one of willingness to pay rather than being forced to pay as a result of a decision of a court or a resolution authority in another jurisdiction.

In the case of a SIFI failure, each legal entity is treated separately even if it is not able to operate as a stand-alone company. Courts have been reluctant to pierce the corporate veil unless there is extreme commingling or other exceptional factors justifying consolidation in insolvency. The result is that only the assets of each member of the group can be used to pay its creditors and its creditors alone; its assets are not available to creditors of other members of the group. The ability to shield assets in this way gives SIFIs a degree of legal protection not unlike the protections enjoyed by sovereigns that arise from their immunities and the difficulty of attaching their assets.

The Lehman case illustrates the effects of such complexity. Lehman consisted of more than 2,900 legal entities. It has nearly 1 million derivatives contracts, most of which had at least two Lehman affiliates as parties to the contract. In order to resolve any one of them, it is necessary not only to determine the validity of the claim of the counterparty on each of the affiliates in the group but also to determine the validity and value of the claims of each Lehman affiliate on the other. This is difficult enough in itself, but it is made harder still by the doubts about the ability to exercise claims over Lehman assets held in custody by Lehman affiliates. In some cases the assets held in custody were rehypothecated. As a result, even if the complex web of countervailing claims could be untangled, it might not be possible to obtain the collateral underlying them.

---

20. See Herring and Carmassi (2010).

21. States are not as complex as SIFIs, but they do have separate administrative subdivisions, provinces, regions, and municipalities. They commonly own their central banks and other separate state entities, which are protected by the veil of incorporation. For example, central bank reserves are insulated from creditor execution in cases in which only the state is liable to the creditor.

Legal complexity arises for a number of reasons, including taxation, regulatory and legal provisions, and a history of repeated mergers and takeovers. Group structures and intragroup relationships are also designed to serve a number of corporate objectives, such as managing risk and ratings and streamlining operations. Although these structures may have advantages for the group, they tend to increase complexity and create contagion by making the viability of one company within the group dependent on others in the same group.

Complexity is extremely pernicious from the perspective of resolution. Yet it will be difficult to deal with because of the strong incentive to minimize taxes and to arbitrage regulation, coupled with the well-established legal doctrine of respecting legal personality. Still, that should not deter efforts to make legal form follow economic function.[22] The most ambitious proposal is presented in Cumming and Eisenbeis (2010), in which the authors propose that each financial institution conduct business from a single legal entity.[23] The FSB's assessments of the recovery and resolution plans required for all globally systemically important financial institutions will examine whether the legal structures of these groups are a serious obstacle to SIFI resolution, but there is strong resistance to suggestions that groups be required to simplify their structures significantly.

Potential Solutions to the Problems of Sovereign and SIFI Debt Resolution

Since the origins of the challenges for sovereign and SIFI resolution are the same—the fact that both are beyond the pale of standard legal resolution procedures grounded in national legislation—the basic nature of the solution must be the same. The solution must develop a framework for resolution that extracts the best features of national resolution regimes and applies them to SIFIs and sovereigns in a way that addresses their idiosyncrasies. The frameworks will have common elements, but the nature of the challenges facing sovereigns and SIFIs is sufficiently different to mean that the frameworks will need to be distinct.

There are essentially two ways to develop international frameworks for resolution of entities that are beyond the pale of national law. One is to negotiate and ratify an international treaty; the second is to rely on incentives for cooperation combined with soft law techniques that establish common principles and

22. See Hüpkes (2009).

23. Blundell-Wignall and others (2009) presents a proposal that is similar in inspiration but less ambitious in that the author would permit separate legal entities in the same group, but the group itself would be treated as a single entity. See also Kay (2009) and U.K. Independent Commission on Banking (2011a and 2011b).

practices to guide resolution. The first is neat, but difficult; the second is realistic, but slow and piecemeal. On balance, the second approach is more likely to produce tangible results and viable arrangements.[24] States are unlikely to relinquish sovereignty over such basic matters as how their tax receipts are used, and even if a treaty were agreed, issues of enforcement would persist.

There are numerous soft law options that could be given momentum through international institutions such as the G-20 and the FSB. The private/public effort to develop collective action clauses is an example of how standard documentation can be changed to address the problem of disruptive litigation by a small minority of disaffected creditors.[25] A similar private/public initiative could be undertaken to address the discontinuities caused by the use of standard event-of-default clauses in master agreements for derivatives contracts. However, to be effective, the use of soft law to create effective frameworks for resolution would need to be accompanied by significant changes in the structure and operation of banks and the nature of sovereign borrowing.

Existing dispute settlement arrangements could be developed to deal with sovereign debt distress. Since debt arises as a result of investment, it is subject to the procedures set out in the Convention of the International Center for Settlement of Investment Disputes (ICSID).[26] Since resolution of a 1997 case involving jurisdiction, public loans have been considered to be an investment, and recently disputes between Argentina and private investors have been submitted to ICSID arbitration. There are several advantages to ICSID procedures. First, there is an "exclusive remedy" rule that means that once consent to ICSID arbitration has been given, the parties cannot seek redress in domestic courts or other arbitration panels and domestic courts may not issue orders to stay ICSID proceedings. ICSID awards are final and binding, and they are not subject to review outside the ICSID convention. Awards are to be recognized and enforced in all states that are party to the convention as if they were judgments of the local domestic courts.

However, ICSID procedures suffer from several significant shortcomings. The first is that submission to ICSID jurisdiction cannot be taken for granted. To be sure, some contracts provide for ICSID arbitration and it may be called for under

24. See Large and Walker (2010), in which the authors argue that soft law standards developed in a manner that promotes buy-in are preferable to externally imposed rules that breed circumvention and regulatory arbitrage.
25. See Group of Ten (2002b).
26. For information on ICSID procedures, see International Centre for Settlement of Investment Disputes (2006).

bilateral investment treaties, but the language in private contracts is sometimes ambiguous, and parties can and do reject ICSID jurisdiction.[27] Second, the same enforcement challenges that arise with judgments by domestic courts arise with ICSID awards. Sovereigns still enjoy limited immunity and have few assets that can easily be seized. Third, ICSID procedures provide satisfaction to aggrieved private parties (and sometimes public parties), but they are not designed to achieve the broad public policy objective of amending policies that gave rise to the failure of the sovereign to meet its debt service obligations.

It is also possible to think of World Trade Organization (WTO) dispute settlement procedures being applied to sovereign debt disputes because, unlike most other procedures, those of the WTO provide for an effective enforcement mechanism. However, these procedures are meant to deal with interstate disputes, and the Paris Club procedures already provide an effective means to restructure bilateral official debt and to address the need for changes in policies that caused the problems. WTO procedures do not have this last feature, and it is not clear how they would be used to resolve disputes among official debtors and private creditors unless the creditors' states became the alter egos of the creditors.

Comity has proved to be an effective means to secure consistent treatment of those subject to the laws of several jurisdictions as long as those jurisdictions adhere to common principles and approaches. If the FSB recommendations for effective resolution regimes were fully implemented, national resolution authorities would then adhere to the same principles and have similar powers.

The development of frameworks for resolution through soft law requires broad agreement on objectives and principles, implicit or explicit political benediction, and continuous close cooperation among authorities to establish confidence that the agreed principles will be upheld in a crisis. The financial crisis that began in 2007 created such momentum with respect to SIFIs. It led to the G-20/FSB efforts to ensure that no institution will be too big to fail. However, there has been no equivalent effort in the area of sovereign debt resolution, though the debt distress of some European countries has now made this a priority. The last effort to make progress in the development of a resolution framework for sovereigns occurred after the Asian crisis that began in 1997. It petered out both because of the episodic nature of sovereign debt crises and because the effort was driven by two different and ultimately incompatible agendas. One was to develop a mechanism that would have ceded sovereignty to a supranational institution;

27. For this reason, there has been an effort to develop standard language in contracts for submission to ICSID jurisdiction.

the other was to develop and refine private law contracting practices with the avowed purpose of achieving the public policy objective of ensuring more orderly sovereign debt defaults.

It is now time to initiate a new process for developing a framework for sovereign debt resolution. Since sovereign and SIFI debt distress are closely interlinked, both by the fact that one exacerbates the other and by the fact that common challenges arise in developing a framework, the efforts should inform each other. The most natural process would be to have them occur under the G-20 umbrella. That process is well under way for SIFIs, and it should be initiated for sovereigns.

Principles and Practices for Sovereign and SIFI Resolution

The slow and gradual effort to develop procedures to resolve the debt distress of sovereigns and SIFIs has led over time to a somewhat amorphous set of principles and practices that govern transnational resolution frameworks. They are the outcome of a process of international cooperation that is shaped by three basic realities.

The first is that individuals, institutions, and states pursue their own interests. The fact that individuals do so is a basic tenet of economics.[28] By contrast, states are often viewed as devices to remedy some of the shortcomings of the pursuit of narrow self-interest by individuals, either by acting to internalize externalities or by restricting or offsetting the detrimental consequences of the pursuit of self-interest. However, in the realm of international cooperation, states pursue their own national interests, which may or may not correspond with the promotion of global welfare.

Second, there are steep differences in the influence of different parties on the outcome of an international agreement. All are not equal, and it is not helpful to think of the process of developing international agreements in terms of the operation of markets since the basic assumption of atomistic agents does not hold.

That leads to the third reality. Agreement will not be reached if any major party is worse off as a result. That is to say, agreement can be achieved only if it is Pareto improving without side payments. Keeping these realities in mind is helpful in developing principles and practices for resolution of transnational entities.

---

28. Behavioral economics, however, starts from a different premise. It holds that seemingly "rational" economic decisions are shaped by psychological, social, and evolutionary factors. See Trivers (2011) for a discussion of how physiological and evolutionary factors cause the human mind to deceive itself.

Following below are some principles and practices that merit consideration in any transnational resolution framework. While it is essential to take into account specific circumstances in applying them, they should have enough generality to apply to both sovereign and SIFI debt resolution.

Principles

Work on the development of frameworks for sovereigns and SIFIs should build on the very considerable efforts that have gone before. Principles for resolution exist implicitly in national insolvency frameworks, though there are significant differences across countries in the weight that they are given and in whether the resulting regimes are debtor or creditor friendly. However, the systemic nature of SIFI and sovereign crises means that greater weight will need to be given to public interest issues—despite the pursuit of self-interest embedded in the process of international cooperation.

Make Systems and Structures Incentive-Compatible and Consistent with Resolution

A basic precondition for making any resolution regime effective is to address the incentive incompatibilities that arise when there is an alternative to using it. Resolution systems will not be used if there is a soft option in the form of hard government money. For SIFIs, that means that the asymmetries in incentives that arise from the socialization of losses and the privatization of gains must be eliminated. Attention has been diverted from these important but difficult reforms by the focus on capital. In principle, capital serves two functions. It provides a buffer to absorb losses, and it changes the incentives of shareholders. In practice, the buffer function predominates. Having a larger buffer implies that wind-downs will not be needed and reduces the urgency of efforts to create an effective insolvency mechanism. It does little or nothing to change the incentives to create complex entities that are difficult to wind down or to make shareholders focus on the strategic orientation of the firm. Shareholders in widely held companies treat shares as investments to be bought and sold as risk and reward change, not as ownership claims that are used to influence business strategy.

For SIFIs, making structures incentive-compatible and consistent with resolution would mean making radical changes in the legal structure of financial groups, in their corporate governance, and even in the extent to which liability is limited through incorporation. Up until the last quarter of the last century, investment banking was conducted through partnerships, whose liability was unlimited. That was the last vestige of a model of banking that aligned incentives and control and that was almost universal until its gradual replacement by limited liability and the separation of ownership and control.[29]

For states, it may mean some voluntary waiving of sovereignty, for example, by issuing debt under the laws of other jurisdictions. It could also involve recognizing that serial restructurings help address the need for changes in conditionality as circumstances change. And it could lead to greater use of restructuring procedures such as those of the Paris Club that entail explicit conditionality, which deters the types of policies that lead to unsustainable debt positions. Such conditionality could be provided by the IMF or in regional arrangements such as those being put in place in Europe. In principle, covenants in debt contracts that provide for recovery when economic prospects improve or link rates of return to macroeconomic or industry-wide indicators could be used to foster continued adherence to prudent economic policies. However, such contracting practices have not worked in the past, and it is unlikely that they will emerge on their own on a scale sufficient to make a significant difference.

Adopt Procedures That Are Impartial and Fair

Stated so baldly, this principle appears so self-evident as to be meaningless. In practice, it would mean that the framework should cover all "large" exposures, irrespective of the nature of the creditor—secured or unsecured, public or private, and domestic or foreign creditors and equity holders; workers with wage claims; and governments with tax claims. In some cases, ways will need to be found to represent classes of claimants—for example, through the formation of creditor committees. Any carve-outs or priorities would need to be justified on public interest grounds.

The impartiality and fairness principle also means that the framework should contain a mechanism such as the Paris Club's comparability-of-treatment provision that ensures comparable treatment across classes of creditors as well as within a class. It should contain conditionality provisions to deal with the time consistency problem, which has an important intertemporal fairness dimension. Fairness also gives the arrangements legitimacy.

---

29. See Haldane (2011) for a useful discussion of changes in control rights over banks and how they have shaped incentives. It is notable that hedge funds, which often are structured so that the lead partner has unlimited liability, have not been a source of systemic risk, at least so far. This is not because unlimited liability makes hedge fund managers so conservative that hedge funds never fail; indeed, entry and exit in this market segment are more frequent than in other segments of the financial market. It is because, as with the investment banking partnerships of the nineteenth and twentieth centuries, the incentive structure leads to a scale and scope of activities that does not imperil the system as a whole.

In practice, this principle implies that similarly situated creditors will be treated equitably and that differences in treatment across classes will be justifiable. However, secured creditors and preferred creditors, for instance, those who provide post-resolution funding, are and should be treated differently from unsecured creditors. Secured creditors may have rights to collateral that are not shared with unsecured creditors. Recognition and enforcement of their differing rights within the context of the insolvency regime create certainty in the market, thereby facilitating the extension of credit. As a general rule, the established hierarchy of claims should be maintained in resolution.

Let Broad Public Policy Considerations Determine Priorities

Priority in bankruptcy should not be the outcome of competition among different stakeholders seeking to maximize their individual interests but should take into account externalities and third-party effects. Giving super-senior status to "debtor-in-possession" funding provided in the course of a restructuring aids resolution. There should be a presumption in favor of it, but if preferred creditors come to hold a large proportion of claims, the only way to make the debt sustainable may involve including those creditors in future restructurings.

Promote Predictability

Well-articulated procedures help make outcomes more predictable, so resolution frameworks should help all affected parties to anticipate what the outcome will be in different circumstances. Predictability in resolution arrangements is important for at least two reasons. First, the absence of arbitrariness is a necessary, though not sufficient, condition for fairness. Second, predictability permits markets to price state-contingent claims more accurately.

Avoid Discontinuities

Designing resolution frameworks so that they consist of a continuum of measures helps to promote predictability and fairness. It also helps markets to function. A resolution framework should therefore permit the gradual scaling up of measures. It should start with an early and radical strategic reorientation or policy adjustment by the board or the government, which should take place before debt restructuring. Moreover, entry into a resolution should not create discontinuities or frustrate transactions essential for the maintenance of the value of a traded portfolio, and it should allow for continuity under an administrator or receiver in the case of SIFI resolution or under an IMF adjustment program in the case of sovereigns.

Maximize the Value of Assets

Maximization of value is one of the objectives of national bankruptcy regimes. Liquidation, therefore, is seen as a measure of last resort, and most resolution takes place in a manner that preserves the value of the bankrupt firm even if the firm ceases to exist as a separate legal entity. In the case of sovereign states and SIFIs, liquidation is not an option. Value maximization relates primarily to the continued provision of essential services or critical functions, not to maximizing the value of shareholders' claims.

Preserve Critical Functions

The principle that critical functions should be preserved is closely allied to the principle of maximization of the value of assets from the perspective of the wider community. It stresses the need to take into account externalities, and it helps in performing the triage needed to make public finances sustainable. It may involve the creation of utilities providing essential infrastructure services, or it may require changes in the structure of companies to permit their orderly dismemberment. It may also involve changes in the operation of key funding markets to maintain their liquidity, depth, and continuity. It could permit or require the central bank to serve as the market maker of last resort in those markets.

Avoid Contagion

The principle that frameworks for resolving transnational debt distress should avoid contagion illustrates their limitations. Reforming bankruptcy arrangements so that there is a continuum of measures rather than a single last-resort measure to deal with default would reduce the contagion that arises from seeing default as a cataclysmic event. However, it would not eliminate the contagion that arises from shifts in risk appetite or from the financial or other economic links of the distressed debtor with other entities.

Balance Individual Rights with the Need to Serve the Public Interest

The primary original purpose of most national insolvency legislation was to reconcile the interests of different classes of individuals—debtors and creditors— while taking into account some wider societal considerations, such as preventing value-destroying competition for the residual assets of the bankrupt entity. Insolvency arrangements must maintain discipline to ensure that debtors make payments in full and on time; in other words, they should deal with moral hazard. At the same time, holdouts should not be able to obstruct a resolution that satisfies the vast majority of stakeholders and will make debt sustainable and preserve critical functions. In the case of both SIFIs and sovereigns, the third-party effects are so great that the balance between protecting individual rights and serving the public interest inescapably tilts toward the latter.

Practices

A wide spectrum of practices can be used to implement the principles discussed above. They include the following:

—restricting contracting practices that augment contagion or create discontinuities, such as the use of a standardized event-of-default clause in CDS contracts, walk-away clauses, automatic closeout upon entry into resolution, and so forth;

—establishing, in law, a continuum of early intervention triggers and strict timelines for actions and implementation of resolution measures;

—taking ex ante measures that promote resolvability and increase predictability of loss allocation in resolution, including by developing recovery and resolution plans combined with changes in operations or alteration of the form of companies that enhance resolvability and by using "bail-inable" debt, and mandatory bail-in requirements; and

—adopting common priority rankings across jurisdictions—for example, by providing seniority or "preferred creditor status" for "debtor in possession" financing to any entity providing it.

Conclusions

The serial SIFI and sovereign debt crises underscore the importance of developing effective frameworks for the resolution of the debts of transnational entities that are beyond the pale of national law. If such a framework had existed for sovereigns, the problems that Greece faces could have been addressed earlier and more decisively, and the contagion involving other members of the euro area could have been contained. Creating such a framework must be a high priority of the international community.

Such frameworks are best developed using soft law. They need to be given political momentum by a process of international cooperation such as the G-20. Efforts are under way to develop such a framework for SIFIs, and a similar endeavor for sovereigns is well worth the effort. The two efforts can and should inform one another because the challenges are similar. The two greatest challenges are preventing contagion and changing the structures and behavior that give rise to debt distress in SIFIs and sovereigns.

A soft law approach must be evolutionary, and each framework will need to be tailored to the specific challenges of SIFI and sovereign restructuring. Nonetheless, certain common principles should apply. First, public good considerations should carry significant weight in the design of insolvency arrangements for sovereigns and SIFIs. The externalities are just too great. Second, since resolution takes many forms and can take place at many stages of distress, there should be a continuum of measures. Markets detest discontinuities, just as nature abhors a vacuum. Finally, bankruptcy should be designed to shape incentives and to change the behavior that leads to insolvency. Private sector "bail-ins" are no better than public sector "bailouts" if they do not fundamentally change behavior. Progress will be slow, but the stakes are high. It pays to persist.

References

Basel Committee on Banking Supervision. 2010. "Report and Recommendations of the Cross-Border Bank Resolution Group." Basel (March).

Blundell-Wignall, Adrian, and others. 2009. "The Financial Crisis: Reform and Exit Strategies." Paris: OECD Publishing (September).

Carbó-Valverde, S., E. J. Kane, and F. Rodríguez Fernández. 2011. "Safety-Net Benefits Conferred on Difficult-to-Fail-and-Unwind Banks in the U.S. and EU before and during the Great Recession." Working Paper 16787. Cambridge, Mass.: National Bureau of Economic Research (February).

Cumming, C., and R. Eisenbeis. 2010. "Resolving Troubled Systemically Important Cross-Border Financial Institutions: Is a New Corporate Organizational Form Required?" In *Issues in Resolving Systemically Important Financial Institutions,* edited by R. Herring. Wharton Financial Institutions Center. Wharton School, University of Pennsylvania.

Financial Stability Board. 2011. "Key Attributes of Effective Resolution Regimes for Financial Institutions." Basel (October).

Group of Ten. 2002a. "Insolvency Arrangements and Contract Enforceability." Contact Group on the Legal and Institutional Underpinnings of the International Financial System. Basel, Paris, and Washington (September).

———. 2002b. "Report of the G-10 Working Group on Contractual Clauses." Basel, Paris, and Washington (December).

Hague Conference Sovereign Insolvency Study Group. 2010. "State Insolvency: Options for the Way Forward." London: International Law Association.

Haldane, A. 2011. "Control Rights (and Wrongs)." Wincott Annual Memorial Lecture. Westminster, London. Bank of England Speeches (www.wincott.co.uk/lectures/Andy_Haldane_2011.pdf).

Herring, R. J. 2011. "The Central Role of Resolution Policy in Dealing with Systemically Important Financial Institutions." Paper presented at the IADI Research Conference, Basel (June).

Herring, R. J., and J. Carmassi. 2010. "The Corporate Structure of International Financial Conglomerates: Complexity and Its Implications for Safety and Soundness." In *The Oxford Handbook of Banking,* edited by A. Berger, P. Molyneux, and J. Wilson. Oxford University Press.

Hüpkes, E. 2005. "Too Big to Save—Towards a Functional Approach to Resolving Crises in Global Financial Institutions." In *Systemic Financial Crisis: Resolving Large Bank Insolvencies,* edited by D. Evanoff and G. Kaufman. Singapore: World Scientific Publishing.

———. 2009. "Form Follows Function: A New Architecture for Regulating and Resolving Global Financial Institutions." *European Business Organization Law Review* 10, no. 3: 369–85.

International Centre for Settlement of Investment Disputes. 2006. "ICSID Convention, Regulations, and Rules." Washington.

International Monetary Fund. 2010. "Resolution of Cross-Border Banks: A Proposed Framework for Enhanced Coordination" (www.imf.org/external/np/pp/eng/2010/061110.pdf).

International Monetary Fund/World Bank. 2009. "An Overview of the Legal, Institutional, and Regulatory Framework for Bank Insolvency." Washington (April 17).

Kay, J. 2009. "Narrow Banking: The Reform of Banking Regulation." London: Centre for the Study of Financial Innovation (CSFI) (September).

La Porta, R., and others. 1998. "Law and Finance." *Journal of Political Economy* 106, no. 6 (December).

Large, A., and D. Walker. 2010. "Underpinning Systemic Stability: The Case for Standards." *Central Banking Journal* (November).

Sturzenegger, F., and J. Zettelmeyer. 2007. *Debt Defaults and Lessons from a Decade of Crisis.* MIT Press.

Trivers, R. 2011. *Deceit and Self-Deception.* London: Allen Lane.

U.K. Independent Commission on Banking. 2011a. "Interim Report Consultation on Reform Options." London: U.K. Independent Commission on Banking (April).

———. 2011b. "Final Report." London: U.K. Independent Commission on Banking (September).

UN Commission on International Trade Law. 2005. *Legislative Guide on Insolvency Law.* New York: United Nations.

———. 2010. *Practice Guide on Cross-Border Insolvency Cooperation.* New York: United Nations.

Willard Group (G-22) Working Group on International Financial Crises. 1998. "Report." (October) (www.bis.org/publ/othp01d.pdf).

Wood, P. R. 2007. *International Loans, Bonds, Guarantees, and Legal Opinions.* London: Sweet and Maxwell.

MORGAN RICKS 4

The Case for Regulating the Shadow Banking System

THE TITLE OF THIS chapter raises at least two questions. First, what is meant by "shadow banking"? Second, what is meant by "regulate"? Neither question has an obvious answer. This chapter uses the term "shadow banking" to refer to a specific activity: *maturity transformation* that takes place outside the depository banking sector. "Maturity transformation" simply denotes the issuance of fixed-principal, very short-term IOUs, with the proceeds invested in longer-term financial assets (typically credit assets). This activity is, of course, the traditional domain of depository banking. The shadow banking system performs virtually the same function, but its short-term IOUs are not formally styled as "deposits."

The term "shadow banking" as used here has no necessary connection to the securitization markets—although shadow banking firms do own large amounts of securitized credit. Nor does the definition given above hinge on collateralization in any formal legal sense. Some of the short-term IOUs issued by shadow banks are collateralized instruments, but many are unsecured. The concept of shadow banking used here does not refer to purportedly "shadowy" or "opaque" areas of the financial markets, such as the derivatives markets. It is not an all-purpose reference to unregulated or lightly regulated parts of the financial system, nor is it intended to encompass the hedge fund industry (although some hedge funds are engaged in shadow banking). Finally, it is not a loose reference to the structured credit business—the tranching of securitized credit through collateralized debt obligations and the like. It is important to be clear about these issues, because the term "shadow banking" is often used to signify very different things. This chapter adopts a precise, functional definition: shadow banking is simply maturity transformation that takes place outside the depository banking sector. To quote Gorton (2010), "the shadow banking system is, in fact, real banking."

What about "regulate"? This term, too, must be used carefully. The term is sometimes used interchangeably with "oversee" or "supervise": it is said that we should bring institutions under the "regulatory umbrella" so that they will no longer be "out of view" of the relevant authorities. But this formulation is incomplete. The long-standing regulatory regime for depository banking encompasses many things: explicit portfolio and activity restrictions; capital requirements; cash reserve requirements; restrictions on affiliations and affiliate transactions; access to public support facilities—that is, the lender of last resort and deposit insurance; a special receivership regime in the event of failure; and so on. In view of this panoply of regulatory tools and functions, the proposition that we should "regulate" the shadow banking system, in and of itself, conveys little information. *How* should we regulate the functional activity of maturity transformation, if at all? What are the components of a coherent regulatory design for this activity—if indeed one is needed?

This chapter argues that maturity transformation is associated with a cognizable market failure, establishing a prima facie case for government intervention. Indeed, such a market failure arguably is the central problem for financial regulatory policy. (To quote University of Chicago economist Doug Diamond, a leading theorist in this area: "Financial crises are always and everywhere about short-term debt.")[1] Panics by holders of short-term IOUs disrupt the credit markets. In particular, a panic produces a sudden negative shock to the supply of financing, thereby significantly diminishing businesses' and consumers' access to credit for consumption and real investment. The result is a substantial disruption to the real economy.

In the area of *depository* banking, our modern regulatory system seems to have had stability-enhancing benefits. In developing a regulatory approach to shadow banking, then, the tools of modern depository regulation might offer a useful starting point. But the key question to ask is *which* of those tools are essential. This chapter argues that the stabilization of maturity transformation seems to depend on the availability of public support facilities: tools like the lender of last resort and deposit insurance. Recent regulatory reforms in the United States have

---

1. Quoted in Panel Discussion on Financial Regulation, Becker Friedman Institute, University of Chicago, November 6, 2010 (http://mfi.uchicago.edu/events/20101106_finregulation/).

not moved in this direction. Indeed, the movement has been decidedly *away* from this approach to stabilizing maturity transformation. This chapter argues that recent reforms are therefore unlikely to be conducive to stable conditions in the shadow banking system.

In this regard, it is important to address the role of "resolution." It is commonly argued that the risks of shadow banking can be significantly mitigated through the use of special administrative resolution techniques. At first blush, the logic appears to be straightforward. The federal resolution regime for depository banks seems to have been associated with relatively smooth bank failures, systemically speaking. So it seems only natural to apply similar resolution techniques to nondepository firms, including firms engaged in shadow banking. That was the basic logic behind the creation in the United States of the new Orderly Liquidation Authority (OLA), a centerpiece of the recently enacted Dodd-Frank Act. Indeed, OLA was modeled closely on the existing U.S. receivership regime for depository banks. The idea was to take this resolution tool, which appears to have served us well in the depository realm, and transport it to the nondepository sector.

However, this logic raises a basic question. It is true that depository failures—which historically were very damaging—have been rendered relatively benign. But was this shift made possible by depository *resolution?* Or was it deposit *insurance?* For they are two very different things. Deposit insurance and lender-of-last-resort authority are specifically directed toward preventing depository banks from defaulting on their short-term IOUs (deposits). By contrast, OLA is an insolvency regime, not an insurance program. The institutional design of OLA contemplates that shadow banking firms will still default on their short-term IOUs in practically all cases. Simply put, if default is the problem, then OLA probably is not the solution.

This chapter sketches the outlines of an alternative regulatory regime for shadow banking, modeled on deposit insurance. Although a full analysis of this alternative is beyond the scope of the chapter, one central point will be emphasized. If maturity transformation is associated with a market failure, then we must consider limiting the types of firms that may finance themselves with short-term IOUs—that is, we must consider requiring firms to obtain a license in order to issue in this market. Logically, that would mean legally disallowing unlicensed parties from funding themselves with these instruments (subject to de minimis exceptions).

This prohibition is, of course, the foundational law of depository banking: firms are legally prohibited from issuing deposit obligations without a special license. In any discussion about regulating shadow banking, the threshold regulatory question is whether this cornerstone prohibition should be extended to encompass the broader universe of short-term IOUs. In a sense, shadow banking can be understood as modern-day "free banking"—a regime under which no special license is required to issue money-like instruments. Like the free banking regime of the mid-nineteenth-century United States, the shadow banking system has shown itself to be unstable, with adverse consequences for the real economy.

This chapter draws on two recent works by the author. The first, Ricks (2011a) ("Regulating Money Creation after the Crisis"), provides some of the conceptual underpinnings for the argument presented here. The second, Ricks (2011b) ("A Regulatory Design for Monetary Stability"), provides a more detailed defense of the insurance-based regime described here. This chapter focuses more directly on the shadow banking problem, and it offers a more pointed critique of recent regulatory policy—particularly OLA.

The Contemporary Monetary Landscape

Shadow banking involves the issuance of fixed-principal, very short-term IOUs. This chapter refers to these instruments as "money-claims"—a generic term that recognizes the monetary character of these instruments. It is useful to begin with a brief overview of the market for U.S. dollar-denominated money-claims. Figure 4-1 depicts the evolution of this market over the past two decades. The red-tinted series (the top nine series in the figure) represent "private" money-claims, in the sense that the issuer (promisor) is a private firm, not a public institution. The blue-tinted series (the bottom five) represent "sovereign" money-claims, meaning that the government is either issuer or guarantor of the instrument.[2]

Each of the instruments shown in figure 4-1 is a fixed-principal, very short-term IOU. Their precise technical features vary in certain respects. Some, like repurchase agreements ("primary dealer repo") and portions of the asset-backed commercial paper market, are collateralized instruments; the others generally are not. Insured and uninsured deposits are issued only by licensed depository banks; the rest are issued by nondepository institutions. Money market mutual fund (MMMF) "shares" function like fixed-principal IOUs and typically are redeemable more or less on demand; unlike the other instruments, their issuers are regulated under the federal investment company laws. Eurodollar deposits are simply U.S. dollar-denominated short-term IOUs issued by financial institutions that

---

2. In the case of short-term agency securities, the guarantee has been implicit.

Figure 4-1. *Gross Money-Claims Outstanding*[a]

Billions of dollars

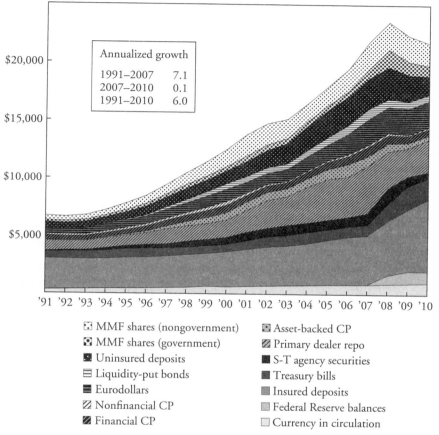

Annualized growth	
1991–2007	7.1
2007–2010	0.1
1991–2010	6.0

⬚ MMF shares (nongovernment)   ◩ Asset-backed CP
◑ MMF shares (government)   ▨ Primary dealer repo
▪ Uninsured deposits   ■ S-T agency securities
☰ Liquidity-put bonds   ▤ Treasury bills
▬ Eurodollars   ▨ Insured deposits
▨ Nonfinancial CP   ▨ Federal Reserve balances
▨ Financial CP   ▢ Currency in circulation

a. Sources are detailed in appendix 4A. In certain cases—particularly Eurodollar deposits—extrapolation was required due to the absence of reliable data; extrapolation methodologies are described in the appendix. This figure uses a one-year maturity cut-off, following market convention for the "money market." However, these instruments are heavily concentrated at the short end of the range. A large majority mature within one month, and probably a majority mature within one *week*.

are domiciled outside the United States. (The "euro" prefix is misleading, as the issuer need not be European.) These formal distinctions are matters of detail and are not important for present purposes. All of these instruments are fixed-principal, very short-term IOUs, and, as discussed below, they share basic functional attributes.

Figure 4-1 gives rise to a few immediate observations. First, the market for U.S. dollar-denominated money-claims is huge, exceeding $20 trillion on a gross basis.[3] (By way of comparison, total outstanding U.S. mortgage debt is around $14 trillion.) Second, this market has grown rapidly over the past two decades. The 7.1 percent annualized growth rate of the market from 1991 to 2007 was significantly in excess of the 5.4 percent annualized growth rate of nominal GDP over the same period. Third, while insured deposits were the single largest individual component of this market throughout the entire period, their share of the total diminished steadily during the years preceding the crisis. Finally, while the market for short-term IOUs is commonly supposed to consist largely of commercial paper issued by nonfinancial firms to finance their working capital, it is immediately apparent that this view is mistaken. The figure shows that nonfinancial commercial paper is only a trivial component of the overall market for money-claims. The market is dominated by sovereign and financial issuers, not by commercial or industrial issuers. The issuers of private money-claims represent the modern shadow banking system.

It is useful to look separately at the private and sovereign components of the money-claim universe. Private money-claims are shown in figure 4-2. Sovereign money-claims—money-claims that are either issued or guaranteed by the federal government—are shown in figure 4-3.

As shown in figures 4-2 and 4-3, over the period from 1991 to 2007, private money-claims grew at an annualized rate of 9.6 percent, far outstripping the 4.0 percent growth rate of sovereign money-claims over the same period. Unsurprisingly, that trend reversed itself in 2008 with the government's intervention during the financial crisis. The quantity of sovereign money-claims increased dramatically from 2007 to 2010. Interestingly, most of this crisis-related growth came not from the Federal Reserve's balance sheet expansion ("Federal Reserve balances")—indeed, figures 4-2 and 4-3 reveal the relatively modest size of the Federal Reserve's balance sheet in relation to the overall

---

3. It should be emphasized that these are *gross* numbers. That is to say, these figures do not net out those money-claims that are held by issuers of money-claims. For example, the figure includes the shares of money market mutual funds; these institutions' assets consist almost entirely of other categories of money-claims that are shown in the figure. Similarly, the figure includes Federal Reserve balances, which are generally owned by the issuers of deposit obligations.

Figure 4-2. *Gross Money-Claims Outstanding, Private*[a]

Billions of dollars

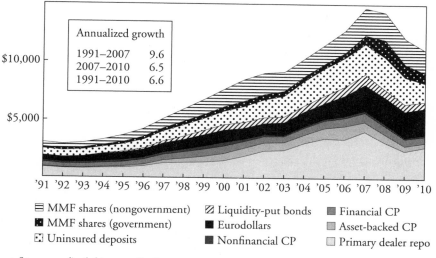

MMF shares (nongovernment) · Liquidity-put bonds · Financial CP
MMF shares (government) · Eurodollars · Asset-backed CP
Uninsured deposits · Nonfinancial CP · Primary dealer repo

a. Sources are detailed in appendix 4A.

Figure 4-3. *Gross Money-Claims Outstanding, Sovereign*[a]

Billions of dollars

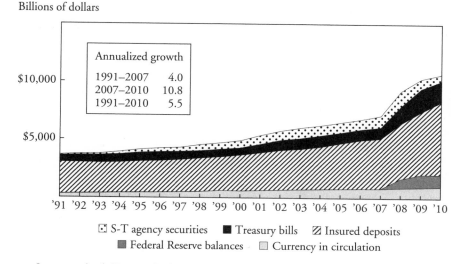

S-T agency securities · Treasury bills · Insured deposits
Federal Reserve balances · Currency in circulation

a. Sources are detailed in appendix 4A.

Figure 4-4. *Gross Money-Claims Outstanding, Private Divided by Total*[a]

Percent

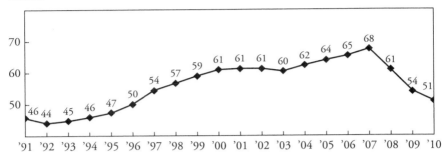

a. Sources are detailed in appendix 4A.

market for money-claims—but rather from emergency increases in deposit insurance coverage.[4] Still, as shown in figure 4-1, the post-crisis growth in sovereign money-claims was insufficient to offset the massive contraction in private money-claims over the same period.

During the years preceding the crisis, private money-claims came to represent a steadily increasing share of the total. Figure 4-4 illustrates that trend and its sudden reversal over the past three years. As shown in the figure, by 2007 private money-claims had come to represent 68 percent of the total, up from 46 percent at the start of the period. A cursory examination of this figure reveals that the periods during which the share of private money-claims increased most rapidly roughly coincide with recent financial "booms" (1996 through 2000 and 2004 through 2007). This shift can be understood as increasing privatization of the money supply.

The proposition that the instruments shown in figure 4-1 have "money-like" attributes was addressed in detail in Ricks (2011a). For present purposes, it is sufficient to postulate that economic agents find it useful to allocate a portion of their wealth to liquid instruments whose value relative to currency is extremely stable.[5] In order to possess this stable-price property, a financial instrument must exhibit very low credit risk and very low interest rate risk. Money-claims are unique in possessing both of these attributes.

4. This increased coverage was attributable to two policy measures: first, the increase in the deposit insurance cap from $100,000 to $250,000 under the Emergency Economic Stabilization Act of 2008, Pub. L. No. 110-343, § 136; and second, the FDIC's emergency Transaction Account Guarantee program, which temporarily removed the deposit insurance cap for noninterest-bearing demand deposit obligations.

5. For a discussion that reaches similar conclusions on this score, see Lucas and Stokey (2011).

In this regard, it is important to emphasize that the term "money-claim" is not synonymous with the term "safe asset" as used in the current literature.[6] That term has come to denote credit instruments that have, or are perceived to have, negligible *credit* risk. Thus, a long-term Treasury security or a long-term AAA-rated obligation issued by a securitization trust would constitute a safe asset under current usage. It is important to note, however, that such long-term instruments can and do fluctuate significantly in price due to changes in market rates of interest.[7] This characteristic is incompatible with the requisite stable-price feature. Accordingly, all long-term instruments are excluded from the term "money-claim" as used in this chapter.

Currently, there exists no cognizable legal or regulatory category corresponding to the term "money-claim" as used here. Instead, the existing U.S. regulatory regime singles out the issuers of *deposit* obligations for special treatment. This chapter takes the position that this distinction is both formalistic and anachronistic. Other money-claims serve a function substantially similar to that of deposit obligations. In essence, they are cash-parking contracts.

This is not to suggest that there are no important distinctions between deposit obligations and other money-claims. On the contrary, two such differences merit special mention. First, demand deposit obligations serve as the predominant medium of exchange in modern economies. Generally speaking, other money-claim categories do not serve this function. Second, deposit obligations are a ubiquitous retail product; a significant proportion of their ownership base consists of relatively unsophisticated consumers. By contrast, most other money-claims are institutional products. In these two important respects, deposit obligations are indeed special.

Yet it does not follow that different regulatory regimes are warranted for deposit issuers, on the one hand, and other money-claim issuers, on the other. As argued below, money-claim issuance (or, equivalently, maturity transformation) is associated with a market failure that justifies government intervention. This rationale applies equally to deposit issuers and to issuers of nondeposit money-claims.

In practice, the functional similarities between deposit obligations and other money-claims are widely acknowledged. Ricks (2011a) describes a variety of

6. For a recent discussion of the importance of this distinction, see Poszar (2011).

7. By way of illustration: if ten-year interest rates increase from 5.0 percent to 6.0 percent, a risk-free bond with a duration of ten years will lose about 9 percent of its market value. Interest rate movements of this magnitude are not an unusual occurrence. From year-end 1990 to year-end 2010, there were fourteen distinct, non-overlapping periods during which ten-year Treasury yields increased by 1 full percentage point.

legal, accounting, and economic contexts in which nondeposit money-claims are treated as functional substitutes for deposit obligations. (To provide just one example: they are designated as "cash equivalents" under generally accepted accounting principles so long as they mature within three months, and their purchases and sales are not required to be recorded in the statement of cash flows—such transactions are treated as exchanges of "cash" for "cash.") It is for this reason that the issuers of nondeposit money-claims have come to be known in recent years, collectively, as the shadow banking system. Like depository banks, shadow banking firms are engaged in the business of maturity transformation, but the money-claims that they issue are not formally styled as "deposits."

Finally, it is noteworthy that, as a matter of emergency policy, the regulatory distinction between deposit obligations and other types of money-claims has been disregarded. As shown in table 4-1, the federal government supported almost every category of private money-claim with emergency stabilization programs in 2008 (compare with figure 4-1).

In addition, the major emergency policy measures that are not reflected in table 4-1—such as capital infusions under the Troubled Asset Relief Program (TARP) as well as the FDIC's massive debt guarantee program for longer-term

Table 4-1. *The Policy Response to the Financial Crisis*

Private money-claim category		Emergency policy measures
Money market mutual fund "shares"	►	Money market mutual fund guarantee (Treasury) Money Market Investor Funding Facility (Fed)
Uninsured deposits	►	Transaction account guarantee (FDIC) Term Auction Facility (Fed) Deposit insurance limit increase (EESA)[a]
Liquidity-put bonds	►	N/A
Eurodollar deposits	►	Central bank liquidity swaps (Fed)
Financial commercial paper Nonfinancial commercial paper	►	Temporary Liquidity Guarantee Program (FDIC) Commercial Paper Funding Facility (Fed)
Asset-backed commercial paper	►	Asset-Backed Commercial Paper–Money Market Mutual Fund Liquidity Facility (Fed)
Primary dealer repo	►	Primary Dealer Credit Facility (Fed) Term Securities Lending Facility (Fed)

a. Emergency Economic Stabilization Act of 2008, Pub. L. No. 110-343, § 136.

debt—were directed primarily toward stabilizing diversified financial firms that rely heavily on money-claim financing. It is no exaggeration to say that practically the *entire* emergency policy response to the recent crisis aimed at stabilizing the market for private money-claims.

The stated purpose of these interventions was not to protect these markets for their own sake but to protect the real economy. These emergency measures were therefore predicated on the assumption that unhindered panic in the money-claim market would do serious economic damage. The basis for that assumption is discussed next.

What's the Matter with Panics?

Defaults by money-claim issuers tend to follow a predictable and well-known pattern. First, one or more money-claim issuers experiences significant portfolio impairments. Some money-claimants begin to withdraw funds from suspect issuers, causing an initial liquidity drain. Other money-claimants sense danger, and the withdrawals escalate into a self-perpetuating run. (In the context of shadow banking, withdrawal simply means declining to roll over money-claims.) Without government liquidity support, the result is default and insolvency proceedings for money-claim issuers. Furthermore, a run on one institution may serve as a "focal point" for money-claimants of other issuers, causing liquidity pressures at relatively healthier firms. Runs thus tend to happen in a correlated fashion, giving rise to panics. This is a standard and fairly uncontroversial account.

Such developments should be expected to have an impact on the supply of newly issued credit to borrowers in the real economy. Under panic conditions, cash parkers remove funds from suspect issuers and seek safety in sovereign money-claims (such as Treasury bills) or in money-claims issued by firms with substantial cash balances. As a precautionary response, money-claim issuers (shadow banks) naturally reduce their exposure to the capital markets and seek to increase their cash reserves. When that happens on a large scale and in a correlated fashion, the result is a shock to the supply of newly issued credit. Such a supply shock should be expected to increase credit costs and reduce the quantity of real credit issued.[8]

---

8. For a related but somewhat different account, see Stein (2012). Stein emphasizes the role of "fire sale" externalities that result from bank runs. In his model, funds removed from the banking system during a run are not immediately reintermediated. As a result, there is less capital "left over for investment in new projects," and the "hurdle rate for new investment" increases. The model is one of a supply shock in the credit markets brought about by run-behavior. See also Diamond and Rajan (2010).

Figure 4-5. *The Liquidity Events*

A. U.S. Asset-Backed Commercial
Paper Outstanding

Billions of dollars

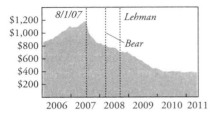

B. Tri-Party Repo Outstanding

Billions of dollars

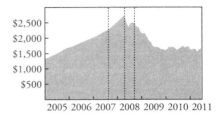

C. U.S. Prime Money Market
Fund Shares Outstanding

Billions of dollars

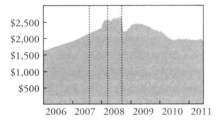

D. Short-Term Funding Spreads[a]

Percent

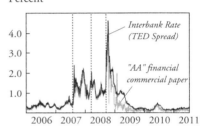

Sources: Panel A: Securities Industry and Financial Markets Association (SIFMA); Excel file ("US ABCP Outstanding") available at www.sifma.org/research/statistics.aspx/. Panel B: FSOC (2011), chart 5.1.17, p. 57; Excel file available at www.treasury.gov/initiatives/fsoc/Pages/annual-report.aspx). Panel C: FSOC (2011), chart 5.3.5, p. 75; Excel file available at www.treasury.gov/initiatives/fsoc/Pages/annual-report.aspx). Panel D: Bloomberg; TED Spread and financial commercial paper rates available through Bloomberg subscription service.

a. Three-month obligations; spread to risk-free rate.

A dynamic like the one described here was evident in the recent financial crisis. Figure 4-5 depicts an unfolding liquidity crisis in the shadow banking system. This liquidity crisis started in August 2007 with a market-wide run on asset-backed commercial paper (ABCP), a class of short-term IOUs issued by conduits that invest in longer-term securities. During the second half of 2007, the volume of outstanding ABCP went into free-fall (panel A) when many investors declined to roll over their positions.

Panel B shows a similar phenomenon occurring a few months later, in a different segment of the money-claim market. It is widely known that the proximate cause of the failure of Bear Stearns was a run on the firm's overnight financing through the giant dealer repo market. Despite the Federal Reserve–assisted rescue of Bear Stearns in March 2008 and despite the Fed's simultaneous establishment of special lending facilities to support the repo market, the period after Bear's failure saw a rapid reduction in repo volumes.

As shown in panel C, the Lehman Brothers default in September 2008 triggered a run on the money market mutual fund sector—one of the core distribution channels for money-claim funding. Practically overnight, investors withdrew nearly half a trillion dollars from prime money market funds. The free fall was halted only after a massive policy response was brought to bear, including a Treasury guarantee of the entire money market mutual fund sector.

As shown in panel D, the costs of money-claim financing skyrocketed during this period. Short-term funding spreads widened dramatically, as cash parkers sought the safe haven of sovereign money-claims in lieu of ABCP, repo, MMMF "shares," and other private money-claims. Naturally, the shadow banking sector responded by going into cash-preservation mode. The result was a drastic reduction in the supply of new credit to real borrowers, as shown in figure 4-6.

The figure shows dramatic reductions in securitization volumes (panel A) and newly originated loans to big corporations (panel B). Notably, the reductions began well before the crisis reached its apex after the fall of Lehman Brothers in September 2008. Furthermore, these volume reductions coincided with significant increases in the cost of credit in virtually every area of the consumer and business credit markets.[9]

As noted above, the panic of 2007–08 was met with a massive federal policy response that included an explosion of Federal Reserve liquidity facilities, as shown in panel C. It also included an array of other emergency measures, including the Treasury money market fund guarantee; a new FDIC program to guarantee senior debt issued by depositories and their affiliates; and, in early October, giant equity infusions into the nation's largest financial institutions through the TARP program.

These emergency measures ultimately proved sufficient to arrest the money-claim panic. By the following May, short-term funding spreads had returned to pre-crisis levels. The measures were accompanied by extraordinary monetary policy initiatives by the Fed, which cut the target federal funds rate to zero and conducted additional expansionary monetary policy through so-called

---

9. This broad increase in credit spreads seems to rule out the hypothesis that the decline in issuance volumes was driven mostly by a decline in *demand* for financing. A reduction in demand would tend to drive spreads down, not up. The evidence is consistent with a supply shock.

Figure 4-6. *The Credit Crunch*

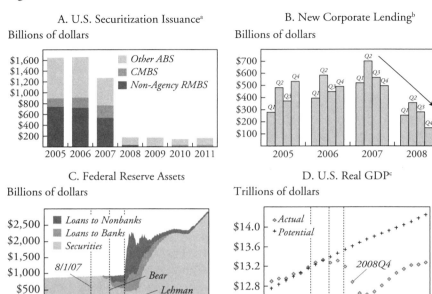

Sources: Panel A: SIFMA; Excel files ("U.S. Mortgage-Related Issuance and Outstanding" and "U.S. ABS Issuance and Outstanding") available at www.sifma.org/research/statistics.aspx. Panel B: Ivashina and Scharfstein (2010). Panel C: Federal Reserve; Excel files available at www.federalreserve.gov/releases/h41/. Panel D: Federal Reserve Economic Data (FRED); "GDCP1" and "GDPPOT" data series available at http://research.stlouisfed.org/fred2/.

a. Excludes agency securitization.
b. U.S. syndicated loan market.
c. Annualized quarterly rates; chained 2005 dollars.

"quantitative easing" initiatives (evident in the buildup of securities in panel C). However, while risk-free rates remained remarkably low by historical standards, these measures were insufficient to avert an abrupt and severe macroeconomic contraction (panel D).

The suggestion here is that the liquidity events shown in figure 4-5 were responsible, in significant measure, for the credit crunch and the ensuing macroeconomic contraction shown in figure 4-6. In other words, this sequence should be interpreted as a causal chain. However, there is at least one other plausible interpretation that must be considered. Perhaps all of these phenomena simply reflected a broad repricing of risk in the capital markets. In its strong form, this view would treat the liquidity event as epiphenomenal, a superficial symptom of the fundamental repricing of credit. The implication is that the credit crunch would have happened anyway, even without the run.

A recent study by Victoria Ivashina and David Scharfstein of Harvard Business School casts doubt on this alternative explanation. Ivashina and Scharfstein (2010), which is essential reading on the credit crunch, examines U.S. financial firms' syndicated lending to the corporate sector during 2007 and 2008.[10] The authors show that lenders with higher amounts of (uninsured) nondeposit financing reduced their syndicated lending activities in the second half of 2008 to a far greater extent than did those with more stable deposit funding (much of which is FDIC-insured). Specifically, a lender with a deposits-to-assets ratio that was 1 standard deviation below the mean reduced its loan originations by 49 percent from late 2007 to late 2008, whereas a lender whose ratio was 1 standard deviation above the mean reduced originations by only 21 percent. Put simply, financial firms that were more susceptible to run behavior cut back on new corporate loan issuance much more severely. The authors conclude that their findings are "consistent with a decline in the supply of funding as a result of the bank run." They further note that "the drop in supply puts upward pressure on interest rate spreads, and leads to a greater fall in lending than one might see in a typical recession."

This discussion offers suggestive evidence that the instability of the shadow banking system had damaging effects on the capital markets and the real economy during the recent crisis. If accurate, this circumstance amounts to a market failure, creating a prima facie case for government intervention. The remainder of this chapter considers alternative modes of intervention. The next section analyzes the likely efficacy of "resolution" techniques, such as those embodied in the new Orderly Liquidation Authority. It is argued that those techniques should not be expected to meaningfully mitigate the damaging effects of shadow banking instability. The subsequent section briefly sketches an alternative approach, one modeled on the modern deposit insurance regime.

"Orderly" Failure and Shadow Banking

It is commonly argued that the shadow banking problem is best addressed through the use of risk constraints (such as portfolio restrictions and capital requirements), perhaps combined with access to central bank liquidity support (the lender of last resort). The difficulties associated with these approaches are discussed in detail in Ricks (2011b). Here it is simply noted that both risk

---

10. A syndicated loan is a large corporate loan provided by multiple financing sources. The authors focus on this market due to the availability of a robust data set of new originations.

constraints and public liquidity support give rise to very significant social costs and that the corresponding benefits are not measurable in any satisfactory way. This circumstance presents legislators and regulators with extremely difficult calibration challenges, leaving them to rely on "gut feel," impressionistic judgments, speculative assumptions, and superficial analyses. The practical significance of this problem would be difficult to overemphasize. A regulatory design that did not rely on such heroic regulatory capacities would obviously be preferable.

In part due to the limitations of these approaches, a major international policy priority has been to develop new insolvency regimes for shadow banks and other nondepository financial institutions. In the United States, one of the centerpieces of the Dodd-Frank Act was the creation of the new Orderly Liquidation Authority for certain financial firms. The goal of this new mechanism is ambitious: as set forth in the statute, it aims "to provide the necessary authority to liquidate failing financial companies that pose a significant risk to the financial stability of the United States in a manner that mitigates such risk and minimizes moral hazard."[11]

Can such a regime be expected to meaningfully address the market failure that is inherent in shadow banking? As noted previously, the statutory scheme of OLA is modeled directly on the existing FDIC receivership authority for depository institutions. This seems sensible; that regime appears to have provided a way to deal with depository insolvencies without imperiling the broader financial system. At first glance, then, this approach might seem to hold the promise of facilitating "orderly" failures of shadow banking entities.

But this proposition needs to be examined more closely. Is it depository receivership or deposit insurance that makes "orderly" depository failures possible? The two are logically distinct. A little history may shed some light here. Prior to the creation of the FDIC, bank failures were handled under insolvency regimes that treated depositors as ordinary creditors. As the FDIC's *Resolutions Handbook* (2003) recounts:

In general practice, between 1865 and 1933, depositors of national and state banks were treated in the same way as other creditors—they received funds from the liquidation of the bank's assets after those assets were liquidated. On average, it took about six years at the federal level to liquidate a failed bank's assets, to pay the depositors, and to close the bank's books— although in at least one instance this process took 21 years. Even when depositors did ultimately receive their funds, the amounts were significantly less than they had originally deposited into the banks.

11. Dodd-Frank Act § 204(a).

With the advent of deposit insurance, it became evident that bank failures could no longer be handled effectively under existing insolvency regimes. A central objective of deposit insurance was to give insured depositors seamless access to their funds when banks failed—to maintain the "moneyness" of deposits. The point, of course, was to prevent default on those monetary instruments, which required a substantial administrative apparatus: the government had to create an agency with the resources, the expertise, and the institutional mandate to achieve that objective. Plainly, the existing management teams of failed banks could not be relied on to administer the deposit insurance regime. The FDIC needed to control the operations of failed banks; it could not stand on the outside looking in.

These two distinct functions—deposit insurance and receivership authority—still go hand in hand. From the *Handbook:*

> In every failing institution transaction, the FDIC assumes two roles. First, the FDIC in its corporate capacity as insurer protects all of the failing institution's depositors. . . . Second, the FDIC acts as the receiver of the failed institution and administers the receivership estate for all creditors. The FDIC as receiver is functionally separate from the FDIC acting in its corporate role as deposit insurer, and the FDIC as receiver has separate rights, duties, and obligations from those of the FDIC as insurer. U.S. courts have long recognized these dual and separate capacities.

Understanding the FDIC's dual roles is important—because the new OLA regime encompasses only one of those roles. OLA is a receivership regime, not an insurance program. And the function of the FDIC as receiver is quite specific. "A receivership," says the *Handbook,* "is designed to market the institution's assets, liquidate them, and distribute the proceeds to the institution's creditors." The objective of this liquidation process is "to maximize the return on the sale or disposition of the receivership estate's assets." It should be evident that the function of depository receivership per se sounds rather similar to the function of the corporate bankruptcy regime. Indeed, the *Handbook* itself notes that "[i]n many ways the powers of the FDIC *as receiver* of a failed institution are similar to those of a bankruptcy trustee." In short, the aim of the FDIC as receiver is to preserve the value of the firm's assets or enterprise in order to maximize recoveries.

But here we run up against a basic question of objectives. Preserving enterprise value in order to maximize recoveries is no doubt a worthwhile policy goal. It is, after all, one of the basic goals of the corporate bankruptcy system.

However, the analysis in this chapter suggests that the distinctive problem associated with shadow banking failures arises not from enterprise value losses but from the disruption to the credit system and the real economy that occurs when money-claimants anticipate a potential *default.*

In their monumental monetary history, Friedman and Schwartz emphasized this very point. They observed that the bank failures that ushered in the Great Depression "had two different aspects." The first consisted of "losses to both [the failed banks'] owners and their depositors, just as the failure of any other group of business enterprises involved losses to their owners and creditors"—in other words, losses of enterprise value. The second aspect was their *monetary* impact—that is, the monetary (and associated credit) contraction that arose when funds were removed from the depository system. Friedman and Schwartz posed a basic question: "Which aspect was the more important for the course of business?" Their conclusion was that "the second was vastly more important than the first." To underscore the point, the authors noted that the losses of bank enterprise value in the early 1930s were "minor" as a fraction of total wealth and "would deserve no more attention than losses of a comparable amount in, say, real estate." In their view, "[t]he bank failures were important not primarily in their own right, but because of their indirect effect." More pointedly:

> If [the bank failures] had occurred to precisely the same extent without producing a drastic decline in the stock of money, they would have been notable but not crucial. If they had not occurred, but a correspondingly sharp decline had been produced in the stock of money by some other means, the contraction would have been at least equally severe and probably even more so.[12]

If this monetary view has merit, then losses of enterprise value are at most a secondary issue when it comes to depository failures. And the discussion above makes clear that the function of the FDIC as *receiver*—on which OLA is modeled— is really about maximizing the enterprise value of failed banks. It is the FDIC as *insurer* that keeps the adverse monetary consequences from taking place.

But does the new OLA regime not give the FDIC access to resources that would enable it to deal with monetary effects as well? For instance, could it not make funds available to honor the money-claims of failed issuers, thereby avoiding any adverse monetary repercussions? Not necessarily. It is true that the FDIC *might* have substantial resources at its disposal under the OLA regime (more on

---

12. Friedman and Schwartz (1963).

this later) and that these resources *might* be used under some circumstances to honor money-claims. Specifically, the OLA legislation gives the FDIC the power to make "additional payments" to third parties if certain conditions are met.[13] Presumably this power could be invoked to honor money-claims, at least some of the time. The FDIC has even hinted at that possibility. In its interim final rule (IFR) regarding OLA implementation, the FDIC made clear that long-term creditors (those with terms exceeding 360 days) will never receive such "additional payments."[14] By inference, that leaves open the possibility that money-claims might sometimes be honored in accordance with their contractual terms, thus neutralizing the monetary impact of failure.

It is important to note, however, the FDIC can make additional payments to creditors only under specified circumstances. In particular, the statute requires the FDIC to conclude "that such action is necessary (I) to maximize the value of the assets of the [firm]; (II) to maximize the present value return from the sale or other disposition of the assets of the [firm]; or (III) to minimize the amount of any loss realized upon the sale or other disposition of the assets of the [firm]."[15] As a textual matter, those conditions have nothing to do with preventing money-claim defaults. On the contrary: they are enterprise value considerations. Certainly these conditions would permit payments under contracts that are needed to keep the business running, such as contracts for ongoing services (paying utility bills, meeting payroll, and the like). But it is far from obvious that pure *funding* contracts—such as money-claims—could ever satisfy any of these criteria. It is worth asking what the status of, say, Lehman Brothers commercial paper—the default on which ignited a run on the money market mutual fund industry—would have been under these standards. It comes down to the FDIC's interpretation.

There is no need to speculate about the FDIC's position. It goes out of its way in the IFR to note that despite the fact that it reserves the right to make additional payments to short-term creditors, no one should count on it. Indeed,

---

13. See Dodd-Frank Act §§ 210(b)(4), 210(d)(4), 210(h)(5)(E).

14. Federal Deposit Insurance Corporation, *Orderly Liquidation Authority Provisions of the Dodd-Frank Wall Street Reform and Consumer Protection Act,* Interim Final Rule, 76 Fed. Reg. 4211 (Jan. 25, 2011) [hereinafter FDIC IFR]. The rule has since been finalized. Federal Deposit Insurance Corporation, *Certain Orderly Liquidation Authority Provisions under Title II of the Dodd-Frank Wall Street Reform and Consumer Protection Act,* Final Rule, 76 Fed. Reg. 41626 (July 15, 2011).

15. Dodd-Frank Act § 210(h)(5)(E). To be precise, this is the standard for transferring claims to a so-called "bridge entity," where they are to be honored. Other avenues are available to make additional payments, but they are subject to more or less the same standards. Incidentally, the FDIC has self-imposed an additional procedural condition: additional payments can be made to a creditor only upon an affirmative vote by the FDIC board of directors, which must make a specific determination that the relevant statutory requirements are met. FDIC IFR at 4215.

according to the IFR, additional payments will be granted with "exceeding rarity."[16] For the avoidance of doubt:

> While the Rule distinguishes between long-term unsecured senior debt and shorter term unsecured debt, this distinction does not mean that shorter term debt would be provided with additional payments under [the applicable statutory provisions]. . . .
>
> Short-term debt holders . . . are highly unlikely to meet the criteria set forth in the statute for permitting payment of additional amounts. In virtually all cases, creditors with shorter-term claims on the covered financial company will receive the same pro rata share of their claim that is being provided to the long-term debt holders. Accordingly, a potential credit provider to a company subject to the Dodd-Frank resolution process should have no expectation of treatment that differs depending upon whether it lends for a period of over 360 days or for a shorter term.[17]

It is possible that this is all an elaborate head-fake. Maybe the FDIC fully intends, as a matter of policy, to promptly honor (in full and on time) the money-claims of issuers that are put into receivership under OLA and believes that it has the statutory authority to do so. (If so, its bluff is unlikely to work forever; you can't fool all of the people all of the time.) As a starting point, however, it seems more sensible to take the FDIC's policy statements at face value.

So what happens to unsecured money-claimants that do not receive additional payments—as will be the outcome "in virtually all cases"? The answer is that they will receive payments based on the value realized, or expected to be realized, from the liquidation of the enterprise in accordance with their creditor priority.[18] More specifically, as a technical matter, the "maximum liability" of the receivership to any claimant "shall equal the amount that such claimant *would have received* if" the failed firm "had been liquidated under chapter 7 of the Bankruptcy Code" or other applicable insolvency laws.[19] In short, unsecured money-claimants should expect to see their claims impaired or extinguished—and they may not receive payouts, if any, for some time.[20]

---

16. FDIC IFR at 4212.
17. Ibid. at 4211–12 (emphasis added). To drive home the point, in its request for comment on the IFR, the FDIC asked: "Are there additional ways to counteract any impression that shorter term debt is not at risk?"
18. Dodd-Frank Act § 210(b)(1).
19. Ibid. § 210(d)(2) (emphasis added).
20. The FDIC "may, in its discretion and to the extent that funds are available, pay creditor claims" after it has determined that they are allowed. Dodd-Frank Act § 210(a)(7). There is no date certain.

For *secured* money-claims (that is, repo instruments), the treatment is somewhat different—but just as problematic from a monetary standpoint. The FDIC has until 5:00 p.m. on the business day following its appointment as receiver to decide whether the repo contract will be honored and, if so, to notify the repo creditor of its decision.[21] If the repo claim is not honored, the repo creditor may terminate the contract and take the collateral. However, it should be clear that any failure to honor repo obligations has adverse monetary consequences. Repo is a money-claim; the collateral underlying it typically is not. If the repo creditor had wanted an asset resembling the underlying collateral, presumably it would have bought that instead. (The fact that repo is collateralized does not imply that the repo creditor is indifferent to the choice between owning the repo and owning the collateral!) Repo creditors do get their collateral quickly, but they must then monetize the collateral if they want to restore their money balances. That means persuading third parties to part with money. If the collateral is very liquid and can easily be sold at little or no fire-sale discount (a big "if" during a panic), then the direct harm to money-claimants under this scenario might be rather small. Nevertheless, the money supply has shrunk.[22] Just as important, as witnessed in the recent crisis, the moment at which repo creditors seize and liquidate collateral from failed money-claim issuers is likely to be precisely the moment at which normally liquid collateral becomes very hard to sell. (If the collateral were so liquid, why did the repo issuer not monetize it to prevent its own demise?) If the collateral cannot easily be monetized, then from a consequential loss perspective repo creditors might be little better off than unsecured money-claimants.

There is yet another problem. Even if the FDIC wants to make additional payments to money-claimants under OLA, it may do so only if the requisite resources are available. The funding provisions of OLA are therefore paramount. In implementing a receivership, the FDIC must borrow from the Treasury

---

21. See ibid. § 210(c)(10)(A). Obligations on those contracts are suspended until that time; see ibid. § 210(c)(8)(F)(ii). In addition, creditors' walkaway clauses are unenforceable; see ibid. § 210(c)(8)(F)(i). This discussion assumes that the repo instrument qualifies as a "qualified financial contract," as should practically always be the case.

22. The FDIC has indicated that it will "exercise care" in valuing collateral and that it "will review [each secured] transaction to ensure it is not under-collateralized" (FDIC IFR at 4212). Any money-claim that is undercollateralized presumptively will not be honored: "[I]f the creditor is undersecured due to a drop in the value of such collateral, the unsecured portion of the claim will be paid as a general creditor claim" (ibid.). Explicitly, the FDIC wants to discourage "overreliance" on "short-term, secured transactions in the repurchase market," which it views as "[a] major driver of the financial crisis and the panic experienced by the market in 2008" (ibid.).

Department—and those borrowings are not unconditional. They are subject to "such terms and conditions as the [Treasury] Secretary may require."[23] That is to say, they are at the discretion of the then-presiding administration—which might very well be sensitive to the political ramifications of authorizing the disbursement of potentially hundreds of billions of dollars in taxpayer funds to honor the money-claims of a failed financial firm.

Furthermore, there are explicit statutory limitations on the size and timing of those borrowings. For the first thirty days of any receivership, unless the FDIC has "calculated . . . the fair value of the total consolidated assets" of the failed firm, the FDIC is not permitted to borrow funds in an amount exceeding 10 percent of the firm's most recently reported "total consolidated assets."[24] Only after the thirtieth day (or sooner if the fair value calculation is completed) can the FDIC borrow more—but even then its borrowing capacity is limited to 90 percent of the "fair value of the total consolidated assets" of the firm "that are *available for repayment*."[25] (Presumably this latter qualifier is intended to exclude from the calculation assets that are subject to a security interest; if so, then the amount of resources available to the FDIC in any liquidation is a *decreasing* function of the amount of repo issued by the firm.) Thus, even if the FDIC wanted to make quick payouts to money-claimants and were satisfied that it had the statutory authority to do so under the additional payments provision, it still would need the concurrence of the executive branch, and it still might run up against statutory borrowing capacity limits.

Finally, there is one other critical, if more subtle, potential impediment: Treasury's ability to provide the necessary resources is subject to the availability of its own funds. If the Treasury Department needs to issue Treasury securities in order to raise the proceeds for a big loan to the FDIC, and if those borrowings would cause the federal government to exceed the then-operative statutory public debt ceiling, then congressional approval would be needed.[26] As witnessed in the recent crisis (not to mention in the summer of 2011), this risk is hardly trivial.[27]

---

23. Dodd-Frank Act § 210(n)(5).
24. Ibid. § 210(n)(6).
25. Ibid.
26. Ibid. § 210(n)(5).
27. The debt ceiling needed to be increased in both of the major pieces of crisis-response legislation that were enacted in late 2008. See Housing and Economic Recovery Act of 2008, Pub. L. No. 110-289, § 3083, 122 Stat. 2654; Emergency Economic Stabilization Act of 2008, Pub. L. No. 110-343, § 122, 122 Stat. 3765. Former Treasury Secretary Henry Paulson has emphasized that the debt ceiling was a key issue in congressional negotiations during the crisis. See Paulson (2010).

To sum up, the position of money-claimants in a Dodd-Frank orderly liquidation is far from secure. Their statutory entitlements are generally similar to what they would be in bankruptcy: they have no legal basis to complain if they receive only the value that they would have received in a bankruptcy liquidation, and they generally have no right to receive any payments at all until the conclusion of the receivership, which might be years away. (Contrast that with the position of insured depositors.) Although it will decline to do so "in virtually all cases," the FDIC might in its discretion authorize additional payments to money-claimants if it satisfies itself that such payments would maximize returns or minimize losses to the receivership. Even then, however, adequate funding must materialize—and it is not obvious that it will do so in a timely fashion or at all. The quantity of funds available for any liquidation is subject to strict numerical limitations, particularly in the first thirty days. The administration needs to agree to supply the necessary funding, and there is a significant chance that the debt limit would need to be increased, requiring an act of Congress.

Needless to say, this approach is very different from the model that the FDIC uses for insured depositories—the one that arguably has prevented insured depositor panics for nearly eighty years. If the "orderliness" of depository failures arises from the fact that insured depositors' claims are seamlessly honored in full and on time—if, as Friedman and Schwartz argued, the basic problem is essentially *monetary* in character—then OLA cannot be said to offer a reasonable prospect of "orderly liquidation."

Sketching an Alternative Regulatory Design

So long as money-claims remain subject to default, it seems unlikely that the problem of runs and panics and the associated adverse economic consequences can be avoided. As discussed above, OLA is not designed to address this issue.

In Ricks (2011b), I proposed a regulatory apparatus to address this problem directly. The elements of the proposal can be described succinctly. Under the proposed design—a "public-private partnership" (PPP) regime for money creation—the government would

—establish licensing requirements for the issuance of money-claims. (Logically, this would mean disallowing unlicensed parties from issuing these instruments, subject to de minimis exceptions.)

—require licensed firms to abide by portfolio restrictions and capital requirements. (In effect, adherence to these risk constraints would be the "eligibility criteria" for the regime.)

—establish an explicit government commitment to stand behind the money-claims issued by licensed firms, making them default-free.

—require licensed firms to pay ongoing, risk-based fees to the government in exchange for this public commitment.

Those who are familiar with the modern regulation of depository institutions will observe that these are precisely the core regulatory techniques that have been used for the depository sector since the establishment of the FDIC in 1933. Specifically: the federal government and state governments issue special charters to depository banks, and unlicensed firms are legally prohibited from issuing deposit liabilities; depository banks are constrained to a narrow range of permissible activities and investments and are subject to capital requirements; the federal government explicitly stands behind (most) deposit obligations through the deposit insurance system; and depository banks pay ongoing, risk-based fees to the government in return for this explicit commitment. In short, U.S. depository banks operate under a public-private partnership regime.

Conceptually, then, the PPP proposal is modest, even conservative. It envisions the modernization of an approach that has been used in the United States for many decades, arguably with reasonable success (albeit with some notable lapses). It is important to note that the proposal is not that deposit insurance be "extended" to cover institutions that are currently ineligible for depository licenses. Instead, the argument begins at an analytically prior position. It starts by revisiting banking law's foundational *prohibition:* existing law forbids the issuance of *deposit* obligations without a special license, but this prohibition does not apply to other categories of money-claim. As argued above, this distinction is both formalistic and anachronistic. In our modern financial system, deposit obligations—once the predominant cash-parking contract—have come to represent only a small fraction of outstanding money-claims. Other money-claims raise the same basic policy problem.

The end result of this functional regime would be to make all money-claims sovereign and default free. In the event of insolvency, licensed issuers would be subject to a special resolution regime under which money-claims would be honored in full and on time, while other providers of financing would see their claims impaired or extinguished. (This resolution regime would be modeled on the FDIC's existing resolution regime for depository banks, under which insured deposit obligations are seamlessly honored.) In effect, the PPP regime would recognize money creation as a public good. The proposal does not contemplate coverage caps, such as the current $250,000 limit on deposit insurance coverage. All money-claims, whether styled as "deposits" or not, would be sovereign obligations.

A natural question is what types of firm should be eligible for licenses—equivalently, what types of asset portfolio should be permitted to be financed with money-claims. Ricks (2011b) provides reasons to think that licensed issuers should be limited to relatively low-volatility portfolios of credit assets. Many business models that currently rely heavily on money-claim financing, such as broker-dealers and certain types of hedge fund, would be ineligible for licenses under this criterion. Such firms would therefore be precluded from issuing money-claims—again, just as firms not licensed as depository banks are now prohibited from issuing deposit instruments. In practical terms, they would be required to "term out" their funding. That is, they would be required to finance themselves in the (debt and equity) capital markets. Funded in this way, these firms would be amenable to ordinary bankruptcy procedures. Furthermore, having dealt with the problem of money-claim panics through the PPP system, the government could credibly deny unlicensed firms access to public support facilities.

Under the proposed design, large portions of the financial industry that currently rely heavily (directly or indirectly) on money-claim funding would be required to term out their financing structures. The effects on the profitability and size of these firms would be very substantial. On a related note, the PPP regime should be expected to result in higher bid-ask spreads in the capital markets, reducing overall capital mobility to some degree. Moreover, the money market mutual fund business model would be rendered uneconomic.[28] These effects are undesirable when considered in isolation. However, the removal of a subsidy is necessarily costly to its beneficiaries.

Without question, the PPP regime raises implementation challenges and risks of its own. In particular, it requires a substantial contingent resource commitment from the government. However, that is true of any government intervention to provide a public good. (And the government's response in the recent crisis should give the lie to the notion that such a commitment does not already exist.) The costs of publicly underwriting the money supply through the PPP system must be weighed against the benefits of monetary stability, which appear to be substantial. Unlike recent regulatory reforms, the PPP proposal contemplates the end of shadow banking—an activity whose existence appears to be incompatible with financial and monetary stability.

---

28. MMMF portfolios consist entirely of money-claims, which would all be federally insured under the PPP regime, reducing their yield. In addition, MMMFs would be required to pay ongoing fees and abide by capital requirements, since their "shares" are themselves money-claims. It is very unlikely that this business model would generate sufficient returns to be viable.

Table 4A-1. *Sources for Money-Claim Figures in Figures 4-1 through 4-4*

Measure	Source	Notes
Currency in circulation	Federal Reserve Economic Data (FRED), available at http://research.stlouisfed.org/fred2/	Year-end data.
Federal Reserve balances	FRED	Year-end data.
Treasury bills	Council of Economic Advisers (2011), table B-87	Year-end data.
Insured deposits	FDIC (2011)	Estimated insured deposits reported by the FDIC; Q4 data.
Short-term agency securities	Bloomberg (Government Sponsored Enterprise [GSE] short-term borrowing); 2010 annual reports for Fannie Mae and Freddie Mac; Federal Home Loan Bank (FHLB) Office of Finance annual reports (discount notes)	FHLB discount notes extrapolated prior to 1998 (as a constant proportion of GSE short-term borrowings). Year-end data except for Freddie Mac 2010, whose short-term debt measure is an average balance.
Primary dealer repo	FSOC (2011), chart 5.2.43	Extrapolated prior to 1995 (as a constant proportion of financial CP); Q4 data.
Asset-backed commercial paper	Federal Reserve Data Download Program; FRED	Pre-2001 data reflect Federal Reserve's old method; 1991 figure was not available, so it was set equal to 1992 figure; December data. Data for 2001–10 reflect Fed's new method; year-end data.
Financial commercial paper	Federal Reserve Data Download Program; FRED	Pre-2001 data reflect the Fed's old method; December data. 2001–10 data reflect the Fed's new method; year-end data.
Nonfinancial commercial paper	Federal Reserve Data Download Program; FRED	Pre-2001 data reflect the Fed's old method; December data. 2001–10 data reflect the Fed's new method; year-end data.

(continued)

Table 4A-1. *Sources for Money-Claim Figures in Figures 4-1 through 4-4* (continued)

Measure	Source	Notes
Eurodollars	FDIC (2011); McGuire and von Peter (2009)	Sum of FDIC's reported foreign office deposits and McGuire and von Peter's $2.2 trillion eurodollar estimate for 2007 extrapolated before and after 2007 (as a constant proportion of the FDIC's reported foreign office deposits); Q4 data.
Government money market mutual funds	ICI (2011)	Year-end data.
Nongovernment money market mutual funds	ICI (2011)	Includes both the nongovernment and tax-exempt categories reported in ICI (2011); year-end data.
Liquidity-put bonds	FSOC (2011)	2005–10 estimates are the sum of the average amounts outstanding of tender option bonds, auction rate securities, and variable rate demand bonds, extrapolated prior to 2005 (as a constant proportion of ABCP); year-end data.
Uninsured deposits	FDIC (2011)	Calculated by subtracting estimated insured deposits from domestic office deposits; Q4 data.

References

Council of Economic Advisers. 2011. *Economic Report of the President*. (www.whitehouse.gov/administration/eop/cea/economic-report-of-the-President/2011).

Diamond, Douglas, and Raghuram Rajan. 2010. "Fear of Fire Sales and the Credit Freeze." BIS Working Paper 305. Bank for International Settlements (www.bis.org/publ/work305.pdf).

FDIC (Federal Deposit Insurance Corporation). 2011. "Quarterly Banking Profile." First Quarter 2011 (http://www2.fdic.gov/qbp/).

Friedman, Milton, and Anna J. Schwartz. 1963. *A Monetary History of the United States: 1867–1960.* Princeton University Press.

FSOC (Financial Stability Oversight Council). 2011. "2011 Annual Report." Washington, D.C.

Gorton, Gary B. 2010. *Slapped by the Invisible Hand: The Panic of 2007.* New York: Oxford University Press.

ICI (Investment Company Institute). 2011. *Investment Company Factbook* (www.ici.org/pdf/2011_factbook.pdf).

Ivashina, Victoria, and David Scharfstein. 2010. "Bank Lending during the Financial Crisis of 2008." *Journal of Financial Economics* 97, no. 3: 319–38.

Lucas, Robert E., and Nancy L. Stokey. 2011. "Liquidity Crises." Federal Reserve Bank of Minneapolis, Economic Policy Paper 11-3.

McGuire, Patrick, and Peter von Goetz. 2009. "The U.S. Dollar Shortage in Global Banking." *BIS Quarterly Review* (March 2009).

Paulson, Henry M. 2010. *On the Brink.* New York: Business Plus.

Poszar, Zoltan. 2011. "Institutional Cash Pools and the Triffin Dilemma of the U.S. Banking System." IMF Working Paper 11/190 (www.imf.org/external/pubs/ft/wp/2011/wp11190.pdf).

Ricks, Morgan. 2011a. "Regulating Money Creation after the Crisis." *Harvard Business Law Review* 1, no. 1: 75–143.

———. 2011b. "A Regulatory Design for Monetary Stability." Harvard John M. Olin Discussion Paper Series 706.

Stein, Jeremy. 2012. "Monetary Policy as Financial-Stability Regulation." *Quarterly Journal of Economics* 127, no. 1: 57–95.

CHARLES W. CALOMIRIS
RICHARD J. HERRING

5

Why and How to Design a Contingent Convertible Debt Requirement

ALTHOUGH DEBATES STILL rage over the causes of the financial crisis of 2007–09, one thing is clear: several of the world's largest financial institutions—including Fannie Mae, Freddie Mac, Citigroup, UBS, AIG, Bear Stearns, Lehman Brothers, and Merrill Lynch—had amassed huge and concentrated credit and liquidity risks related to subprime mortgages and other risky investments, but they maintained equity capital that was too small to absorb the losses that resulted from those risky investments. In other words, relative to risk, equity capital proved inadequate to insulate these firms, and many others, from insolvency when their risks were realized.[1]

Internal bank risk management and external prudential regulation and supervision failed precisely because they did not correctly compute and require the appropriate amount of equity *relative to risk*. The regulatory failure was not that equity capital requirements were too low, per se. After all, as of mid-2006, Citigroup's ratio of the market value of equity relative to the market

For helpful comments, the authors wish to thank, without implicating, Wilson Ervin, Mark Flannery, Charles Goodhart, Andrew Haldane, Tom Huertas, George Pennacchi, Kenneth Scott, Matthew Willison, and Peter Zimmerman. We are also grateful to the participants in the Brookings-Nomura-Wharton Conference on Financial Markets for comments on an earlier draft.

1. By "equity capital" we refer here and elsewhere in this chapter to the economic value of equity (which we later proxy with a moving average of the market value of equity) rather than the book value of equity.

value of assets was nearly twice that of Goldman Sachs; and yet, Citigroup, not Goldman Sachs, was the institution whose losses produced insolvency. The difference occurred because Citigroup's risk exposures, including off-balance sheet risks associated with implicit liability to clean up problems in special-purpose entities and special investment vehicles, were disproportionately larger than those of Goldman Sachs.

Examples of failures to constrain risk within a firm's capacity to bear loss abound. Chief executive officers and boards appeared to have lacked an effective framework or the willingness to apply the appropriate tools to measure risk correctly or to constrain aggregate risk within prudent limits.[2] Ellul and Yerramilli (2010) finds that banks that rewarded risk managers more prior to the crisis not only saw smaller crisis-related losses but also had lower ex ante volatility, which provides strong evidence that management decisions not to prioritize and empower risk management were a central contributor to the crisis.

This defect can take many forms within a bank's risk management system: overreliance on risk decisions taken at a low level in many product lines and trading desks without consideration of how such exposures might interact under various macroeconomic conditions; a tendency to follow the herd in an attempt to grow revenues and market share rather than question the adequacy of capital to absorb risks inherent in particular strategies; reluctance to question fundamental assumptions about basis risks and hedges; disregard for the risk inherent in the centuries-old challenge of funding long-term assets with short-term liabilities and for liquidity risk more generally; a tendency to override limits when they conflicted with revenue goals; the inability to track aggregate exposures over complex legal structures and product silos in any reasonable amount of time; and failure to risk-adjust the price of internal transfers of funds and compensation more generally.

As a result of these sorts of errors of risk management, the bonuses and compensation that many financial firms granted were real, but the profits used to justify those payments were not. Not only did stockholders suffer as a result of these errors, ultimately taxpayers were obliged to bail out insolvent large institutions or face the possibility of significant spillover costs to the rest of the financial system.

---

2. See Coffee (2010) for the view that these apparent failures in corporate governance may, in fact, be the consequence of pressure from institutional shareholders for managers to take greater exposures to risk. To the extent that this view has merit, our proposal addresses it by creating substantial dilution risk for shareholders, including the CEO who is also at risk of losing both his equity interest and his institution-specific human capital.

Examples of these problems may be found in the bankruptcy of Lehman Brothers (Valukas 2010), the losses sustained by UBS (UBS 2008) and AIG (Eisenbeis 2009; Special Inspector General for TARP 2009), the collapse of Northern Rock (Kirkpatrick 2009), the forced merger of Bear Stearns (Kirkpatrick 2009; SEC 2008), and the collapse of Indy-Mac, Washington Mutual (WaMu) (Kelly 2008; Office of the Inspector General 2010), and Wachovia (Corston 2010), as well as the string of losses reported by Citibank (Special Inspector General for TARP 2011), Merrill Lynch, and Bank of America (SEC 2010). The studies of these individual experiences have questioned whether anyone, including corporate board members, senior management, and supervisors, even comprehended their institutions' exposure to subprime mortgage risk.

These failures to maintain adequate capital and to exercise effective governance of risk are all the more remarkable because regulators and supervisors have been focusing on the problems of risk measurement and capital budgeting for more than two decades. Risk-based capital is precisely the measure that the Basel Committee says that it has been targeting all along when setting its minimum standards for capital. Obviously, despite widespread agreement that risk-based capital was the key concept on which to focus prudential regulation of capital, both bank risk managers and supervisors failed to measure risk correctly and failed to require capital commensurate with that risk.

Why did the regulatory system perform so badly? The failure was not the result of the inadequate richness of the conceptualization of risk. The Basel Accord on Minimum Capital Requirements (1987) has undergone numerous refinements, including a major amendment in 1996 to take account of market risks and a complete renovation of risk measurement with the announcement of Basel II in 2004. Principles for enhancing governance of risk have been addressed in a series of supervisory studies (BCBS 1997; BCBS 1999a; BCBS 1999b; BCBS 2005; BCBS 2006; BCBS 2008; BCBS 2010a; BCBS 2010b; Joint Forum on Financial Conglomerates 1998; and Davies 2003). Indeed, "The Core Principles of Banking Supervision" (BCBS 1997) incorporates sound corporate governance of risk as a key principle.

There were two central reasons that prudential regulation failed to require financial institutions to maintain adequate capital. First, incentive problems distorted the measurement of risk; second, they discouraged the timely replacement of lost equity capital. With respect to the first of these problems, the process for measuring risk, on which capital requirements are based, encourages the understatement of risk. Under existing rules, banks and rating agencies control the measurement of risk used by regulators. Bankers and rating agencies, however, suffer from conflicts of interest that offer them benefits when they understate risk. Banks that understate their risk enjoy lower capital requirements; rating agencies that do so receive larger fee income, allocated through a competitive process known as "ratings shopping." Given their reliance on banks' internal models of risk and on rating agency opinions, prudential authorities have no credible, independent information to serve as a basis for forcing banks to raise their internal assessments of risk.

When bank risk is not measured correctly, it cannot be managed properly. If banks have a strong incentive to understate their risks, then even they may fail to understand the magnitude of risk mismeasurement, which will prevent them from taking appropriate measures to penalize excessive risk taking within their firms.

With respect to the second problem—the failure to replace lost capital in a timely fashion—it is instructive to consider how long it took Citigroup and other financial institutions to deplete their capital during the recent financial crisis. As shown below, many months passed between the initial financial shocks of the crisis—the first revelations of the spring of 2007, the August 2007 run on asset-backed commercial paper, the Bear Stearns bailout of March 2008—and the systemic collapse of mid-September 2008. During the year and a half leading up to the systemic collapse, roughly $450 billion in capital was raised by global financial institutions. Clearly, global capital markets were open, and there were many willing investors, especially hedge funds and private equity funds, as well as wealthy individuals. But many of the financial institutions most deeply affected by the crisis prior to September 2008, despite persistent and significant declines in the market value of their equity relative to assets, chose not to raise sufficient capital.

A top executive at one of those banks confessed to one of us over breakfast during the summer of 2008 that despite the need to replace lost equity, the price of his bank's stock was too low. Issuing significant equity in the summer of 2008 would have implied substantial dilution of stockholders—including existing management. Institutions that had suffered large losses preferred to wait, hoping for an end to the crisis in the summer of 2008 and the elevation of risky asset prices that would accompany that market improvement. After the bailout of Bear Stearns, they also believed that if their situation deteriorated severely, the government would be likely to step in. That further undermined any incentive to replace equity capital promptly, much less preemptively. On balance, the best strategy was to wait and hope for the best.

Of course, these two problems—ex ante risk mismeasurement and mismanagement and ex post failure to replace lost equity—are related. If banks realized that they would be forced to replace lost capital in a timely fashion, then they would have a greater incentive to manage risk properly and maintain adequate equity capital commensurate with that risk in the first place because they would face the prospect of a significant cost (in the form of stockholder dilution) from having to replace lost equity capital in a troubled market.

If regulation failed because of distorted or inadequate incentives to measure and manage risk and to postpone the replacement of lost capital, then it follows that a central focus of reform should be to address those two incentive problems. How can we change bankers' incentives so that they will improve the accuracy of their risk assessment, manage risk better, and replace lost equity capital faster?

In this chapter, we show how a properly designed requirement for convertible contingent capital (CoCos) can provide unique incentives that will, first, motivate systemically important financial institutions (SIFIs) to implement strong systems of risk governance to measure and manage risk and, second, raise additional capital or sell assets in a timely fashion, when necessary, to minimize the chance of violating minimum capital adequacy standards. In addition, our proposed requirement would supplement an institution's capacity to bear loss. Finally, a suitably designed CoCo requirement would supplement supervisory oversight with market discipline. Of course, other complementary reforms of prudential regulatory standards would also be desirable (see Calomiris 2011), but we show that they are not substitutes for CoCos, which play a unique role in improving incentives for risk management and the maintenance of adequate capital, especially for large, "too big to fail" institutions.

Why Equity Capital Requirements Are Not Enough

Basel III (BCBS 2011) has placed emphasis on requirements for more and better-quality capital and more intensive supervision. Do the increases in capital contemplated by the Basel Committee offer a solution to the two crucial problems of risk mismeasurement and failure to replace lost capital in a timely fashion? Will the contemplated enhancement of supervision solve these two problems? History does not provide much reason to be optimistic about either of the proposed solutions.

Although the emphasis on increasing shareholders' equity is a move in the right direction, these reforms will not solve the fundamental problems of accurate risk measurement and maintenance of adequate capital. The measure of shareholders' equity employed by Basel is an accounting measure that inevitably lags its true economic value, thus avoiding timely recognition of loss. The ability to avoid timely recognition of loss encourages banks to understate risk, since they will not be forced to raise dilutive equity in the wake of losses. And, after unrecognized losses occur, banks' incentives for risk management can become even more distorted, since the temptation to gamble for resurrection can lead thinly capitalized banks to increase their risk exposure. Why does the Basel approach to capital requirements produce errors and lags in the recognition of loss?

The measure of shareholders' equity continues to rely on accounting principles that, while they vary from country to country, combine book values and "fair values" when measuring capital compliance.[3] This approach inevitably delays the recognition of losses and permits banks and supervisors—both of whom may stand to benefit from postponing the recognition of loss—to conceal losses in a number of ways.[4] Bankers can be very creative in their use of complex transactions to disguise losses. Supervisors face substantial challenges in detecting and preventing manipulation of book values through gains trading (recognizing capital gains on positions that are held at book value while deferring the recognition of losses), which is a common practice. The bankruptcy of Lehman Brothers (Valukas 2010) revealed another device to exaggerate capital adequacy measures—the so-called Repo 105 or 108 transactions, which disguised repos (a collateralized borrowing) as a removal of assets and thus a reduction in the size of the balance sheet.

The agility of firms in devising strategies for regulatory and accounting arbitrage makes it unlikely that supervisors will ever be able to keep up. Effective regulation is a continual contest between those who are being regulated and those who are supervising, who are less well paid and less well informed. Even when regulators attempt to close a loophole, regulatees usually find another in only a matter of weeks. The innovation known as a Re-Remic provides a good example of the process (IMF 2009a). Because resecuritized securitizations (collateralized debt obligations, or CDOs) were a major source of loss during the crisis, the regulatory authorities attempted to patch the regulatory framework by increasing the risk weights for resecuritized debt in July 2008.[5] The Basel Committee raised the capital charge on BB-rated tranches of resecuritizations from 350 percent to 650 percent and on the AAA-rated tranches of resecuritizations from 20 percent to 40 percent.

3. This, of course, creates problems in comparing capital adequacy across countries. For example, countries that follow international financial reporting standards take a much stricter view of netting off-balance sheet positions than does U.S. generally accepted accounting principles (GAAP), so that the leverage for the five major U.S. dealers in derivatives is substantially understated relative to that of their European peers.

4. For evidence of such understatements of loss during the recent crisis, see Huizinga and Laeven (2012).

5. The Basel Committee (BCBS 2009) has defined a resecuritization as a securitization in which "at least one of the underlying exposures is a securitization exposure."

Within weeks financial engineers had found a loophole. By resecuritizing a Remic that had been downgraded from AAA to BB, they could create a new special-purpose vehicle called a Re-Remic that would allow the old securities to be exchanged for newly tranched securities of which, say, 30 percent would be rated BB because they would take the first loss and that would enable the remaining 70 percent of the new securities to be rated AAA. The BB-rated tranche could be sold to a hedge fund or other investor interested in distressed debt or held by the banks. In the latter case, the result would be a reduction in tier 1 capital required against the position from 14 percent (= 350% * 4%)[6] to 8.92 percent (= 40% * 70% * 4% + 650% * 30% * 4%). The Re-Remic could even include a trigger clause so that if the newly minted AAA securities were subsequently downgraded, they could be re-subdivided into two "exchange classes." Through that means, 65 percent of the original portfolio of securities could retain an AAA rating and another 5 percent could be allocated to a BB-rated first-loss tranche. But still the amount of required capital to be held against the position would be 9.37 percent (= 65% * 40% * 4%* + 35% * 650% * 4%) rather than the original 14 percent.

Not only can supervisors be caught unaware of losses, they also may prefer to pretend that they are unaware. "Forbearance"—especially the ever-greening of loans to borrowers who would otherwise be delinquent, just enough to keep current on their debt service payments—remains a constant challenge for supervisors, who often find themselves under substantial political pressure to delay bank loss recognition.

We emphasize that delayed recognition is not only a technical challenge. Supervisors are subject to substantial political pressure, and that pressure often leads them to prefer to forbear and "play for time" rather than enforce capital adequacy requirements. The purposeful delays by the U.S. authorities in the 1980s and by the Japanese and Mexican authorities in the 1990s are some of the most visible examples of a widespread phenomenon that has been documented time and time again. Supervisors also may lack incentives to enforce the spirit of prudential rules because they are likely to be challenged in judicial or administrative proceedings or legislative hearings for any action that forces an institution to recognize losses, especially when there is some hope that losses will be reversed in time. In some countries, supervisors have been personally liable and subject to criminal penalty for such supervisory errors, and that legal liability is often used to threaten supervisors against taking aggressive actions. The result of these measurement and incentive problems is that supervisory

6. Four percent is the minimum amount of tier 1 capital required against risk-weighted assets, and 350 percent is the new risk weight applied to BB-rated securitizations.

action is often delayed until losses become indisputable rather than when they actually occur.

Given the information and incentive problems that face supervisors, there is little reason to have confidence in new supervisory powers to bring about timely recognition of loss. For example, Britain's Financial Services Authority, which was widely regarded as one of the most effective, forward-looking supervisory authorities in the world, provided an especially egregious example with regard to its oversight of Northern Rock. Just weeks before its collapse, Northern Rock was permitted by its supervisors to adopt the advanced internal measurements approach to computing its regulatory capital requirement. This regulatory decision permitted Northern Rock to reduce its required capital by 30 percent, which it intended to pay out to its shareholders.

Accounting loss recognition lags were substantial during the recent crisis. For example, Duffie (2009) notes that "Citibank, a SIFI that did receive a significant government bailout . . . had a Tier 1 capital ratio that never fell below 7% during the course of the financial crisis and was 11.8% at roughly its weakest moment in December 2008, when the stock-market capitalization of Citibank's holding company fell to around $20 billion dollars, or about 1% of its total accounting assets." Moreover, we have seen, the thin layer of equity capital maintained by most financial institutions can be overwhelmed by sudden losses that occur in a crisis, especially if they respond by selling illiquid assets into thin markets.

The International Monetary Fund (2008) has shown that all of the banks that required bailouts in the crisis reported higher-than-average levels of capital in the last period before the intervention. Indeed, the recent crisis showed that all three components of the regulatory capital adequacy ratio are fundamentally flawed: one, the measure of capital in the numerator did not reflect an institution's ability to absorb loss without going through some sort of resolution process; two, the risk adjustment of assets in the denominator did not reflect some of the most important risks that banks faced; and three, the minimum acceptable level of capital so reported was much too low.

The ease with which banks, especially SIFIs, can evade capital regulation and engage in regulatory arbitrage suggests a need for creating some form of reliable, incentive-based regulation that makes maximum use of available information (including market-based information) to force them to recognize and replace lost capital and to measure and control their risks more effectively. The current approach of understating risk ex ante, disguising loss ex post, and seeking to avoid dilutive equity issues when they are needed most, leaves SIFIs with few options if that risky gamble does not pay off—apart from appealing for a bailout accompanied by the implicit threat that their demise will cause chaos if they do not receive a bailout.

Of course, one could argue that making initial book equity capital requirements much higher would solve some of the incentive problems that distort risk measurement and risk management, even without properly incentivizing the timely replacement of capital. Recently, several academic proposals for reform have called for significant increases in bank equity requirements. Clearly, if banks maintained, say, 50 percent of their financing in the form of book equity, it would be almost certain that bank stockholders, rather than taxpayers, would pay the full cost of any understated risks gone wrong. Would that approach encourage proper risk management by banks? Would it produce banking system outcomes consistent with the public interest?

We do not think so. First, a draconian increase in equity requirements would raise the costs of finance for banks. That increase in cost would translate into a contraction of banking activity—including bank lending. A recent paper, Admati and others (2011), argues that more equity finance might not substantially increase the funding cost of banks. We do not agree. Equity is costlier to raise than debt for fundamental reasons associated with asymmetric information and with managerial agency costs.

With respect to the first of these, Myers and Majluf (1984) showed that adverse selection costs of raising external equity result from asymmetric information and that information problems add to the cost of equity relative to debt. Those costs are reflected both in negative returns upon the announcement of an equity offering and in the much higher underwriting costs firms pay to issue equity rather than debt, which reflect the attempts by issuers to overcome asymmetric information problems during their "road shows" (Calomiris and Tsoutsoura 2011).[7] The literature on bank "capital crunches" documents that shocks to bank equity capital have large contractionary effects on the supply of lending precisely because lost equity is costly to replace, as assumed by Myers and Majluf (Bernanke 1983; Bernanke and Lown 1991; Kashyap and Stein 1995 and 2000; Houston, James, and Marcus 1997; Peek and Rosengren 1997 and 2000; Campello 2002; Calomiris and Mason 2003; Calomiris and Wilson 2004; and Cetorelli and Goldberg 2009).

The negative signaling effects of equity offerings (as modeled in Myers and Majluf 1984) will tend to be mitigated if equity offerings are mandated by regulation rather than chosen voluntarily, but that does not imply that higher

---

7. "Road shows" refers to investment bankers' meetings with institutional investors to explain the motives for raising capital and to allay any concerns that they may have about the prospects of the issuer.

regulatory capital requirements would eliminate the negative signaling effects of an issuance in equity to meet those higher requirements. First, even if all banks went to the equity market at the same time to raise equity, banks whose managers know that they are in better condition will have an incentive to expend more on underwriting to ensure that investors receive credible information of their superior condition. Those expenditures contribute to the costs of equity capital requirements. Second, there will still be differences among banks in the extent to which they choose to raise equity, which means that signaling costs from announcing equity offerings will still be present. For example, some banks (those with high-quality risky assets whose value might be very hard to reveal to outsiders) may decide to avoid equity offerings and meet their higher equity ratios by selling some of their less-opaque assets instead. For both of those reasons, higher equity capital requirements do not eliminate the information costs and attendant adverse selection risks that make equity offerings costly.

In addition to the asymmetric information costs of raising equity, very high equity ratios can have undesirable consequences for managerial efficiency. Although a moderate increase in equity requirements can encourage better risk management by bankers, a dramatic increase could have the opposite effect. As argued in Kashyap, Rajan, and Stein (2008), too much equity can exacerbate agency problems within a bank because reduced leverage and new stock offerings could produce a more entrenched status for bank managers by insulating them from market discipline if leverage is low and ownership is more fragmented.

Whether the tax benefits of debt (the deductibility of interest in corporate taxation) should be included when measuring the relative *long-run* costs of equity finance has been hotly debated (see, for example, Admati and others 2011). But even if tax savings matter only from a transitional perspective, it is beyond doubt that if banks were permitted to raise capital in part through CoCos,[8] they would likely choose to issue capital faster—and thus to restrict loan growth less— during the transition to higher capital. Given the desirability of improving access to credit as one of the means of promoting economic recovery, transitional issues are far from trivial.

All of this is not to say that we oppose a significant increase in capital requirements. We believe that a significant increase is necessary (see Admati and others 2011 and Miles, Marcheggiano, and Yang 2011), but we recognize that there are negative—not just diminishing—social returns to achieving a higher amount

---

8. The CoCo that we propose is designed to be converted from debt to equity only in rare circumstances. Thus, we would argue the tax authorities should permit the deduction of interest on CoCos, like interest on straight debt, for tax purposes.

of capital solely by raising equity capital requirements beyond some point. In our view, raising equity requirements on SIFIs to 9.5 percent of risk-weighted assets, as under Basel III, makes sense, and we could also see legitimate arguments for raising capital even higher, but a draconian increase in equity capital requirements would not be desirable because the risk of default at SIFIs can be reduced in less costly ways. But we also emphasize that the moderate increase in the required capital ratio under Basel III would not be sufficient, per se, to allay all ex ante concerns regarding the adequacy of capital to cover potential losses on assets, much less enough to ensure the adequacy of capital after a significant loss. That is especially so when one recognizes the ability of financial institutions that wish to target a high probability of default on their debts to raise their levels of risk to more than compensate for any moderate rise in capital requirements.

Furthermore, it is hard for regulators to determine the appropriate amount of capital for a bank, and that amount changes over time as risks change. A given amount of equity, even if appropriate today, may not be the right amount tomorrow. Because a properly designed CoCo requirement creates incentives for banks to issue equity to maintain the right amount of capital (equity plus CoCos) relative to risk, CoCos not only encourage timely replacement of lost capital and better management of risk but also encourage banks to respond to increased risk with higher capital.

The limitations of equity capital requirements as a prudential device that we have identified—problems of measuring and enforcing book capital requirements, the asymmetric information and managerial efficiency costs of excessive reliance on equity requirements, the manifestation of those costs in inadequate credit supply, the social costs of potentially inadequate capital, and the need to respond to losses and increases in risk through timely increases in capital—all motivate our proposal for a contingent capital requirement. Our proposed contingent capital requirement retains deductible debt finance as the dominant form of bank finance. Above all, it ensures that management would face strong incentives to manage risk, set capital appropriately, and replace any significant loss of equity capital with new equity capital offerings on a timely basis.

CoCos also have merit in comparison with equity requirements alone with respect to political economy and fair treatment of bank shareholders. Banks that currently benefit from the safety net will undoubtedly resist any increase in capital requirements because, due to implicit and explicit government protection of their liabilities, they already benefit from the lower borrowing costs that they would gain by raising more equity. When faced with a choice between issuing CoCos or equity, however, they should prefer CoCos. CoCos permit banks to continue to exploit the tax shield provided by the asymmetry of treatment between interest and dividends in the tax codes of most countries.[9] Thus, the issuance of CoCos need not result in value loss to shareholders while the forced issuance of equity (given the bank's assets) automatically does (through the reduced tax shield, as well as any funding cost effects related to adverse selection costs of raising equity and agency costs of reduced leverage).

Design Choices of the Various CoCo Proposals

The essential idea of a CoCo has been widely discussed for a number of years by a number of authors. Despite numerous differences in design and specific intent, virtually all versions of CoCos have the common goal of establishing a contractual structure that results in an increase in bank capital in adverse states of the world. That can occur either directly through contractual convertibility or indirectly through incentives to voluntarily raise new equity capital. Recapitalization restores the bank to a viable position of capital adequacy and thereby avoids regulatory resolution. Table 5A-1 in the appendix shows how a number of the proposals vary with regard to three critical features: the amount of CoCos required to be issued; the trigger for conversion from bonds to equity; and the conversion rate, or the amount of equity to be issued when the CoCos are converted.

The differences across proposals with respect to these three key design aspects reflect differences in the weights that the various CoCo proposals attach to the following objectives: one, providing a contingent cushion of common equity that results from the conversion of debt when the CoCo is triggered, which we label the "bail-in" objective; two, providing a credible signal of default risk in the form of the observed yield spread on convertible debt prior to any conversion, which we label the signaling objective; and three, incentivizing the voluntary, preemptive, and timely public issuance of equity (or rights offerings) into the market as a means of avoiding highly dilutive CoCo conversion, which we label the equity-issuance objective.

---

9. Albul, Jaffee, and Tchistyi (2010) suggest that a plausible way to limit the tax shield benefit from issuance of CoCos might be to permit a full deduction for "interest payments that correspond to the coupon on similar, straight bank debt, but to exclude any part of the [CoCo] coupon that represents compensation for the conversion risk. As McDonald (2010) notes, tax deductibility may have political value by virtue of eliminating a reason for banks to oppose contingent convertibles." Although CoCos are of value even without the tax shield, if banks are deprived of a tax benefit that is available to other institutions, some business is likely to migrate from the banking sector to the shadow banking sector, where it is more difficult to monitor and regulate. Of course, the first best solution to this problem would be to eliminate the asymmetry in the tax treatment of dividends and interest payments.

The particulars of the design characteristics of our proposal reflect our view that the primary objective of a CoCo should be the equity-issuance objective. Our recommendations regarding the amount, trigger, and conversion terms of CoCos all reflect our view that the central objective of CoCos should be to incentivize the prompt, voluntary issuance of equity into the market in response to significant losses of equity by a SIFI. Rather than focusing on facilitating a more orderly liquidation of assets, as advocates of the bail-in objective propose, or on creating a convertible debt instrument that would credibly suffer substantial default risk via conversion and therefore provide useful, forward-looking perceptions of default embedded in market signals, we focus on providing institutions with a strong incentive to strengthen risk management and take remedial measures to raise equity long before they face a substantial risk of insolvency.

As recognized by D'Souza and others (2009), the incentive to issue equity preemptively is strengthened when the size of CoCos is large, when the trigger is credibly and observably based on market prices at a high ratio of equity to assets (long before serious concerns about insolvency arise), and when the conversion ratio is dilutive of existing common shareholders (creating a conversion dilution "sword of Damocles" that makes the prospective dilution from issuing preemptive equity into the market appear desirable by comparison).[10] Under those conditions, a SIFI experiencing significant loss and approaching the point at which dilutive conversion would be triggered would choose to issue significant equity into the market, possibly combined with asset sales that would raise the market value of its outstanding equity relative to assets, thereby avoiding the conversion trigger.

To be effective for this purpose, a large amount of CoCos must be required (otherwise the threat of dilution from conversion will not be as great) and the dilutive conversion rate, in combination with the size of the CoCos being converted, must result in more dilution of common stockholders than the alternative preemptive stock offering. By "dilutive CoCo conversion," we mean a conversion that will leave the holders of CoCos with at least as much value in new equity as the principal of the bonds that they surrender.

D'Souza and others (2009) emphasizes that CoCos designed to result in substantial dilution upon conversion not only encourage banks to voluntarily raise preemptive equity capital to avoid CoCo conversion but also have another practical advantage as debt instruments: the strong incentives for management to avoid

---

10. This can be viewed as a reversal of the debt overhang problem, in which shareholders are reluctant to issue equity because most of the gains will go to creditors. Our approach provides incentives for shareholders to issue equity preemptively in order to avoid massive dilution.

conversion mean that CoCos are likely to trade more like fixed-income instruments than ordinary convertibles. Thus, CoCos are likely to hold greater appeal to institutional investors,[11] who tend to prefer low-risk debt instruments.[12] In Huertas's colorful phrase: "To the common shareholder, contingent capital holds out the prospect of death by dilution and it can be anticipated that shareholders would task management to undertake the necessary measures to avoid dilution" (Huertas 2009, p. 5).

Given the strong incentives embedded in our version of CoCos to promote timely equity offerings, we believe that our CoCos would almost never actually convert into equity. They would play little role in "bail-ins" or in signaling CoCo holders' losses (which, in equilibrium, should be expected to be nearly zero). Of course, if a bank experienced a sudden and complete loss of market confidence (say, as the result of accounting fraud á la Enron or WorldCom), then the SIFI likely would be unable to avoid conversion through a preemptive equity offering. Although we value the ability of CoCos to absorb losses under such circumstances, our main interest is in creating very strong incentives for managers to take corrective action while they still have multiple options for doing so.

Not only would the corrective action of a preemptive stock issue or asset sale preserve high ratios of equity to assets in the wake of significant shocks ex post, but the knowledge of the existence of CoCos and the anticipation of the possibility of facing dilutive CoCo conversion would create strong incentives for management to maintain high ratios of capital, accurate measures of risk, and effective controls on risk at SIFIs. CoCo conversion would be a CEO's nightmare: not only would existing stockholders who are diluted by the conversion be calling for his head, but he would also face an onslaught of sophisticated new block holders of stock (institutional investors who formerly were CoCo holders) who are likely to be eager to sack senior management for their demonstrated incompetence.

11. Some insurance companies and bond mutual funds, which have been substantial holders of subordinated debt in the past, have protested that their regulators will not permit them to hold CoCos because they may convert to equity. But if the conversion occurs, the equity could be quickly sold and reinvested in bonds; therefore, that does not seem to be an insuperable constraint.

12. D'Souza and others (2009) runs simulations to show that the strong incentives for CoCo issuers to avoid conversion would make conversions extremely rare; thus, they would have yields quite close to those of traditional subordinated debt. During the Brookings-Nomura-Wharton Conference on Capital on Financial Markets, at which an earlier draft of this chapter was presented, Shigesuke Kashiwagi reported on the results of a survey of more than 150 institutional investors around the world, conducted by Nomura. The survey was designed to gauge the appetite of institutional investors for contingent capital instruments. The survey showed that 74 percent of respondents were either "relatively comfortable" or "very comfortable" with their ability to value Crédit Suisse Buffer Capital Notes (an early example of a CoCo). Of the 150 respondents, 46 percent had purchased Crédit Suisse Buffer Capital Notes and 50 percent had purchased varieties of CoCos issued by Lloyds Bank and Rabobank.

The literature on CoCos has become vast in a short period of time (see Murphy and Willison 2011 for a review). For example, Doherty and Harrington (1995), Flannery (2005), Kashyap, Rajan, and Stein (2008), D'Souza and others (2009), Huertas (2009), Duffie (2009), Pennacchi (2010), Pennacchi, Vermaelen, and Wolff (2009), Bolton and Samama (2010), and Hart and Zingales (2010) have highlighted the potential value of requiring some form of contingent equity capital infusion for banks through conversion of existing debt, insurance contracts, or a rights offering as a buffer against loss. The Dodd-Frank Act mandates the Federal Reserve to study the scope for use of some minimum amount of contingent capital as part of regulatory capital requirements.[13] BCBS (2011) sets out standards that CoCos must meet to qualify as tier 1 or tier 2 capital. The Swiss have specified a requirement for CoCos. Several banks have begun issuing one or another version of them. European Commission (2011) proposed standards for debt bail-ins to avoid the use of taxpayer funds. Requiring a minimum amount of subordinated debt instruments that convert automatically into equity in adverse states of the world prior to reaching the regulatory insolvency intervention point has been embraced by numerous regulators as a credible means of promoting market discipline, which would have several advantages relative to traditional subordinated debt (sub debt).[14]

13. See section 112 (a).2.I of the Dodd-Frank Act.

14. A long tradition in the theory of capital regulation suggests that some form of credibly unprotected subordinated debt would be useful to include as part of a bank's capital requirement because of its role as a disciplinary device. The primary motivation behind the subordinated debt idea (Horvitz 1983; Guttentag and Herring 1987; Calomiris 1999; Shadow Financial Regulatory Committee 2000; Herring 2004) is that requiring a bank to issue a minimum amount of junior, unprotected debt, which would suffer first loss in the event of an insolvency, publicizes market perceptions of default risk. That could inform bank supervisors about the condition of a bank and make supervisors more likely to act rather than forbear from disciplining banks (since the signal is public). Junior debt yields are especially useful as indicators to policymakers since the FDIC is in a senior position relative to junior debt. Thus, observing the yields on junior, subordinated debt provides a helpful indicator of market perceptions of the risk borne by the FDIC. If supervisors can detect risk in a timely fashion, bank failures will be less likely because, first, banks will have to react to supervisors' concerns by limiting their risk and raising their equity capital once they suffer losses that increase their default risk on debt; second, banks that are unable to prevent continuing deterioration in their condition will be subject to credible prompt corrective action (PCA) to prevent them from becoming deeply insolvent. Indeed, the advocates of sub debt requirements, therefore, have traditionally seen a sub debt requirement as a complement to PCA. PCA envisions rule-based interventions by regulators (triggered by indicators of weakening bank condition) to require that banks increase capital and reduce risk prior to becoming insolvent. The problem in practice is that intervention, which is triggered by book value ratios, typically has not been sufficiently prompt to permit any effective corrective action to be taken.

In response to the mandate within the Gramm-Leach-Bliley Act of 1999 that required the Federal Reserve and the Treasury to study the efficacy of a sub debt requirement, a Federal Reserve Board study reviewing and extending the empirical literature broadly concluded that sub debt could play

CoCos are superior to straight sub debt as a form of required capital from several perspectives. First, by making subordinated debt convert into equity prior to bank insolvency, CoCos eliminate the potential, politically charged issue of deciding to impose losses on debt holders after intervention—something most regulators were reluctant to do in the recent crisis. Since CoCos will have already converted to equity, they will share in any losses suffered by equity holders, and so the issue of imposing loss is removed from consideration. CoCos, unlike straight subordinated debt, will credibly protect deposits against loss in adverse times to some extent.

Second, because CoCos would credibly remain in the bank and suffer losses in insolvency states, ex ante the prices of CoCos will accurately reflect their true risks. Given the widespread practice of bailing out subordinated debt during the crisis, sub debt can no longer serve this function.

Third, in the event that conversion is triggered, CoCos provide a better buffer against losses to depositors, counterparties, and senior debtors than subordinated debt does, since they will cease to accrue interest once they convert and therefore alleviate liquidity pressures on the bank to some extent.

Fourth and most important, if properly structured (as discussed above), CoCos will give incentives to boards and senior managers to replenish any significant losses of equity on a timely basis and thereby also strengthen controls over risk and corporate governance.

Of course, if an institution waits too long or if it experiences a sudden, dramatic loss of market confidence (as in the Enron collapse), it may find that equity markets are closed to it or that it can sell assets only at distressed prices. That is why SIFIs are likely to launch new issues or sell assets long before they approach the CoCo conversion point, particularly if the CoCo trigger is set high enough

---

a useful role as a signal of risk. Despite that conclusion, no action was taken to require a sub debt component in capital requirements; instead, the Fed concluded that more research was needed. The development of the credit default swap (CDS) market and recent research showing that CDS yields contain important information about bank risk not otherwise available to supervisors (Segoviano and Goodhart 2009) have added further interest in finding ways to harness the information content of sub debt for regulatory purposes. Other observers, however, have noted that actual sub debt yields and CDS spreads were quite low during the financial boom of 2005–07, indicating that they would not have provided a timely signal of increased bank risk in 2006 and early 2007. On the other hand, advocates of sub debt requirements have noted that outstanding bank sub debt in 2006 and 2007 was not credibly unprotected and, in fact, was bailed out during the crisis in most cases. Indeed, all of the subordinated debt of Fannie Mae and Freddie Mac was bailed out. In that sense, the failure of sub debt to signal problems could simply reflect correct expectations by market participants that the debts that they were holding were not effectively at risk.

so that this point is reached long before insolvency (when it may be too late to issue new shares).[15]

Setting an Appropriate Trigger and Related Issues

An appropriate trigger must be accurate, timely, and comprehensive in its valuation of the issuing firm (D'Souza and others 2009), and it should be defined so that it can be implemented in a predictable way so that CoCo holders can price the risks inherent in the instrument at the time of its offering. The latter point has been emphasized by the ratings agencies that refuse to rate CoCos in which the conversion is contingent upon the decision of a regulator or of bank management.[16]

Some proposals for contingent capital (for example, D'Souza and others 2009; Hart and Zingales 2010) assume that book values of the institution's equity relative to its assets would be the appropriate conversion trigger for CoCos. But book value is an accounting concept, subject to manipulation, and is inevitably a lagging indicator of deterioration in a bank's balance sheet.[17] The problem of using book value as the trigger is not just one of managerial dishonesty.[18] As we argue above, regulators and supervisors have shown time and again that they are hesitant to opine negatively about SIFIs in a way that will become public. Such forbearance leads to protracted delays in recognizing problems. Thus, a central purpose of employing non-equity capital is to reinforce official supervision with market discipline.

What market-based measures could be employed as the trigger? The two obvious candidates are credit default swap (CDS) spreads and stock price movements. CDS markets seem less desirable for the purpose of deriving triggers for two

15. One problem frequently noted by Charles Goodhart—which does not apply to our proposal—arises with CoCos that aim to achieve the bail-in objective. Bailing in debts via conversion when banks are near the insolvency point may make it harder for banks to raise funds as they near that low CoCo trigger. In other words, since bail-in CoCos are intended to give haircuts to debt holders, they will not be keen to buy them when the prospect of a haircut is near. Under those conditions, equity issues also may not be feasible. Goodhart worries that bail-in CoCos, therefore, could be destabilizing for banks nearing financial distress and thus would either be counterproductive or not enforced. Our emphasis on CoCos with high triggers, which dilute stockholders in favor of debt holders, does not suffer from this problem.

16. This point is valid and may be an important constraint because some institutions that would be natural holders of CoCos are not permitted to hold unrated securities.

17. For example, the Japanese banking system was insolvent for almost a decade while still satisfying its minimum book value capital requirements under the Basel standards.

18. It may also involve the complicity of accounting firms in window-dressing transactions as shown in the Lehman Brothers case.

reasons. First, the markets are relatively shallow and thus may be more susceptible to manipulation. Second, the pricing of risk is not constant over time; an
observed spread at one point in the business cycle under one set of market conditions can be indicative of a higher level of risk than that same spread observed
at another time under a different set of business conditions (see, for example,
Bekaert, Hoerova, and Lo Duca 2010).

Equity values, if used properly, would provide the best source of information
for designing a trigger. Indeed, some of the best-known cases of large-firm failures that surprised rating agencies and regulators were signaled long in advance
by a *severe and persistent decline in the aggregate market value of their equity.* KMV's
ratings of WorldCom's and Enron's debt were relatively successful in predicting
their defaults. The reason for its success was that the KMV model was based
on the Black-Scholes approach to measuring default risk as a function of leverage (measured using market values) and asset risk (also derived from observed
stock returns volatility). Similarly, market value information about Lehman provided an early warning of its problems. Valukas (2010) notes that, evaluated on
a market value basis,[19] the substantial and protracted decline in Lehman's share
price rendered it insolvent on several occasions during July and August 2008.
If Lehman had been required to issue CoCos with a trigger based on its market
value of equity, this substantial and protracted market decline in the equity value
of Lehman would have produced conversion of debt into equity long before
insolvency.

As we have noted, the existence of a properly designed CoCo requirement
would also incentivize all financial firms to voluntarily raise equity capital
in large amounts before hitting the CoCo trigger. Lehman postponed a significant issuance of equity capital during the summer of 2008, apparently in
the belief that the crisis would pass and its share price would rise. If it had
faced the prospect of CoCo conversion, its behavior during that summer likely
would have been quite different. D'Souza and others (2009) shows that even
under extreme assumptions about the potential decline in share prices in reaction to the announcement of an equity offering, the dilution effects on stockholders could be much lower from an equity offering than from a triggered
conversion, provided that the CoCos subject to conversion are of sufficient
size and provided that they convert on sufficiently favorable terms to the holders of the CoCos. Managers who maximize the value of shareholders' claims

---

19. Valukas (2010) derived the market value of assets by adding the equity market capitalization and
the market value of liabilities, making use of the balance sheet identity to infer the market value of assets,
which could be compared with the face value of Lehman's liabilities.

in the firm always have a strong incentive to prevent the triggering of the conversion of CoCos by strengthening the governance of risk and, if necessary, preemptively issuing equity into the market or selling assets, *so long as the dilution effect of the CoCo conversion is sufficiently large.* Even managers who are not maximizing shareholder value per se will want to avoid the potential corporate governance consequences of a massive CoCo conversion, which would almost certainly lead to a shareholder revolt led by preexisting shareholders and joined by former holders of CoCos who have become shareholders. That might improve the market for corporate control, which is virtually dormant for most highly regulated institutions.

Of course, there is cause for concern that stock market prices may be unreliable measures of true value. Declining equity values are reliable only as rough measures of a SIFI's health if they are sufficiently persistent and severe, and even then they offer only a rough indication of the firm's financial health. Fortunately, that indication is good enough to serve as an effective trigger for CoCos. We suggest employing a ninety-day moving average of the ratio of the market value of equity relative to the sum of the market value of equity plus the face value of debt to smooth fluctuations in share prices and reduce the noise in market value signals.[20] We define this ratio as the quasi-market-value-of-equity ratio, or QMVER.[21] That would also make it more difficult for speculators to force a CoCo conversion through a coordinated bear run on a bank's stock.[22] Figure 5-1 provides an example of the smoothing effect of the ninety-day moving

20. Given the practical difficulties of pricing bank debt on an ongoing basis and given the fact that in equilibrium, the structure of CoCos that we propose would result in little risk of conversion, we believe that it is not worthwhile to attempt to price bank debt when determining the denominator of the QMVER, hence our reliance on a "quasi" market-value-of-equity ratio rather than a true one. Because the market value and face value of debt are likely to remain reasonably close to one another (except in the case of major interest rate shocks), we do not regard this as an important deficiency. Furthermore, one can argue that using the face value of debt when setting a QMVER trigger is conservative, since it does not allow the ratio to rise as the result of decreases in the value of debt related to increased *default* risk.

21. In principle, liabilities could be adjusted for movements in the risk-free rate but not for movements in the risk premium. So long as monetary conditions are stable, however, that is a second-order refinement of a straightforward measure that would tend to undermine its transparency.

22. Albul, Jaffee, and Tchistyi (2010) finds that holders of CoCos will have an incentive to manipulate the equity price only if the ratio of the equity conversion value to CoCo value is high enough to make the conversion profitable for the holders of CoCos. In contrast, bank equity holders have an incentive to manipulate equity prices only if the ratio of equity conversion value to CoCo value is low enough to make the forced conversion profitable for them. Note that if the trigger is a long moving average, the resources required to manipulate the share price over a sufficiently long period would be very substantial. Moreover, a sustained departure from the equilibrium price is likely to attract speculators who can profit from resisting the attempt to manipulate share prices.

Figure 5-1. *The Smoothing Effect of a Ninety-Day Moving Average on the*
Quasi-Market-Value-of-Equity Ratio, April 2006–April 2010

Market cap to quasi–market value of assets (percent)

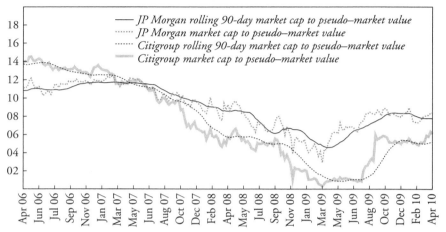

Source: Authors' compilation based on data from CRSP database.

average on the QMVER of Citigroup and JPMorgan Chase during the period
April 2006–April 2010.

Would a trigger based on the QMVER be desirable based on the criteria of
predictability, timeliness, comprehensiveness, and accuracy? Clearly, it is a comprehensive measure of firm value (in fact, the market capitalization of a bank is
the comprehensive measure of value, which includes, in principle, the value of
tangible and intangible assets as well as off-balance sheet positions).

Because market values of the shares of SIFIs are continuously observable
in broad, deep, resilient secondary markets—markets that continued to trade
actively even during the depth of the financial crisis (when many other markets
ceased to function)—a trigger based on equity valuation will be timely. There is
an obvious trade-off between the greater timeliness of a short moving average
period and the greater reliability of the signal from a longer time period. We
suggest ninety days for the moving average, based on the experience from the
recent crisis, which suggests to us that ninety days offers plenty of time for policymakers to respond to low-frequency disruptions (like the August 2007 run on
asset-backed commercial paper) and also plenty of time for banks to respond to
declines in equity value by raising new equity in the market.

With respect to the latter point, we note that between September 2007 and September 2008, some $450 billion in capital was raised by financial institutions. A typical road show for a fully marketed seasoned equity offering is measured in weeks. Although many seasoned equity offerings nowadays are executed on an expedited basis, especially by large firms, it is probably reasonable to assume that the due diligence required to issue equity into the market during a time of severe loss would require the offering to be fully marketed, with a somewhat protracted road show. Hence, we think that a thirty-day moving average window for the trigger may be a bit short if the intent is to motivate share offerings in the wake of equity value losses.

A trigger based on the QMVER would also make the valuation of CoCos more predictable. We do not mean to imply, of course, that stock market returns are predictable but rather that markets are able to forecast the time-varying variance of those returns and therefore to make reasonable inferences about the probabilities of different potential states, including movements into the neighborhood of the trigger. That is useful for pricing CoCos and bank stock, since the potential effects of dilution—both from CoCo conversion and from preemptive equity offerings to prevent CoCo conversion—would factor into both the pricing of CoCos and bank equity in the presence of a CoCo requirement. The ability to model conversion when it is based on observable functions of market equity prices is a highly desirable feature of the QMVER trigger.

Will the QMVER be a sufficiently accurate measure of financial condition? Yes, so long as the demands placed on the measure are not excessive. Equity prices are not perfectly reliable, and they are especially unreliable in detecting small valuation changes over short periods of time. They also may be subject to manipulation. For those reasons, it is useful to sacrifice some degree of timeliness by relying on a moving average. But for the purpose of constructing a credible, predictable, comprehensive, and reasonably accurate measure of large swings in the market value of a SIFI, the market value of the firm is the only real possibility. So long as the user does not seek to achieve false precision, equity is reliable.

For example, suppose a trigger were defined as follows: the CoCo will convert from debt to equity if the ratio of the market capitalization of the bank to the quasi–market value of the bank falls to 4 percent. Assuming that the bank started with a prudent ratio of market cap to the quasi–market value of assets, a decline to this trigger point would provide a reasonably accurate measure of a sustained decline in the value of the firm. Since the share prices are ninety-day moving averages, no SIFI could reasonably argue that the decline in the value of its equity was the product of market manipulation or irrational shareholder behavior.

Is there cause for concern that CoCo holders might try to force conversion through a coordinated bear run on a bank's stock? We believe that the long moving average, the liquidity of the equity market, and the ability of banks to issue equity in response to price declines (discussed further below) would prevent such a strategy from yielding a profit. Nevertheless, as an added precaution against any possibility of market manipulation, we suggest limiting investments in CoCos to qualified nonbank institutional investors and requiring that any such investor be prohibited from simultaneously holding a bank's CoCo and shorting its equity position.[23] That prohibition would not limit short selling in a bank's equity, but it would prevent CoCo holders from coordinating a short-selling strategy designed to force CoCo conversion.

Many policymakers and academics have argued in favor of cyclical variation in capital standards, which has also been embodied in the buffer component of the Basel III approach to capital requirements. That topic is beyond the scope of this chapter, but suffice it to say that by fixing the minimum proportion of CoCos relative to the quasi–market value of the firm's assets, our approach would incentivize firms to raise capital during booms, when they can do so most cheaply, and would encourage banks to be more cautious about funding unsustainable lending booms with overly optimistic, small capital buffers. In that respect, CoCo requirements could automatically help to achieve one of the central objectives of cyclical variation in capital standards. Similarly, time-varying capital requirements for equity and CoCos would allow firms to reduce outstanding CoCos somewhat in recessions, if they experience cyclical declines in the size of their balance sheets.

Because the trigger for CoCo conversion would occur while the SIFI is still demonstrably solvent and because preemptive equity issues prior to hitting the trigger would result in further increases in equity, it is arguable that the CoCo requirement would make insolvency extremely unlikely. Nevertheless, unusually severe shocks do occasionally happen; therefore, it is still important to have available a prompt corrective action regime, as well as an effective system of resolution to go with it.

For the same reasons that a ratio of market value to the quasi–asset value of the firm would serve as the best trigger for CoCo conversion, it would also serve as the best trigger for PCA. If the CoCo conversion trigger occurred at 4 percent, then the PCA trigger should start if the firm breaches the 4 percent ratio again after the recapitalization achieved by the CoCo conversion.

---

23. Our proposal also prohibits banks from purchasing CoCos—both their own and those issued by other banks.

If CoCos convert, how quickly should the firm have to reissue a new batch of CoCos? Under our proposal, CoCo conversion would happen only for firms that experience a sudden and lasting loss of the confidence of the equity market. Such firms are likely to become distressed and enter into resolution. But if they do not, they should be required to place new CoCos into the market within a reasonable period of time—say, within a year (see also Flannery 2009).

Should CoCo conversion be triggered by systemwide losses of capital or other macroeconomic indicators? While indexation of bank debts to systemwide states of the world can be justified from a variety of perspectives (Diamond 1984; Hellwig 1998; Gersbach 2010), for CoCos to incentivize the appropriate management of risk and capital at each bank, there should be a link between the individual bank's circumstances and the triggering of CoCo conversion. For that reason, systemwide triggers—which are potentially useful for some purposes—are not useful for CoCo requirements of the type that we envision.

The Right Amount and Conversion Ratio for the CoCos

Because the comparative efficacy of CoCos as an incentive device depends crucially on their dilutive effects on equity holders, it is important that CoCos be issued in sufficient quantity, especially relative to the amount of equity capital required (since relative dilution is key to ensuring preemptive offerings of equity). For that reason, we suggest—alongside a roughly 10 percent requirement for the ratio of the book equity relative to book assets—a similar magnitude for the required ratio of CoCos relative to book assets. For purposes of seeing how such a requirement might have worked during the recent crisis, in which banks were required to hold a minimum of 2 percent common equity relative to risk-weighted assets (both measured in book value terms), it seems plausible to propose that the minimum required amount of CoCos consistent with our proposal would have been set at roughly 2 percent of the quasi–market value of the firm's assets.[24] Under those assumptions—employed for illustration only— we note that a 4 percent trigger would set off a conversion of CoCos equal to

24. The crisis showed that the definition of the numerator, the risk-weighted denominator, and the minimum acceptable ratio were completely inadequate. Nonetheless, for this retrospective examination of the crisis it is interesting to see whether the quasi-market-value-of-equity ratio would have been informative in separating SIFIs that would require intervention from SIFIs that did not. Basel III will require a much higher level of equity, and the issuance of CoCos should be larger as well.

2 percent of the quasi–market value of the bank's assets. That would imply a huge potential dilution of equity holders. To maximize the incentive effects from the threat of dilution upon conversion, all of the required CoCos should be converted when the ratio hits the trigger.

Similarly, to ensure incentives for preemptive equity offerings, the conversion ratio should be set so that stockholders face significant dilution from conversion. Conversion should require a sufficient number of shares per face value of CoCos so that the post-dilution market value of shares received is greater than the face amount of the CoCos.[25]

To be concrete and to ensure adequate incentives for timely equity offerings while the bank still has access to the equity market, we propose the following combination of CoCo design features (summarized in table 5-1): Commensurate with the current Basel III book equity requirement for SIFIs—which envisions as much as a 9.5 percent tier 1 equity requirement relative to risk-weighted assets—we propose that the amount of CoCos be set at 10 percent of book assets. To ensure adequate dilution risk to shareholders, we propose that all CoCos convert upon hitting the trigger with a conversion ratio that is 5 percent dilutive of equity holders (relative to face value). We suggest an 8 percent QMVER trigger for CoCo conversion based on a ninety-day moving average.

---

25. Two issues of contingent capital—one by Rabobank (a cooperative) and the other by Lloyds—have proven to be significantly more expensive than subordinated debt. But it is important to note that those issues present a very different incentive to the managers than that contemplated in this proposal. In the case of Rabobank, which is a mutual, there are no shareholders to be diluted and the conversion terms are extremely unfavorable to the holders of CoCos—an 85 percent reduction in the value of their claims upon conversion. On the other hand, the Lloyds issue of CoCos was part of an exchange in stressed circumstances. Moreover, the issuance of the bonds during the crisis probably increased their cost. A more interesting experiment is the February 2011 issue of CoCos by Crédit Suisse. This issue, made by a bank that fared comparatively well during the crisis, is designed to buttress the new Basel III capital requirements. Although many institutional investors (especially regulated insurers and bond mutual funds), who have been the main buyers of hybrid capital instruments, have warned that they cannot hold the bonds without changing their investment mandates to allow them to hold equity-linked debt, Crédit Suisse reported a large number of inquiries from wealthy individuals seeking higher yields, as well as hedge funds and other asset managers hoping to exploit (Hughes 2011) "the . . . price anomalies inherent in a nascent market." Clearly the traditional holders of hybrid capital (instruments that the tax authorities are willing to treat as tax deductible but the regulatory authorities have been willing to count as capital for regulatory purposes) are reluctant to exchange them for CoCos, because the regulators have shown by their actions during the recent crisis that they will protect holders of hybrid capital from loss, preferring instead to shift the losses to taxpayers. When the $2 billion Crédit Suisse issue was made, it proved to be an overwhelming success. The CoCos featured a coupon of 7.875 percent and would be converted if the common equity tier 1 ratio of Crédit Suisse fell below 7 percent. Crédit Suisse received orders exceeding 11 times the amount on offer.

Table 5-1. *Summary of Key Features of Proposed CoCo Requirement*

Feature	Recommendation
Primary goal	Prompt recapitalization.
Minimum amount of CoCos	10 percent of book value of assets.
Trigger	QMVER of 8 percent, using a ninety-day moving average of market value.
Conversion ratio	5 percent dilutive of the market value of stockholders' shares relative to the face value of their shares.
Conversion amount	All CoCos are converted on reaching the trigger.
Holders	Qualified nonbank institutional investors holding no short equity positions in the common equity.
PCA trigger	If 8 percent trigger is reached twice.
Time to replace converted CoCos	One year.

Does Our CoCo Proposal Suffer from a "Multiple-Equilibria" Problem?

Some authors have challenged whether CoCos of the type that we propose are feasible. In particular, Sundaresan and Wang (2010)—hereinafter SW—argues that CoCos with market value triggers can suffer from a multiple-equilibrium problem unless conversion is carefully designed to avoid any dilution of preexisting holders of common stock. In their model, dilutive CoCo conversion leads to the possibility of more than one potential time path of stock prices for any given time path of asset values. SW concludes that such multiple equilibria in share prices can make it impossible to price CoCos and also lead to potentially destabilizing bear runs on bank stocks, as small perturbations in market prices might lead market participants to switch from a belief in one equilibrium to another. SW concludes, therefore, that CoCos should not both be based on market equity triggers and convert into equity at ratios that favor CoCo holders (that is, conversion ratios in which the face value of CoCos is converted into more shares than the equivalent amount of equity, using the equity price at the date of conversion). That conclusion, applied to our proposed CoCo requirement, is incorrect, but their analysis helps to motivate the specific design features of a proper CoCo requirement, which we develop here.[26]

---

26. Concerns about multiple equilibria have encouraged some CoCo proponents to design triggers based on book value ratios or to give banks an option to convert rather than require conversion (as in Bolton and Samama 2010). Those design choices are problematic. As we have already noted, a book value

Following SW, we assume a bank with the following (all values are defined in market value): assets = $100; senior bond (or deposits) = $80; and CoCos = $10. One share of equity exists, and the total initial market value of equity is $10. In the absence of a CoCo, the bank's equity share would be valued at $10, but in the presence of a CoCo with a market value trigger and a dilutive conversion feature, $10 is only one of the possible values of the equity share. The following example illustrates the problem identified by SW. We assume that the CoCo conversion trigger is set based on a market value of equity of 5 percent or less of assets, which in the SW example translates into a stock price at $5 per share or less. The conversion ratio is assumed to be dilutive of preexisting shareholders. Specifically, we assume that the $10 in CoCos converts into three shares of stock if the stock price is $5 (the trigger price)—a nondilutive conversion would require a conversion ratio of CoCos into two shares of equity when the equity price is $5. SW shows that there are two rational expectations equilibria: one in which the stock price is $10 per share and no conversion takes place and another in which the stock price is $5 and conversion takes place.

Those are both rational expectations equilibria because expectations are fulfilled by equilibrium prices. If the market believes that the price should be $5 per share, conversion will happen. The new number of shares will be four, so the original owners of the bank, who owned 100 percent of the bank's equity prior to conversion, now own only 25 percent. The new amount of equity will be $20, since $10 in CoCo debt was canceled upon conversion. The price per share of equity will be $5. If the market believes that the price should be $10, then conversion will not occur (since the market value of equity does not hit the 5 percent trigger). There are two rational expectations equilibria: if the market believes the price is $5 per share, then that belief will turn out to be true, and if the market believes the price is $10, then that belief will turn out to be true.

Note, however, that this example from SW makes another significant, implicit assumption: that the market knows that the bank would take no action to prevent the low-stock price equilibrium of a $5 share price from occurring. In other words, SW implicitly requires that the bank refrain from issuing new equity into

---

trigger depends on the behavior of management and supervisors (which is not easily predictable) and thus makes the probability of CoCo conversion difficult to quantify. Giving banks the option to convert creates a different problem: during a crisis, if banks believe that asset prices are temporarily depressed, they may prefer not to convert, thus reducing the benefit of adding new capital to the bank. Furthermore, in a model in which banks have the option to convert, the existence of CoCos will not encourage preemptive offerings of equity. Here we show that neither a book value trigger nor a bank option for conversion is necessary to deal with the potential problem of multiple equilibria.

the market if the price of equity begins to fall toward the lower equilibrium value of $5.

To see why this implicit assumption is important, consider the following amendment to the SW example. We make all the same assumptions employed in SW but make two additional assumptions: one, it is possible for the bank to issue new shares prior to conversion if the price of shares in the market starts to move toward the lower equilibrium price; two, a moving average trigger is used, whereby the triggering of conversion occurs only if the stock price falls to the trigger value or below for a finite length of time.

Under these assumptions, if the share price begins to fall below $10, the bank could issue one share of common stock into the market, say, at any price between $10 and $5 a share. To be concrete, suppose that the stock price falls to $5 and that the bank issues one share of stock into the market at $5 a share. Doing so raises both the value of assets and the value of equity by $5. Because the trigger for CoCos is defined in terms of the *ratio of market value of equity relative to assets (the QMVER), at a $5 share price, conversion will not take place,* since the offering of a new share has raised the new QMVER above 5 percent.

Note that without conversion, the lower equilibrium price of $5 a share is no longer a rational expectations equilibrium, since the expectation of conversion that underlay the $5 price will not be realized. Indeed, the price of equity would rebound to $7.50 a share (which contradicts the $5 equilibrium assumption) if the share price had actually fallen to $5, prompting the bank to issue the single share into the market. But this out-of-equilibrium offering and price volatility should not occur, since the $5 share price is no longer a rational expectations equilibrium; therefore, there is no reason to expect that the price would ever have fallen to $5 in the first place. The bank will never have to issue into the market at $5 a share, since $10 is now the unique equilibrium price and arbitrage in the market will ensure that the market price will never fall below $10. Clearly, the bank will want to announce and follow this share-issuance policy, since it would avoid the dilutive conversion of CoCos that occurs in the lower price equilibrium.[27]

Several clear lessons emerge from this analysis. First, in light of the possibility of multiple equilibria, it is especially desirable to put a moving average process into the definition of the trigger, requiring, as in the example above, that the QMVER trigger be hit over a period of time, not just at a moment. Second, when

---

27. As early as 2009, many advocates of CoCos with dilutive conversion were pointing precisely to the incentives CoCos can create for timely issuance of common stock to prevent dilutive CoCo conversion (D'Souza and others 2009). Indeed, as we emphasize, this feature of CoCos has been central to the discussion of why they would be helpful in preventing "too big to fail" bailouts.

considering the necessary length of time for that moving average, it is important to make sure that the period is long enough to allow management time to arrange for a preemptive equity offering to prevent conversion. We believe that a ninety-day moving average would allow plenty of time for a stock offering. In empirical evidence below, we show that using a ninety-day moving average during the crisis of 2007–09 would have provided ample opportunity for banks that were losing equity value to have issued equity to restore their QMVERs.

Third, CoCo triggers should be set relative to the QMVER, *not* the share price. Stock offerings could change the price per share (as could a stock split); obviously, it is the total equity buffer that should matter from the perspective of the CoCo trigger, and that should be set as a proportion of assets.

In summary, we have shown that our CoCo proposal does not suffer from the SW multiple-equilibria problem. A substantial CoCo requirement (requiring banks to maintain a significant proportion of their balance sheet financing in the form of CoCos), with a dilutive conversion ratio, triggered by a smoothed QMVER trigger (which we define as the ninety-day moving average) would not produce multiple equilibria in the pricing of bank stock.[28]

How the CoCos Requirement Would Have Worked in 2007–08

Figure 5-2 illustrates how the proposed CoCo trigger would work. As the QMVER falls, approaching the trigger, a firm like A (line A) would issue equity (or sell assets) to avoid hitting the trigger. If for some reason a firm like B is unable or unwilling to issue equity or sell assets, the conversion of CoCos is triggered (line B). That will result in massive dilution of existing shareholders, who will undoubtedly be angry, and the new shareholders who formerly held CoCos are likely to be unhappy as well. Shareholder dissatisfaction on this scale is likely to lead to the ouster of the existing management and the installation of a new management team that will strengthen the governance of risk. And so CoCo conversion might enhance the virtually moribund market for corporate control of regulated financial institutions—an important element of market discipline that is largely ineffectual among regulated banks. It will certainly add further motivation to management to take corrective action before reaching the trigger.

---

28. Our solution to the multiple-equilibria problem is different from that in Pennacchi, Vermaelen, and Wolff (2010) and Pennacchi (2010). In that proposal, incumbent stockholders have the right to purchase converted equity at a nondilutive price from new (post-conversion) stockholders. That option avoids multiple equilibria, but because it eliminates the cost of dilution on incumbent stockholders, it also dampens the incentive to raise new capital to replace lost capital or to manage risk better ex ante, which we see as central advantages of our proposal.

Figure 5-2. *How a CoCo Trigger Might Work*

Market cap to quasi–market value of assets (percent)

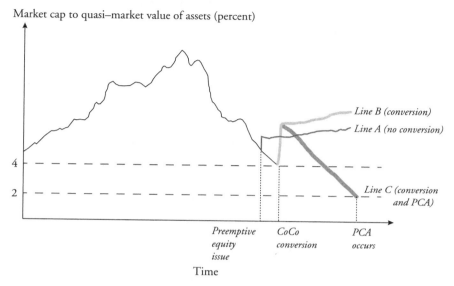

Source: Authors' illustration.

The doubling of capital and reduction in liquidity pressures (and perhaps a new management team) may buy the firm enough time to successfully restructure. Finally, firm C may be unable to use the additional capital and time to accomplish restructuring or recapitalization; therefore, its value will continue to decline until prompt corrective action is triggered (line C).

Figure 5-3 shows the movement of the ratio of the ninety-day moving average of the market cap to the quasi–market value of assets from April 2006 to April 2010 for five SIFIs that did not require government support. It is important to emphasize that this simply illustrates the ability of the QMVER ratio measure to distinguish between soundly managed institutions and weaker institutions; it does not show what would actually have happened if all institutions had been subject to a CoCo requirement.[29] Note that none of these institutions fell below

29. In the presence of our proposed CoCo requirement, the rate of decline in the QMVER would be higher than in the absence of the requirement. Stock prices would take into account the small probability of conversion, and as the QMVER approached the trigger and that probability increased, two effects would reduce stock prices: the dilution that existing shareholders would suffer from conversion, and the loss of tax savings from the deductibility of interest. Those effects, however, would be small, since the probability of conversion would remain small (banks would endogenously prevent the QMVER from getting too close to the trigger value by issuing equity).

Figure 5-3. *Ratio of the Ninety-Day Rolling Market Cap to the Quasi–Market Value of Assets for the Five SIFIs That Did Not Require Substantial Government Intervention, April 2006–April 2010*[a]

Market cap to pseudo–market value of assets

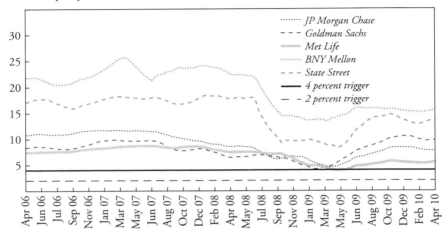

Source: Authors' compilation based on data from the Center for Research in Security Prices (CRSP) database.

a. For large American financial institutions that did not receive Supervisory Capital Assessment Program (SCAP) infusions.

the 4 percent ratio. If the CoCo requirement had been in place, only Goldman Sachs and MetLife might have triggered a conversion. The prospect of dilution, however, would almost certainly have caused the managers of both firms to issue more equity or sell assets to avoid hitting the trigger.

Contrast figure 5-4, which shows the movement of the ratio of the market cap to the quasi–market value of assets for ten banks that required substantial government support, were forced to merge, or entered bankruptcy, with figure 5-3, which shows the comparable ratio for banks that did not require substantial government support. Note that all of these firms breached the 4 percent ratio and in most cases did so many months before they were subject to intervention. It is especially noteworthy that Bear Stearns, Lehman Brothers, and AIG—all of which appeared to catch the supervisory authorities by surprise and were subject to different interventions, hastily improvised over sleepless weekends—had, in fact, fallen below the 4 percent trigger several months earlier. It is possible that a CoCo requirement might have induced those firms to adopt higher standards of risk governance and make more aggressive attempts to raise capital or sell assets.

Figure 5-4. *The Ratio of the Ninety-Day Rolling Market Cap to the Quasi–Market Value of Assets for Ten Banks That Required Substantial Government Intervention, April 2006–April 2010*[a]

Market cap to pseudo–market value of assets

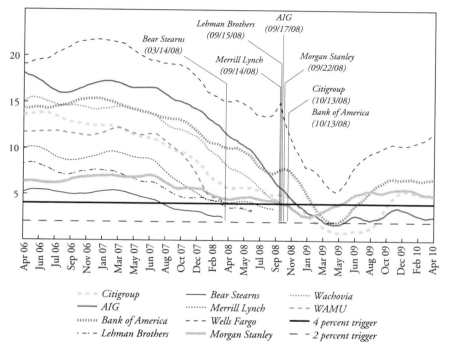

Source: Authors' compilation based on data from CRSP database.
a. U.S. SIFIs that failed were forced into mergers or received major SCAP infusions.

At a minimum, it would have bought them additional time to prepare for an orderly resolution and would have been a clear warning to regulators to refine their rapid resolution plans.

Note that figure 5-5 shows a similar pattern for the European banks that required large-scale intervention. In almost every case, the 4 percent ratio was breached long before intervention was hastily arranged.

In summary, a 4 percent trigger based on the ratio of the market cap to the quasi–market value of assets might have been an effective device for preventing the collapse of all of these troubled SIFIs during the 2008–09 crisis. Moreover, each of these institutions would have faced strong incentives to strengthen pre-emptively the corporate governance of risk and, if necessary, issue equity or sell

Figure 5-5. *Ratio of the Ninety-Day Rolling Market Cap to the Quasi–Market Value of Assets for Select European Banks That Required Substantial Government Intervention, April 2006–April 2010*

Market cap to pseudo–market value of assets (percent)

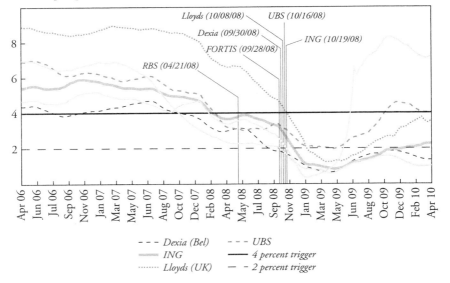

assets to avoid triggering their CoCos months earlier. And the supervisors could not have claimed to be taken by surprise at the sudden collapse of the firms. Although we illustrate our counterfactual with a 4 percent trigger, we propose an 8 percent trigger in our suggested CoCo requirement, which would have worked even better to prevent the post–September 2008 collapse because it would have created strong incentives for voluntary equity issues by banks long before September 2008.

In particular, our proposed CoCo requirement would have reduced the damage from the two largest failures—those of AIG and Lehman Brothers. Although counterfactuals are speculative by definition, at least three reasons suggest that such a system would have been effective if AIG and Lehman Brothers had been identified as SIFls. First, the issuance of CoCos would have enhanced market discipline and limited their risk taking.

Second, both firms crossed the CoCo trigger six to eight months before their demise. Since Lehman was heavily owned by its managers and employees, the prospect of dilution would have surely concentrated their minds on raising new equity, while they still had access to equity markets, or on selling lines of business or assets. Even if they had hit the conversion trigger, however, the automatic recapitalization would have given them more time to find a private solution to their problems, which might have involved a merger, a restructuring, an additional recapitalization, or a change in management. At a minimum, it would have warned the supervisors and resolution authorities of impending trouble so that there would have been no necessity to engage in desperate measures over a sleepless weekend. Breaching the PCA trigger would have conserved liquidity by restricting dividends, share buybacks, and bonuses.

Third, the primary supervisor and the college of supervisors would have had warning to prepare for the challenges that they would face in a resolution.

Fourth, even if the proposed CoCo requirement had not prevented the disorderly failures of Lehman Brothers and AIG, the consequences of those failures for other financial institutions—and for the financial system as a whole—would have been far milder under our proposed requirement. If other large financial institutions had been encouraged by CoCo requirements to maintain higher capital ratios in 2007 and 2008, the severe consequences of the collapse of money markets might have been averted. After all, the collapse of interbank deposit, repo, and asset-backed commercial paper markets reflected ballooning counterparty risks among these global intermediaries. If large banks had issued sufficient capital in response to their losses in 2007 and early 2008, counterparty risk would have been contained.

Since regulation of book capital ratios and supervision has proven so ineffectual, it is high time to place a greater emphasis on market signals that discipline SIFIs. CoCos, suitably designed, can be an ideal instrument for channeling such discipline in a way that strengthens the stability of the financial system.

Conclusion

We have developed a proposal for a contingent capital (CoCo) requirement and shown that CoCos can play a unique role alongside a standard minimum book-value-of-equity-ratio requirement. If properly designed, a CoCo requirement can provide a more effective solution to the too big to fail problem by ensuring adequate capital relative to risk, and it can do so at a lower cost than a simple equity requirement. A proper CoCo requirement can provide strong incentives for the prompt recapitalization of banks after significant losses of equity or for the proactive raising of equity capital when risk increases. Correspondingly, it can provide strong incentives for effective risk governance by regulated banks, and it can reduce forbearance (supervisory reluctance to recognize losses).

Different proposals for CoCo requirements reflect different purposes, including facilitation of bail-ins, signaling of bank risk, and encouragement of timely voluntary offerings of equity into the market by banks that have suffered significant loss. We argue that the third of those purposes is the most important, especially for dealing with the too big to fail problem.

The emphasis on the need to incentivize the timely issuance of equity informs our discussion of the proper design of CoCo contracts that would be implemented by the CoCo requirement. We show that, to be maximally effective, a large amount of CoCos (relative to common equity) should be required; CoCo conversion should be based on a market value trigger, defined by using a moving average of a quasi-market-value-of-equity ratio; all CoCos should convert if conversion is triggered; and the conversion ratio should be dilutive of preexisting equity holders. (We summarize the details of our proposal in table 5-1.)

Our proposed CoCo requirement does not suffer from a potential problem of multiple equilibria. Judging as best we can from the experience of the recent crisis, our proposed requirement would have been very effective in encouraging the timely replacement of lost capital early in the crisis. Arguably, if a CoCo requirement had been in place in 2007, the disruptive failures of large financial institutions and the systemic meltdown after September 2008 could have been avoided.

Table 5A-1. *A Selective Survey of the Literature on Critical Features of CoCos*

Source	Amount of CoCos to be issued	Trigger for conversion	Terms for conversion
Doherty and Harrington (1995)	Authors use the term "reverse convertible debt." Issue will be the optimal amount of leverage for the firm. All debt will be converted when the trigger is reached.	At the discretion of shareholders.	The value of new shares given to bondholders is less than the face value of the debt.
Huertas (2009)	An amount equal to some specified proportion of risk-weighted assets. From the diagram on p. 4, that appears to be the same proportion as that of core tier 1 capital to risk-weighted assets.	Finding by regulators that the core tier 1 capital ratio has fallen below a specified level.	Implicitly all contingent capital will be converted. Although Huertas stresses the importance of the threat of dilution, he does not specify the terms for conversion.
D'Souza and others (2009)	The amount issued should be large enough that the firm can be recapitalized even in dire circumstances. (Back tests suggest that CoCos equal to 6 percent of risk-weighted assets would have avoided government intervention in the 2007–09 crisis.)	A "true" measure of capital above the solvency point. Authors reject market values as too volatile and accounting measures as too slow to reflect deterioration. Prefer SCAP-like stress test that would calculate a two-year forward capital ratio for the firm.	Conversion terms must be sufficiently dilutive to original shareholders to motivate them to raise equity before hitting the trigger. The more dilutive the terms of conversion and the higher the trigger point, the lower the cost of issuing CoCos because they are less likely to be converted.

(continued)

Table 5A-1. *A Selective Survey of the Literature on Critical Features of CoCos* (continued)

Source	Amount of CoCos to be issued	Trigger for conversion	Terms for conversion
Dudley (2009)	Amount should be large because cost should not differ much from cost of straight debt and shareholders must face the potential for automatic and substantial dilution. Full amount issued will be converted when the trigger is reached.	Trigger could be tied to deterioration in the condition of a specific bank and/or to the banking system as a whole. It also could be tied to regulatory measures of capital, but Dudley prefers market measures because they tend to lead regulatory-based measures.	"The conversion terms could be generous to the holder of the contingent capital instrument" (p. 7). Conversion terms should be set so that debt holders could expect to get out at or close to par value.
Duffie (2009)	Duffie assumes the full amount would be converted when the trigger is reached.	The trigger that converts debt to equity should be set to eliminate the debt claims before a liquidity crisis is likely to begin and with a strong enough impact on the balance sheet to forestall a self-fulfilling presumption of a liquidity crisis. Duffie rejects a regulatory capital trigger. Favors a tangible common equity trigger if restricted to accounting measures. Advocates a market value trigger but warns that unless a moving average is used, a market trigger can precipitate a "death spiral."	Debt conversion should be accompanied by another sort of contingent capital that will immediately improve the cash position of the bank. Duffie favors a rights offering.

Flannery (2009)	Flannery uses the term "contingent capital certificates" (CCCs). Firms would not be required to issue CoCos, but CCCs could be used to offset the required amount of equity capital. Some of the CCCs would be converted to equity to replace lost equity value. Supervisors determine the minimum equity capital ratio and trigger point. SIFIs cannot hold any CCC for their own account. Since conversion may be partial, it must rely on an allocation mechanism: convert shortest remaining maturities first; sell with various seniorities so that some bonds must convert fully before others can begin to convert; select bonds randomly within a common maturity or common seniority tranche; select CCCs by lottery.	Would convert into equity if firm's capital falls below some critical, prespecified level. Conversion trigger must be expressed in terms of contemporary value of equity and scaled by the book value of assets.	The contemporary market price determines how many shares the holders of CCCs obtain. The terms for conversion should ensure that they suffer no capital loss. Conversion must happen the day after the trigger is reached. If the firm is insolvent because of a sudden collapse in asset prices, covenants in CCCs must specify a conversion price that wipes out original shareholders.
Rajan (2009)	Banks should issue sufficient CoCos so that, when converted, they will dilute the value of old equity substantially.	Two triggers: the system is in crisis based on objective indicators such as aggregate bank losses; and the bank's capital ratio falls below a certain value.	The number of shares the debts convert into should ensure substantial dilution of old equity.

(continued)

Table 5A-1. *A Selective Survey of the Literature on Critical Features of CoCos* (continued)

Source	Amount of CoCos to be issued	Trigger for conversion	Terms for conversion
Squam Lake Working Group (2009)	Banks must be required to issue CoCos because they will otherwise issue other debt securities more likely to shift costs of risky activities to government. When conversion is triggered, presumably all CoCos are converted.	Two triggers: declaration by regulators that the financial system is suffering from a systemic crisis; and bank is found in violation of covenants in its CoCo contract expressed as a ratio of tier 1 capital to risk-weighted assets.	Authors fear that a conversion rate based on market values would trigger market manipulation. They prefer to convert each dollar of debt into a fixed quantity of equity shares rather than a fixed value of equity.
Hart and Zingales (2010)	Authors reject CoCos, arguing that by limiting defaults, CoCos will provide more resources for inefficient managers to waste, while a default would force an inefficient business to restructure and incompetent managers to be replaced. They argue instead for direct issues of equity triggered by CDS price of a bank's debt exceeding a specified threshold.	An example suggests the trigger might be that a bank's CDS price exceeds 1 percent, on average, over the previous month. Authors express concern about finding an appropriate CoCo trigger. If based on accounting numbers, it is likely to trigger remedial action that will lag actual deterioration in bank assets. If conversion is triggered when market prices are low, managers could deliberately talk down the bank's value to activate the trigger and obtain equity on the cheap.	Direct issuance of equity would substitute for conversion of debt. Presumably sufficient equity must be issued to reduce the CDS price below 1 percent.

Albul, Jaffe, and Tchistyi (2010)	Full amount will be converted. Authors also stipulate that CoCos should be substituted for straight debt. They do not specify the amount to be converted.	Conversion is triggered when capital reaches a "distressed level," but regulatory benefits are greater the higher the trigger at which conversion occurs.	No exact ratio is given, but authors emphasize that the conversion ratio of CoCos into shares should not motivate either holders of CoCos or shareholders to manipulate share prices.
McDonald (2010)	Amount of CoCos issued has an initial value equal to the initial value of equity. All will be converted when dual triggers are reached. If CoCos are not converted, bonds would be retired gradually and randomly as maturity approaches to avoid large gains that could occur from manipulation at maturity.	Conversion with a dual price trigger: the bank's shareholders' equity price must fall below a threshold *and* an index of financial firms' stocks must breach a prespecified threshold. The rationale is to ensure that conversion is permitted only during a financial crisis. Market price triggers should reduce pressure on regulators and accountants at critical times.	Conversion occurs into a fixed number of shares at a premium price (so that the value of the shares upon conversion is lower than the par value of the bonds) in order to minimize concerns about share price manipulation and equity death spirals. Author expresses concern that unprofitable stock price manipulation might create a profit if trader also holds a position in market-triggered CoCos. Author believes fixed-share conversion is most likely to deter such behavior.
Pennacchi (2010)	Assumes that all contingent capital converts to equity when a threshold is breached. (Partial conversion introduces additional complications because the value of shareholders' equity at conversion will depend on the value of unconverted CoCos.)	Trigger is stated as ratio of market value of equity to face value of deposits.	If threshold is stated in terms of market value of original shareholders' equity and contingent capital converts at a discount to face value, the resulting total capital will be less than if the conversion were at par. To correct for this, a higher

(continued)

Table 5A-1. *A Selective Survey of the Literature on Critical Features of CoCos* (continued)

Source	Amount of CoCos to be issued	Trigger for conversion	Terms for conversion
			threshold should be used when conversion is at less than par than when conversion is at par. Concludes that CoCos would be a low-cost means of mitigating financial distress and would reduce a bank's moral hazard incentives so long as the conversion threshold is set at a relatively high level of original shareholders' equity.
Coffee (2010)	Amount of CoCos issued should be set relative to a firm's short-term debt in an amount large enough that short-term creditors will not fear insolvency. May be negotiated case by case.	Multiple triggers for partial conversion set relative to substantial declines in share price. For example, 25 percent of CoCos might be converted with a 25 percent decline in share prices since the time that the CoCos were issued. Another 25 percent would convert if the share price decline reached 50 percent, and the balance would convert if the share price fell by 75 percent.	Conversion would be for an equal face value of cumulative, senior, nonconvertible, preferred stock with voting rights. The intent is to dilute equity to deter excessive risk taking and to create a class of voting preferred shareholders who would be rationally risk averse and would curb pressures for excessive risk taking.

Sundaresan and Wang (2010)	Full amount will be converted. Amount issued not specified. Upon conversion, dividends are automatically suspended.	Trigger price and conversion ratio cannot be chosen independently.	Mandatory conversion must not result in any value transfer between equity and CoCo holders. The authors conclude that only one conversion ratio is an equilibrium, and it depends on the design of the CoCo. The CoCo must be designed so that the coupon payments are indexed so that the CoCo always sells at par. In this case, the conversion ratio is simply par value divided by the trigger level of the stock price at which mandatory conversion will occur.
Swiss State Secretariat for International Financial Matters (2011); Swiss Commission of Experts (2010)	The authors envision two kinds of CoCos with two different triggers. Up to 3 percent of buffer capital (= 8 percent of risk-weighted assets) may be composed of CoCos. The progressive component of capital requirements is to be composed of 6 percent CoCos. That leads to a total capital requirement of 19 percent of risk-weighted assets, comprising at least 10 percent common equity and up to 9 percent CoCos.	CoCos with a trigger of 7 percent of risk-weighted assets serve as a capital buffer. CoCos with a trigger of 5 percent of risk-weighted assets should ensure the necessary capital reserve to finance the maintenance of systemically important functions and to see to the orderly resolution of the remainder of the bank in the event of threatened insolvency.	Conversion rate is not specified explicitly; appears to be 1 unit of equity for 1 unit of convertible debt.

References

Admati, Anat R., and others. 2011. "Fallacies, Irrelevant Facts, and Myths in the Discussion of Capital Regulation: Why Bank Equity Is *Not* Expensive." Working Paper. Stanford University.

Albul, Boris, Dwight Jaffee, and Alexei Tchistyi. 2010. "Contingent Convertible Bonds and Capital Structure Decisions." Working Paper. Haas School of Business, University of California–Berkeley (March 26).

BCBS (Basel Committee on Banking Supervision). 1997. "Core Principles for Effective Banking Supervision." April.

———. 1999a, "Supervisory Lessons to Be Drawn from the Asian Crisis." Basel Committee on Banking Supervision Working Paper 2 (June).

———. 1999b. "Enhancing Corporate Governance for Banking Organisations." Consultative Document (September).

———. 2005. "Enhancing Corporate Governance for Banking Organisations." Consultative Document (July).

———. 2006. "Enhancing Corporate Governance for Banking Organisations." Consultative Document (February).

———. 2008. "Report of the Senior Supervisors Group." Consultative Document. Basel.

———. 2009. "Enhancements to the Basel II Framework." Basel: Bank for International Settlements (July).

———. 2010a. "Principles for Enhancing Corporate Governance." Consultative Document (March).

———. 2010b. "Principles for Enhancing Corporate Governance." Consultative Document (October).

———. 2011. "Basel Committee Issues Final Elements of the Reforms to Raise the Quality of Regulatory Capital." Press release (January 13).

Bekaert, Geert, Marie Hoerova, and Marco Lo Duca. 2010. "Risk, Uncertainty, and Monetary Policy." Working Paper 16397. Cambridge, Mass.: National Bureau of Economic Research (September).

Bernanke, Ben S. 1983. "Nonmonetary Effects of the Financial Crisis in the Propagation of the Great Depression." *American Economic Review* 73: 257–76.

Bernanke, Ben S., and Cara S. Lown. 1991. "The Credit Crunch." *BPEA*, no. 2: 205–48.

Bolton, Patrick, and Frederic Samama. 2010. "Contingent Capital and Long-Term Investors: A Natural Match?" Working Paper. Columbia Business School (October).

Calomiris, Charles W. 1999. "Building an Incentive-Compatible Safety Net." *Journal of Banking and Finance* 23 (October): 1499–520.

———. 2011. "An Incentive-Robust Programme for Financial Reform." *The Manchester School* 79: 39–72.

Calomiris, Charles W., and Joseph R. Mason. 2003. "Consequences of Bank Distress during the Great Depression." *American Economic Review* 93: 937–47.

Calomiris, Charles W., and Margarita Tsoutsoura. 2011. "Underwriting Costs of Seasoned Equity Issues: Cross-Sectional Determinants and Technological Change, 1980–2008." Working Paper. Columbia Business School.

Calomiris, Charles W., and Berry Wilson. 2004. "Bank Capital and Portfolio Management: The 1930s 'Capital Crunch' and the Scramble to Shed Risk." *Journal of Business* 77: 421–55.

Campello, Murillo. 2002. "Internal Capital Markets in Financial Conglomerates: Evidence from Small Bank Responses to Monetary Policy." *Journal of Finance* 57: 2773–805.

Cetorelli, Nicola, and Linda S. Goldberg. 2009. "Banking Globalization and Monetary Transmission." Federal Reserve Bank of New York Staff Report No. 333 (revised February).

Coffee, John C. Jr. 2010. "Systemic Risk after Dodd-Frank: Contingent Capital and the Need for Regulatory Strategies beyond Oversight." Working Paper. Columbia University Law School.

Corston, John. 2010. "Systemically Important Institutions and the Issue of 'Too Big To Fail.' " Statement before the Financial Crisis Inquiry Commission, Washington, September 1.

Davies, Howard. 2003. "Corporate Governance in Financial Institutions." Speech delivered to International Monetary Conference, Berlin, June 3.

D'Souza, Andre, and others. 2009. "Ending 'Too Big To Fail.' " New York: Goldman Sachs Global Markets Institute (December).

Diamond, Douglas. 1984. "Financial Intermediation and Delegated Monitoring." *Review of Economic Studies* 51: 393–414.

Doherty, Neil, and Scott Harrington. 1995. "Investment Incentives, Bankruptcies, and Reverse Convertible Debt." Working Paper. Wharton School, University of Pennsylvania (March).

Dudley, William C. 2009. "Some Lessons from the Crisis." Remarks at the Institute of International Bankers Membership Luncheon, New York City (October 13).

Duffie, Darrell. 2009. "Contractual Methods for Out-of-Court Restructuring of Systemically Important Financial Institutions." Submission requested by the U.S. Treasury Working Group on Bank Capital.

Eisenbeis, Robert. 2009. "An Interesting Hearing: AIG." Vineland, N.J.: Cumberland Advisors Commentary (March).

Ellul, Andrew, and Vijay Yerramilli. 2010. "Stronger Risk Controls, Lower Risk: Evidence from U.S. Bank Holding Companies." Working Paper 15178. Cambridge, Mass.: National Bureau for Economic Research (July).

European Commission. 2011. "Commission Seeks Views on Possible EU Framework to Deal with Future Bank Failures." Consultation Document. Brussels (January 6).

Flannery, Mark J. 2005. " 'No Pain, No Gain': Effecting Market Discipline via 'Reverse Convertible Debentures.' " In *Capital Adequacy beyond Basel: Banking, Securities, and Insurance,* edited by Hal Scott. Oxford University Press.

———. 2009. "Stabilizing Large Financial Institutions with Contingent Capital Certificates." Working Paper. Federal Reserve Bank of New York (October 5).

Gersbach, Hans. 2010. "Can Contingent Contracts Insure against Banking Crises?" Working Paper. ETH Zurich.

Guttentag, Jack, and Richard Herring. 1987. "Restructuring Depository Institutions." Working Paper. Wharton School. Reprinted in *Competitive Markets and the Thrift Industry: Proceedings of the Thirteenth Annual Conference, December 10–11, 1987.* San Francisco: Federal Home Loan Bank of San Francisco.

Hart, Oliver, and Luigi Zingales. 2010. "How to Make a Bank Raise Equity." *Financial Times* (February 7).

Hellwig, Martin F. 1998. "Banks, Markets, and the Allocation of Tasks in an Economy." *Journal of Institutional and Theoretical Economics* 154: 328–45.

Herring, Richard J. 2004. "The Subordinated Debt Alternative to Basel II." *Journal of Financial Stability* 1: 137–55.

Horvitz, Paul. 1983. "Market Discipline Is Best Provided by Subordinated Creditors." *American Banker* (July 15).

Houston, Joel, Christopher James, and David Marcus. 1997. "Capital Market Frictions and the Role of Internal Capital Markets in Banking." *Journal of Financial Economics* 46: 135–64.

Huertas, Thomas. 2009. "Too Big to Fail, Too Complex to Contemplate: What to Do about Systemically Important Firms." Paper presented at the Financial Markets Group, London School of Economics, September 15.

Hughes, Jennifer. 2011. "Credit Suisse Deal Offers Truer Test of CoCos." *Financial Times* (February 14).

Huizinga, Harry, and Luc Laeven. 2012. "Bank Valuation and Accounting Discretion during a Financial Crisis." *Journal of Financial Economics* (forthcoming).

IMF (International Monetary Fund). 2008. "Detecting Systemic Risk." *Global Financial Stability Report.* Washington (April).

———. 2009a. "Restarting Securitization Markets: Policy Proposals and Pitfalls." *Global Financial Stability Report.* Washington (October).

———. 2009b. "Responding to the Financial Crisis and Measuring Systemic Risks." *Global Financial Stability Report.* Washington (April).

Joint Forum on Financial Conglomerates. 1998. "Supervision of Financial Conglomerates" (February).

Kashyap, Anil, and Jeremy Stein. 1995. "The Impact of Monetary Policy on Bank Balance Sheets." *Carnegie-Rochester Conference Series on Public Policy* 42: 151–95.

———. 2000. "What Do a Million Observations on Banks Say about the Transmission Mechanism of Monetary Policy?" *American Economic Review* 90: 407–28.

Kashyap, Anil, Raghuram Rajan, and Jeremy Stein. 2008. "Rethinking Capital Regulation." Paper presented at the Federal Reserve Bank of Kansas City Symposium "Maintaining Stability in a Changing World," Jackson Hole, Wyoming, August 21–23.

Kelly, Tom. 2008. "WaMu Failed to Heed Lesson Learned in '80s." Part 1: "The Largest Bank Failure in U.S. History." *Inman News* (October 7).

Kirkpatrick, Grant. 2009. "The Corporate Governance Lessons from the Financial Crisis." *OECD Financial Market Trends* 2009/1.

McDonald, Robert L. 2010. "Contingent Capital with a Dual Price Trigger." Working Paper. Northwestern University (February 15).

Miles, David, Gilberto Marcheggiano, and Jing Yang. 2011. "Optimal Bank Capital." External MPC Unit Discussion Paper 31. Bank of England.

Murphy, Gareth, and Matthew Willison. 2011. "Precautionary Contingent Capital." Bank of England.

Myers, Stewart C., and Nicolas Majluf. 1984. "Corporate Finance and Investment Decisions When Firms Have Information That Investors Do Not Have." *Journal of Financial Economics* 5: 187–221.

Office of the Inspector General. 2010. "Evaluation of Federal Regulatory Oversight of Washington Mutual Bank." Department of the Treasury, Federal Deposit Insurance Corporation (April).

Peek, Joe, and Eric Rosengren. 1997. "The International Transmission of Financial Shocks: The Case of Japan." *American Economic Review* 87: 495–505.

———. 2000. "Collateral Damage: Effects of the Japanese Bank Crisis on Real Activity in the United States." *American Economic Review* 90: 30–45.

Pennacchi, George. 2010. "A Structural Model of Contingent Bank Capital." Working Paper. University of Illinois College of Business (April 23).

Pennacchi, George, Theo Vermaelen, and C. P. Christian Wolff. 2010. "Contingent Capital: The Case for COERCs." INSEAD Working Paper 2010/55/FIN. Fontainebleau, France.

Rajan, Raghuram. 2009. "More Capital Will Not Stop the Next Crisis." *Financial Times* (October 1).

SEC. 2008. "SEC's Oversight of Bear Stearns and Related Entities: Broker-Dealer Risk Assessment Program." Report No. 446-B. Office of Inspector General (September 25).

———. 2010. "Investigation of the Circumstances Surrounding the SEC's Proposed Settlements with Bank of America, Including a Review of the Court's Rejection of the SEC's First Proposed Settlement and an Analysis of the Impact of Bank of America's Status as a TARP Recipient." Case No. OIG-522. Office of the Inspector General (September 30).

Segoviano, Miguel A., and Charles Goodhart. 2009. "Bank Stability Measures." International Monetary Fund Working Paper 09/4. Washington.

Shadow Financial Regulatory Committee. 2000. *Reforming Bank Capital Regulation*. Washington: AEI Press.

Special Inspector General for TARP. 2009. "Factors Affecting Efforts to Limit Payments to AIG Counterparties." Washington: Office of the Special Inspector General for the Troubled Asset Relief Program (November 17).

———. 2011. "Extraordinary Financial Assistance Provided to Citigroup, Inc." Washington: Office of the Special Inspector General for the Troubled Asset Relief Program (January 13).

Squam Lake Working Group on Financial Regulation. 2009. "An Expedited Resolution Mechanism for Distressed Financial Firms: Regulatory Hybrid Securities." Working Paper. Council on Foreign Relations, Center for Geoeconomic Studies (April).

Sundaresan, Suresh, and Zhenyu Wang. 2010. "Design of Contingent Capital with Stock Price Trigger for Conversion." Staff Report 448. Federal Reserve Bank of New York (April 23).

Swiss Commission of Experts. 2010. "Final Report of the Commission of Experts for Limiting the Economic Risks Posed by Large Companies." (September 30) (www.sif.admin.ch/dokumentation/00514/00519/00592/index.html?lang=en).

Swiss State Secretariat for International Financial Matters (SIF). 2011. "Too Big to Fail: Economic Risks Posed by Big Banks." Bern, Switzerland (January 21).

UBS. 2008. "Shareholder Report on UBS's Write-Downs." Zurich (April 18).

Valukas, Anton. 2010. "Report of Anton R. Valukas, Examiner for United States Bankruptcy Court, Southern District of New York." Vol. 5 (March).

DOUGLAS J. ELLIOTT 6

Governance Issues for Macroprudential Policy in Advanced Economies

THE RECENT SEVERE financial crisis is leading policymakers around the world to adopt a new set of tools to manage their nation's economy. Authorities may be able to cushion the blow from dangerous financial crises by using a "macroprudential" approach that fits between monetary policy for the economy as a whole and traditional regulation of individual financial institutions (now referred to as "microprudential" regulation to distinguish it from the new approach). There are multiple definitions of "macroprudential," but the core concept is to manage factors that could endanger the financial system as a whole even if it would not be obvious that they were serious threats when viewed in the context of any single institution. If risks such as excessive exposure to housing credit are common to many financial institutions simultaneously, they can, together with a high degree of interconnectedness between financial institutions, create

The author would like to gratefully acknowledge the support of the City of London Corporation and the helpful comments on previous drafts provided by a number of experts, including Martin Baily, Charles Goodhart, Don Kohn, Bob Litan, and several people who would prefer to remain anonymous. Any errors, of course, remain my own. I would also like to thank Natalie McGarry for her able research assistance. Finally, the views expressed are my own and do not necessarily represent those of the Brookings Institution or its staff or those of the City of London Corporation or its staff.

163

systemic risks even though each individual institution appears sound, when the potential for financial contagion is ignored.[1]

This chapter examines one of the key issues in more detail: how should macro-prudential authorities be structured and governed? Macroprudential policy has rarely been used in advanced economies in recent decades, and the structures to set policy in this area generally are very new or have not yet been formed. Even when an existing body is taking on macroprudential responsibilities, their nature will require new governance approaches. A number of questions therefore arise:

—Should macroprudential policy be conducted by a single authority, multiple authorities, or a committee?

—Which authority or authorities should be in charge of policy?

—In practice, what entities will conduct macroprudential policy in the major financial centers?

—What objectives should the macroprudential authority pursue?

—What tools should be available to the macroprudential authority?

—How should macroprudential authorities decide whether, when, and how to take action?

—To what extent should authorities use subjective judgment?

—How should macroprudential policy be coordinated with monetary policy?

—How should macroprudential and microprudential policy be coordinated?

—How should policy be coordinated internationally?

—How would authorities deal with regulatory arbitrage?

—How can proper accountability for macroprudential decisions be ensured?

—What other structural issues are important for sound governance?

—What is the optimal strategy for communicating macroprudential actions and their effects?

—How can the authorities counteract political pressure not to puncture bubbles?

—What are the major risks facing the macroprudential authorities?

Should Macroprudential Policy Be Conducted by a Single Authority, Multiple Authorities, or a Committee?

As with monetary policy, high-level macroprudential policymaking needs to be decided by a single body. A country would not set up multiple central banks with authority over different parts of its financial system, and it would be awkward—

---

1. Those unfamiliar with macroprudential policy may wish to read the author's comprehensive primer on the topic, written for nonspecialists (see www.brookings.edu/papers/2011/0311_capital_elliott.aspx). Parts of this chapter draw directly from that primer, although most of the chapter consists of new material.

and potentially disastrous—to have multiple authorities making separate decisions about the state of the credit cycle and the need for macroprudential intervention. However, there is room for the authority to be vested either in a single body or in a committee that makes a coordinated overall decision, and different countries have chosen different paths in this regard. Execution of any decisions could also fall onto different bodies, depending on the tool or tools chosen for use by the macroprudential authority.

A number of the pros and cons of setting up a single macroprudential authority rather than a committee follow below.

Advantages of Using a Single Authority

Coherence of decisionmaking. A single authority is more likely than a committee to take a coherent point of view of macroprudential policy. (Of course, anyone who has dealt with bureaucracies knows that this is not an absolute difference but a matter of degree. Even a single body can include seriously dissenting viewpoints.) Coherence is important for multiple reasons. First, incoherence will generally exhibit itself in the taking of partially conflicting policy actions, which reduces the effectiveness of the intended actions. Second, signaling effects are one of the paths by which macroprudential policy, like monetary policy, becomes effective; signals have less effect when they are unclear. Third, macroprudential policy is new enough that authorities will need to learn from their mistakes; learning is easier if there is a coherent policy to judge. Fourth, accountability is difficult to ensure in the absence of clarity.

Reduced probability of infighting. Conflicts between different bureaucracies and ideological views are likely to be fewer and less severe within a single authority than a committee, although, again, this is a matter of degree.

Ability to act. Committees often find it difficult to move forward in the absence of a strong consensus. That could be especially troublesome in boom periods, when the macroprudential authority needs to slow down excessive activity, resulting in lower profits for many parties and potentially lower economic activity. "Taking away the punch bowl" is seldom popular, so some committee members probably will push strongly against it or wish to slow or dilute the action. One way to reach consensus is to delay or hobble a necessary action.

Greater independence. Related to the last point, there will be strong pressures not to slow down a boom. Those pressures become harder to resist when there are multiple points of pressure, as would undoubtedly be true with a committee.

If one of the authorities represented on the committee has been captured by its regulated constituency—or is simply politically weak and therefore in a poor position to resist pressure—the committee will find it even harder to act.

Disadvantages of Using a Single Authority

Potential for groupthink. A single authority may develop a particular way of looking at the world that blocks out contrary facts and beliefs. In contrast, a committee structure could increase the range of ideas and information sources that are given weight in the deliberations.

Potential for an autocrat to take control. The head of a single authority may gain a position in which he or she can totally dominate the internal debate, a possibility that is especially strong if the head controls the careers of all or a majority of those on the decisionmaking committee of the single authority. This can create a more extreme version of groupthink in which the decisions are really those of a single, possibly inflexible, person.

Less credibility. If a committee of key regulators and policymakers were able to reach a consensus, the combined weight of the various members might make it easier to stand up to political pressures and doubts than would be the case with a single authority.

Less flexibility. A committee might find it easier to reverse itself if it made a mistake than would a single authority. That is not guaranteed, of course.

On the whole, I would recommend a single authority in order to combat the great difficulties that the body would face in taking painful actions during boom periods, which is probably the greatest single problem facing such authorities in these early days of macroprudential policy. However, there are clearly arguments on both sides of the ledger, as listed above.

Whichever option is chosen, single authority or committee, the detailed governance structure should be designed to minimize the disadvantages of that option. For example, the Financial Policy Committee (FPC) being set up under the Bank of England is a committee that will have external members with considerable clout and independence.[2] That should reduce the problems of groupthink and careerism that otherwise endanger structures with a unitary authority. It pro-

2. The FPC will be described in the future tense in this chapter because the enabling legislation has not yet been put in place. However, an interim FPC currently operates along the lines envisioned for the ultimate version.

vides some of the benefits of a committee without taking on the disadvantages of dispersed authority so strongly.

A committee structure, on the other hand, needs a strong chair and various organizational strengths, such as its own research support and independent funding, as has largely been structured into the Financial Stability Oversight Council (FSOC) in the United States. These will hopefully aid the committee to reach independent decisions and to stick to its guns in the face of political pressures.

Which Authority or Authorities Should Be in Charge of Policy?

The first question in choosing which authority or authorities to take charge of macroprudential policy is the extent of the role of the central bank. Again, there are pros and cons to a powerful central bank role.

Advantages of a Strong Central Bank Role

Overlap of macroprudential and monetary policy. As discussed below, the two types of economic policy have a number of overlapping areas. In particular, very loose monetary policy can set off a "search for yield" in financial markets that can stimulate a financial bubble. For its part, macroprudential policy could gum up the monetary transmission mechanisms and reduce the effectiveness of monetary policy decisions. The overlaps are not so large as to warrant a single unified policy, but they are sufficient to call for careful coordination, which is easier if the central bank plays a major role in macroprudential policy.

Political independence. Central banks have generally earned a great deal of independence from political influence, as a result of years of failed experiments in politically directed monetary policy. Macroprudential policy needs the same kind of independence, since one of its roles also is to "take away the punch bowl."

Credibility. In most advanced economies, the central banks have established strong and credible organizations, which could help macroprudential policy withstand onslaughts from those who might suffer when necessary restraints are placed on credit booms.

Strong analytical resources. Macroprudential and monetary policy issues are similar enough that the strong intellectual resources available at the central banks would be helpful in tackling the difficult complexities that arise as macroprudential policy grows from infancy.

Disadvantages of a Strong Central Bank Role

Subservience to monetary policy goals. Decisionmakers at a central bank might consciously or unconsciously favor monetary policy goals at the expense of macroprudential policy requirements. Wherever the decisions are made, authorities will need to deal with the overlap of monetary and macroprudential policy. Central bank decisionmakers who have a powerful role may find strong incentives to shortchange macroprudential policy.

Tainting of monetary policy decisions. In theory, the problem could run the other way. A central bank might become so enamored of macroprudential policy that it would aid those policies by tightening or loosening monetary policy inappropriately. In practice, that is unlikely to be a major problem for many years because the credibility of monetary policy as an approach has already been established while macroprudential policy is relatively new.

Excessive power in a single body. There is always a tension between the political independence necessary for effective central banking and the benefits of democratic control of major economic decisions. Handing still more power to a non-elected central bank would make the problem even more severe, although not necessarily unmanageable. In some political systems, there could also be a real risk of cronyism—for example, through regulatory capture by private sector banks. Excessive power would be a still greater risk in situations in which the central bank already plays a major supervisory role in addition to conducting monetary policy.

Potential erosion of a central bank's independence or credibility with regard to monetary policy. Macroprudential policy has the potential to become unpopular when used to force higher safety margins in the financial system in order to restrain a boom or prepare for the subsequent bust. It has the further disadvantage that it may not be given any credit if a bust is actually avoided or does relatively little harm because of policy actions taken. The greater the number and the importance of potentially unpopular roles that a central bank takes on, the more risk that its central role in monetary policy management is undermined.

Whatever choice is made about the strength of the central bank's role, there clearly needs to be strong coordination with the macroprudential authority. Therefore, if there is a committee structure, it should almost certainly include the central bank. Beyond that, it would be sensible to include microprudential regulators, for their expertise and also because there is a significant overlap between macroprudential and microprudential policy. In particular, most of the tools available to execute macroprudential policy, such as minimum capital requirements, are traditionally used by microprudential regulators, and it will remain necessary for them to use those tools. Using the same tools for two sets of purposes requires careful coordination.

If there is a single macroprudential authority and it is not at the central bank, it would be desirable to establish the single macroprudential authority as a new authority. In theory, if there is a single microprudential authority, or a dominant one, then that body could also take on macroprudential authority. However, I believe that the risk would be too high that the new macroprudential goals would become subservient in practice to microprudential goals. There are enough surface similarities between macroprudential and microprudential policies that it would be easy to fall into old habits and pay insufficient attention to the new role.

In Practice, What Entities Will Conduct Macroprudential Policy in the Major Financial Centers?

The United States, the United Kingdom, and the European Union have each set up bodies to conduct or coordinate macroprudential policies going forward. Interestingly, the structure that each has chosen is quite different from the others. In the United States, the Financial Stability Oversight Council (FSOC) has the power to make most macroprudential decisions and implementation is often left to the Federal Reserve Board or, to a lesser extent, to other regulators. The FSOC is composed of fifteen members, primarily the heads of the major national regulatory bodies, but with some representation, generally nonvoting, of state regulators, insurance regulators, and financial experts. The secretary of the treasury serves as the chair of the FSOC, and the chair has greater power than required to just run the meetings. For example, no nonbank financial institution can be designated as systemically important without the chair's assent. The Dodd-Frank Act also created the Office of Financial Research (OFR) within the Treasury Department to provide technical expertise to the FSOC, especially in regard to data gathering and analysis and overall analysis of financial stability. Congress clearly intended the OFR, despite being within the Treasury, to have a somewhat independent role, since the OFR director is protected by a fixed six-year term and shielded from pressure to revise congressional testimony to reflect overall administration views.

The FSOC's mandate is to preserve financial stability, and it has wide-ranging power to deal with large banks and with systemically important nonbank financial institutions. It is therefore in a position to actively conduct macroprudential policy, including by leaning against the prevailing wind. However, in the United States there currently appears to be more emphasis on the reduction of systemic risk generally and less focus on the cyclical aspects of macroprudential policy, although that could change.

The United Kingdom has chosen to concentrate macroprudential authority—and financial regulatory authority more generally—at the Bank of England. Consistent with that approach, legislation is being pursued to create the Financial Policy Committee (FPC) at the bank with the clear macroprudential objective of leaning against the wind, in addition to reducing systemic risk more generally. There is already an interim FPC that provides guidance to the bank while awaiting final legislation. The interim committee includes prominent external members, as will the ultimate committee, so it will not be purely a creature of the Bank of England. One aspect of the legislation is that Parliament will very likely specifically authorize the bank to use, or direct the use of, only certain tools as part of its policy. The bank can always make recommendations on the use of tools outside the authorized list, which would still carry considerable weight, particularly in areas in which the authority with ultimate responsibility has a reporting relationship to the bank.

The European Union has created the European Systemic Risk Board (ESRB), which is intended to encourage appropriate macroprudential actions by the national regulators. It describes its mission, in part, as being

> responsible for the macroprudential oversight of the financial system within the Union in order to contribute to the prevention or mitigation of systemic risks to financial stability in the Union that arise from developments within the financial system and taking into account macroeconomic developments, so as to avoid periods of widespread financial distress.[3]

At this initial stage of its development—it is less than a year old—its powers, which include the authority to make its advice public, are purely advisory. If it follows the path of many other EU-wide institutions, however, it is likely to accrete considerably more decisionmaking power over time.

The ESRB is a large body; it has thirty-seven voting members (twenty-seven heads of national central banks, plus ten others) and almost another thirty nonvoting members. Many outside observers assume that the smaller Steering Committee, which has fourteen members and is weighted more toward heads of

---

3. ESRB, "Mission, Objectives, and Tasks" (www.esrb.europa.eu/about/tasks/html/index.en.html).

EU-wide institutions, will end up dominating decisions. The ESRB is located in Frankfurt with the European Central Bank, and it will rely considerably on the ECB for technical assistance.

What Objectives Should the Macroprudential Authority Pursue?

Clearly, macroprudential authorities should focus on the stability of the financial system. Unfortunately, that is difficult to measure precisely, although the failure to achieve it can become quite obvious. It may be possible in the years ahead to develop good, objective measures of systemic stability, but for now considerable subjective judgment is required.

It is critical, however, that "financial stability" not be defined purely as the absence or near-absence of the risk of a systemic crisis. The term must encompass the need for the financial system to be a stable provider of the necessary credit to keep the economy moving forward. A narrow focus on the risk aspect of financial stability could lead to excessively high safety margins that reduce risk, but at a very high cost. For example, one could certainly make the regulated system much safer by requiring capital ratios of, say, 80 percent, but that would mean a far smaller regulated sector, providing much less credit.

What Tools Should Be Available to the Macroprudential Authority?

There are quite a number of instruments that could be used by themselves or in combination to execute macroprudential policy, which are discussed in detail in appendix A, taken from Elliott (2011b). They include the following:
   —countercyclical capital requirements
   —dynamic loan loss provisioning
   —countercyclical liquidity requirements
   —limitations on leverage in asset purchases
   —loan-to-value (LTV) ratios for mortgages
   —loan-to-income (LTI) ratios for mortgages
   —minimum margins/haircuts on secured securities lending
   —administrative caps on aggregate lending
   —reserve requirements
   —constraints on currency mismatches
   —credit controls
   —taxation
   —monetary policy

This listing focuses on instruments for managing systemic risks that vary with the state of the credit cycle. In addition, macroprudential authorities may be granted the ability to force changes in the structure of systemically important institutions or types of financial transactions in order to reduce overall systemic risk without regard to the state of the cycle. In the United States, the FSOC, in combination with the Federal Reserve in its supervisory capacity, has considerable power in this regard.

In theory, macroprudential authorities could also be given crisis management powers, but I agree with most analysts in placing those powers outside the macroprudential role, which is generally conceived of as dealing with prevention rather than resolution. Macroprudential authorities should be able to provide good advice and technical support to a crisis resolution authority but should not lead the process. Crisis resolution is much closer in nature to microprudential supervision and also could well involve the use of fiscal powers that do not naturally belong with a macroprudential authority.

A key decision in setting up any macroprudential authority is to determine which tools will be made available to the authority. In this regard, it is important to note that many, if not all, of the tools listed above will not be controlled directly by the macroprudential authority. Most likely, the authority will be allowed to *suggest* to regulators that they use any one or more of the tools that they themselves control, although politics may cause even suggesting the use of some tools to be off limits. The real question is when the macroprudential authority will be allowed to *direct* an action by other regulators, such as increasing the minimum capital requirements for banks or creating or enlarging a countercyclical capital buffer.

In general, a competent macroprudential authority would benefit from having a wide range of potential instruments. That said, there could be reasons to exclude some tools from the list. For example, a legislature may not wish to hand over authority on taxation, even of a limited nature, to an unelected body. Monetary policy, for its part, will almost certainly remain with the central bank, and it is unlikely that the macroprudential authority will be allowed to direct the monetary authority on instruments such as overall interest rates. Finally, allowing the macroprudential authority to place aggregate limits on total lending or other forms of credit controls may be viewed as ineffective or too dangerous for most modern economies with sophisticated financial systems.

If the legislature wishes to keep macroprudential authorities focused on a few key instruments, an approach that I generally do not favor, then there is at least an argument for allowing a subset of the tools that are most generally useful, including countercyclical capital requirements, but excluding the others initially. Having only a subset available may well make the authority less effective, but it could limit potential unintended consequences and may make it easier for markets and the public to understand what the authority will do.

There is also the question of how narrowly the macroprudential authority will be allowed to focus its action. In particular, the use as a macroprudential tool of maximum loan-to-value ratios on mortgages would presumably be more effective if it could be varied across a country, depending on the degree to which a given region or city is experiencing a housing boom.[4] Cutting things a different way, certain types of lending may develop in a dangerous manner at a time when other types are saner.

There are a number of trade-offs between the increased potential effectiveness of making very focused use of macroprudential tools and the governance and communications issues created by that approach. The narrower the ability of the authority to focus its actions, the more it will, in effect, be creating winners and losers by its actions and hence the more powerful it will become. Central banks have been able to achieve a great deal of independence in their conduct of monetary policy in part because their actions affect broad swaths of the economy equally. It is true that their actions may benefit lenders at the expense of borrowers, or vice versa, but at least those are very broad categories and monetary policy moves between restraint and easing frequently enough for the choices to balance out to a considerable extent. (A given central bank could still have an overall bias that favors borrowers or lenders, of course.)

Especially in its early days, macroprudential policy that creates distinct groups of winners and losers may well find itself under strong political attack. Unfortunately, there is likely to be an asymmetry here, because losers from government actions are often considerably more vocal than winners, who are essentially receiving a benefit that they did not expect. Perhaps even more likely is that there will be focused losses for a specific group or groups coupled with much more dispersed benefits to society as a whole. For example, a macroprudential authority might decide that there is a dangerous housing boom in the nation's largest city but not elsewhere and accordingly lower the maximum loan-to-value ratio for mortgages within the city limits. Those affected are likely to complain loudly about the unfairness created by arbitrarily choosing their city when they perceive similar problems just over the city's borders or in the second-largest city

4. The Republic of Korea apparently sets mortgage standards that differ within relatively small geographies for just this reason.

and when they see pockets of their own city that are not experiencing a boom. Similarly, there is a risk that much of the benefit might be undone by changes in lending behavior that effectively move the bubble into the next most congenial location, such as just across the city's borders.

Such risks do not mean that macroprudential authorities should always move in a broad manner. They serve only to point out that trade-offs must be made and that they need to be considered in deciding what powers a new macroprudential authority should have.

How Should Macroprudential Authorities Decide Whether, When, and How to Take Action?

The details of the decisionmaking process are outside the scope of this chapter, but the macroprudential authority must be set up in a manner, and with the resources, that ensures that it has the following:

A framework to judge credit conditions and asset price levels. Macroprudential policy is intended to "lean against the wind" when economic forces are feeding bubble conditions or creating a credit bust. Therefore, there must be a framework to evaluate wind speed and direction and likely near-term changes in both. Most analysts agree that, given the current state of forecasting, subjective judgment must be used in addition to the various proposed quantitative analyses.

A process to determine which tools to use when action is required. If the authorities are vested with multiple macroprudential powers, as they should be, then there must be a way to decide which tools to use, to what degree, when action is needed. (See Elliott 2011b for a detailed discussion of this issue. Appendix B excerpts a suggested set of questions for macroprudential authorities to consider in this regard.)

A framework for imposing the chosen changes to safety margins. For example, how should countercyclical capital requirements be raised or lowered? The most straightforward approach is probably that suggested by the Basel Committee— adding a countercyclical capital buffer to the minimum capital requirements resulting from the rest of the Basel rules. The buffer can be thought of either as a number of percentage points tacked on top of the otherwise required ratios of capital to risk-weighted assets or as a multiple of those ratios. For example, capital requirements could be increased by 10 percent simply by multiplying all existing ratio requirements by 1.1, or the total requirements could be increased by, say, 1 percentage point. In theory, a separate set of calculations could be used to determine the total level of capital needed, but there are compelling reasons to retain the Basel structure rather than create a competing set of rules. An alternative regime could lead to confusion and to odd decisionmaking processes if the new set of rules appeared to be about to bind the banks due to overall financial conditions that might lead to macroprudential action.

A way of deciding how much to move the requirements and within what time frame. As with an analysis to determine whether a move is necessary, quantitative measurements, supplemented by subjective judgment, are necessary to indicate the new level of capital requirements.

Clear means of communicating the decisions and their rationales. Although it will be difficult, it is critically important to ensure that macroprudential decisions are understood by politicians, regulators, banks, financial markets, and other key constituencies. Lack of clarity could lead to confused reactions and market volatility as well as undermine the prospects for achieving the necessary public and political support. This is discussed further below.

Access to the data necessary to ensure that the macroprudential authority is able to obtain all of the above. Macroprudential authorities will be prodigious consumers of data about the financial system and, to a lesser extent, about the rest of the economy. They will need the legal power to ensure that the data they need are available to them, either from other regulatory authorities or from the financial industry directly. Nearly everyone agrees on the desirability of using existing regulatory data sources when possible to avoid imposing unnecessary burdens on the financial industry, but that will not always be feasible. Sometimes it may be necessary to collect information directly or to require regulatory authorities to gather additional information for the use of the macroprudential authorities.

To What Extent Should Authorities Use Subjective Judgment?

It is hard at this point in the development of macroprudential theory to imagine a set of formulas good enough to eliminate the need for the authorities to make judgment calls, even though doing so clearly has its own drawbacks. However, the use of judgment has the great advantage of allowing authorities to take into account information that is not contained in the models, including the possibility that an asset price boom is driven by a genuine economic development and not an investment fad. Authorities also may be aware that other factors, such as world economic conditions, are likely to damp down the boom without the need for macroprudential actions.

In Kannan, Rabanal, and Scott (2009), the authors conclude from their simulation analyses that

> using a macroprudential instrument designed specifically to dampen credit market cycles would also be useful. But expectations should be realistic about what can be achieved with such an approach. In particular, it is often difficult to accurately identify the source of the shock driving house price booms. Invariant and rigid policy responses raise the risk of policy errors that could lower, not raise, macroeconomic stability. Hence, discretion would need to be applied.[5]

Tucker (2009) states that it is

> doubtful that macroprudential instruments could be operated as a rule. To steer the banking system towards increasing its resilience to incipient problems in a stretched sector, a whole series of judgments would have to be made. Whether the rate of credit growth seemed excessive; whether terms were overly lax; or whether the "bubble bursting" would materially damage banks.[6]

The IMF comes to the same conclusion, stating that "[t]hese results suggest that policy reactions to indicators of potential financial vulnerability should be neither automatic nor rigid—policymakers need room for discretion."[7]

However, subjective judgments can be wrong, they can be biased, and they can be harder to explain and defend. There is a fair chance that authorities' predictive ability would be higher if they used subjective judgment than it would be if they used only a formula, but there would also be the danger that the authorities would fall into the very human trap of buying into the same prevailing fallacies about the causes of an asset price bubble as the rest of society. Worse, political pressure might be harder to resist when applying subjective judgment. It is not just a question of defending a decision but also of the human trait of convincing ourselves of those beliefs that will minimize conflict with others.

5. Kannan, Rabanal, and Scott (2009, p. 5).
6. Tucker (2009, p. 9).
7. IMF (2009).

Certainly, however, there would also be the issue of convincing politicians and the public that the authorities were acting appropriately. In the beginning, this could go either way. A formula provides an objectivity that might be helpful, but a formula that has not yet proven itself might be less convincing than the arguments of experts.

In its consultative document on countercyclical capital buffers, the Basel Committee acknowledges that national regulators need to use subjective judgment. In order to increase the consistency and effectiveness of actions across the world, the committee proposed five principles to guide decisions on the use of countercyclical capital buffers (the only instrument that they fully endorsed at that point):

Principle 1: Buffer decisions should be guided by the objectives to be achieved by the buffer, namely, to protect the banking system against potential future losses when excess credit growth is associated with an increase in systemwide risk. [The committee notes that the buffer, as such, "is not meant to be used as an instrument to manage economic cycles or asset prices." That does not mean that it would have no effects on those cycles or prices but that its fundamental purpose is to achieve stability in the financial system.]

Principle 2: The credit/GDP guide [a particular analytical measurement suggested in the report to measure excessive credit growth] *is a useful common reference point in taking buffer decisions. It does not need to play a dominant role in the information used by authorities to take and explain buffer decisions. Authorities should explain the information used, and how it is taken into account in formulating buffer decisions.*

Principle 3: Assessments of the information contained in the credit/GDP guide and any other guides should be mindful of the behaviour of the factors that can lead them to give misleading signals.

Principle 4: Promptly releasing the buffers in times of stress can help to reduce the risk of the supply of credit being constrained by regulatory capital requirements.

Principle 5: The buffer is an important instrument in a suite of macroprudential tools at the disposal of the authorities.[8]

8. Basel Committee (2010, pp. 7–9).

How Should Macroprudential Policy Be Coordinated with Monetary Policy?

If regulatory authorities other than central banks play a significant role in macro-prudential policy, then it will be important to ensure that they coordinate their actions appropriately with their central bank. As an obvious example, it would be unfortunate if tough new macroprudential policies were put in place to stop a potential bubble at the same time as the central bank slammed on the brakes for the economy as a whole, unless the situation were truly so troublesome as to merit action on both fronts.

Conventional monetary policy actions have considerable effects on credit activity and asset prices through a variety of transmission channels, which are explained in appendix C. They include the following:

—changes in the supply and demand of short-term funds

—indirect, and occasionally direct, effects on intermediate and long-term interest rates

—effects on currency exchange rates, which are sensitive to interest rates

—changes in asset prices in general, especially of interest-sensitive assets

—effects on risk aversion and the perception of risk levels

—impacts on capital levels of financial intermediaries

—changes in levels of bank reserves held at the central bank.

Many of these transmission channels directly affect banks and other financial firms in important ways, while all of them have at least important indirect effects. In particular, prolonged low interest rates have been shown to encourage financial institutions and other market participants to take levels of risk that they would otherwise have shunned, levels that can become truly quite excessive in extreme cases.[9] There is an ongoing debate about whether that fact should lead monetary authorities to hold rates higher than they otherwise would at times of overexuberance in the financial markets. Opponents of this approach generally assert either that it is too hard to detect bubbles or that the damage to the wider economy from higher interest rates more than offsets the benefits of taming the financial cycle, or that both claims are true. The debate is too complicated to be adequately covered in this chapter; see Bean and others (2010) for a review of the arguments. However, it is worth noting that the more one believes in an active monetary response to financial

---

9. See Altunbas, Gambacorta, and Marques-Ilbanez (2008), for example.

crises, the less likely one would be to support macroprudential tools that work by affecting the financial system widely. That does not mean, however, that such a belief would be inconsistent with more focused uses of macroprudential policy, such as dealing with bubbles confined to a single sector, such as housing.

Working in the other direction, substantially increasing the required macroprudential safety margins could make it harder for monetary policy easing to be effective. For example, interest rate easing may not translate into significantly greater lending if capital, liquidity, and loan-to-value requirements are all set at levels that discourage such lending.

Because of the various interlinkages, the most effective overall economic policy would require coordination with macroprudential actions that also affect credit provision in significant ways. Similarly, the information required to implement the necessary macroprudential actions overlaps to a considerable extent with that needed for monetary policy, making it highly desirable that all authorities share their information and thought processes.

Finally, macroprudential regulators and monetary authorities both need politicians and the public to accept their actions, lest they eventually lose their independence to make these decisions. If one group is pushing the economy in a particular direction that appears to be at odds with that of the other group, it could do harm to both. Of course, the risk for macroprudential regulators is probably greater, because they will have quite a new mandate and little history to show that their approach is useful.

Coordination must involve appropriate exchanges of information about the state of the financial system and of systemically important institutions, with particular emphasis on those aspects that represent the greatest dangers. Ideally there would also be an open exchange of views about the economy and the financial system. There should be frequent communication at the staff level between the various authorities, complemented by more formal discussions, perhaps once a quarter or more frequently if danger looms.

How Should Macroprudential and Microprudential Policy Be Coordinated?

Most financial regulation concerns the safety and soundness of individual financial institutions, both because it seeks to prevent the collapse of individual entities and because individual solvency is at the core of systemic solvency, although apparent safety at each separate institution is not an absolute guarantee of systemic safety. With the advent of macroprudential policy, "safety and soundness" regulation is often referred to as "microprudential." (I will switch between the two terms, for the sake of variety and because "microprudential" is an ugly word.)

There is a clear need for macroprudential and microprudential authorities to coordinate their actions. First, the large majority of the tools used for macroprudential purposes are the same as those used for microprudential reasons; they are just used for different reasons and sometimes in different ways. As a practical matter, the safety and soundness regulators will generally have the responsibility of ensuring that each financial institution meets the combined macro- and microprudential requirements. There is no point in wasting resources by having the macroprudential authority do individual audits to ensure compliance.

Second, there are overlapping areas of judgment in which macro- and microprudential authorities could find themselves working at cross purposes. The most concerning area relates to the transition from a period of credit expansion to a credit bust. For illustration, assume that microprudential authorities were requiring a core capital ratio of 10 percent and that macroprudential authorities had foreseen a credit bust and added a countercyclical buffer of 5 percentage points, for a total of 15 percent. As the bubble bursts and the credit bust begins, the macroprudential authorities might wish to remove the entire buffer, allowing the total requirement to drop to 10 percent again. However, safety and soundness regulators might be too nervous to let the requirement drop back to normal levels and might move the minimum requirement under their control up to 12 percent or even up to 15 percent.[10]

There is a potential similar problem during a boom period. Microprudential regulators might come to realize that core capital levels are too low, perhaps because financial institutions are gaming the system or because additional information comes to light or the overall economic environment changes. If macroprudential regulators have created a significant countercyclical buffer, then the safety and soundness regulators might not be willing to expend the political capital to raise the core levels or might find it too difficult to do so.

The clear implication of these examples and others is that the two sets of authorities need to coordinate in order to achieve their separate purposes while accessing some of the same tools. Sometimes there may simply be an inherent

10. There is a similar concern that market nervousness might force financial institutions to retain the higher levels. This potential response of markets and microprudential regulators at the time a bubble bursts is an argument for macroprudential buffers to be built to a sufficient level during a boom that the effective total safety margins will drop afterward even if there is some counteraction by markets and regulators.

conflict between the two sets of goals, but most of the time there will be a way to accomplish both, since the two types of regulators are focused on different issues.

There is an argument for enhancing coordination by housing the macro-prudential authority within the same body that regulates safety and soundness. That is not an unreasonable argument, but I view macroprudential policy as more like monetary policy than microprudential policy with respect to its scope and thought processes, although it has similarities to both. It should be possible to have the necessary coordination through good information sharing and regular high-level discussions. If a committee is running macroprudential policy, then clearly safety and soundness regulators should be represented.

A related communications issue also arises. It is important that communications to the financial industry and the public about the required levels of various safety margins make clear which part serves microprudential and which part serves macroprudential objectives.

How Should Policy Be Coordinated Internationally?

A large part of the world's financial system operates on a global rather than a national or local basis. Unfortunately, that adds the need for an additional governance structure, at least in terms of international coordination mechanisms and agreed rules of the road relating to actions that have international ramifications. Some, such as the Institute of International Finance (IIF), have recommended the creation of an international macroprudential body, perhaps associated with the Financial Stability Board, in order to aid coordination. However it is accomplished, coordination across countries will be needed for multiple reasons.

For example, regulators in a given country may determine that their credit markets are starting to boom to a dangerous extent and that it is time to raise capital requirements and/or deploy other macroprudential tools. However, there is a risk that lenders in other countries might step in to fill the gap. They might be able to do so by lending through branches operating in that country, or their total capital might be sufficient for them to comfortably redeploy some of it to the booming country. They also have the alternative in some cases of lending to companies that are based in the booming nation but can borrow outside it, either directly or through foreign subsidiaries.

It therefore becomes important that there be global coordination of macroprudential activities. At the extreme, that could in theory mean treating the globe as one large market and having all relevant countries move in tandem. However, such global coordination not only would be too difficult but also would almost certainly be counterproductive, given that national economies and financial systems remain different enough that the right medicine for one country can be poisonous to another. The task becomes one of ensuring that the differences in macroprudential choices across borders do not cause excessive damage to the policies each nation needs to employ for its own purposes.

One method that has been proposed is for other countries to honor the macroprudential choices of host countries. Thus, if the United Kingdom, for example, were to raise capital requirements on its domestic loans, then other countries should also raise capital requirements on U.K. loans being made by their own banks. A global bank would thereby find that its total capital requirements were based on a weighted average of the requirements relevant to its business in the various countries in which it operates. Unfortunately, there would remain considerable potential for "gaming" the different capital standards across countries, such as, in this example, by finding ways to reclassify what is essentially a U.K. domestic loan as a loan in a country with lower capital requirements.

The Basel III agreement endorsed by the Group of Twenty (G-20) leaders calls for national regulators to honor each other's macroprudential decisions, at least within the range of a countercyclical capital buffer of up to 2.5 percent of risk-weighted assets. It will be necessary to find appropriate coordination mechanisms for the other macroprudential tools that authorities will use. A few of them require no real coordination, such as limitations on loan-to-value ratios for mortgages, since the underlying contracts under local law are at issue. However, most other tools could be undercut by internationally active lenders and borrowers if the right mechanisms are not found to discourage it.

How Would Authorities Deal with Regulatory Arbitrage?

Dealing with regulatory arbitrage could be an especially difficult issue in practice, and the approach taken would depend considerably on the specific circumstances and legal authorities involved. One type of regulatory arbitrage would be the development of major nonbank financial institutions that lie outside the macroprudential framework. The best response might be either to begin regulating these institutions as banks, both for safety and soundness and macroprudential reasons, or to adapt the macroprudential responses to encompass them as well. If neither action makes sense, then arbitrage would create constraints within which macroprudential policy would have to operate, yielding second-best solutions at times.

Another potential difficulty would cross borders, with one nation using a macroprudential policy that is very different from that used by another, which would affect cross-border lending behavior. As noted, it probably makes sense to defer to the macroprudential decisions of other countries, so that if, for example, mortgage lending in the United Kingdom were deemed by the British to need restraining, then lending by banks of other countries that lend in the United Kingdom should be placed under similar restraints. However, there might be more complicated interlinkages that are harder to unravel. They would likely matter only if macroprudential policy varied a great deal across borders—which argues for a bias toward broadly similar policies in today's globally interlinked world.

Nonetheless, for both good and bad reasons, there will be differences in macroprudential policy among major trading partners, and it will be necessary for lines of communication to be open and for the authorities in different countries to be willing to listen to the concerns of their peers. Of course, virtually the same points could be made in regard to monetary policy. Differing national approaches remain an area of serious concern, and sometimes suspicions arise that one country is engaging in "beggar thy neighbor" policies by influencing exchange rates or other economic variables that lead it to benefit at the expense of others. There is no reason to expect easy answers that will always work in such cross-border issues; all that can be done is to design a system to minimize the damage from divergent policies.

It would be about as difficult theoretically to coordinate macroprudential policies as it already is to coordinate monetary policies. It would probably be even more difficult in the beginning, given the uncertainties and different views about the policy framework that would exist initially. The broad idea would be to respond in a similar manner across the globe to similar financial circumstances. If there were a global bubble in commodities fueled in part by excessive credit, then it would be in the interest of most countries to deflate that burgeoning bubble and to increase the effectiveness of the response through coordination of policies.

The task would not be easy, however. There might well be a difference of opinion between those countries that primarily produce commodities and those that primarily consume them about whether a bubble is forming. Or, a particular set of countries might be experiencing a housing bubble while other nations are not. Even in those countries in which a bubble had formed or was forming, the bubble could well be at different stages of development or the countries could be experiencing it to different degrees; as a result, the danger in each case might vary considerably, depending on the local housing and financial systems. Given the various differences, coordination could be difficult.[11]

11. There are parallels with the theoretical discussions in monetary policy concerning optimal currency areas. See, for example, Lafrance and St-Amant (1999) and Benigno (2004).

That said, there are certain aspects of coordination that would virtually always be useful and important. Regulators should share information about the state of the financial system in their countries, especially regarding any potential dangers. Major financial institutions with substantial cross-border activities must be observed from the multiple viewpoints of the different national regulators in order to ensure that an integrated picture is available for macroprudential decision-making. (There is already one mechanism, "colleges" of supervisors for each of the most critical global institutions; they operate on a somewhat informal and consensual basis.) It would also be useful for any major macroprudential steps to be communicated in advance of implementation to regulatory colleagues in other countries, in case they see implications that are not obvious to a given national regulator.

How Can Proper Accountability for Macroprudential Decisions Be Ensured?

Macroprudential authorities must be accountable to public representatives for their decisions, just as monetary policy officials are. The right approach is probably similar in both cases. The authorities must make clear decisions that they then communicate, along with their reasons for making them. It is also desirable for them to make periodic reports to their governments, as the Fed does in its appearances before congressional committees to explain its monetary policy stance. In the end, the body politic has the ability to rescind or limit the independence and authority of these bodies and could legitimately choose to do so if the authorities appeared to be making too many wrong decisions when viewed with the benefit of hindsight.

In the United Kingdom, Parliament decides what macroprudential tools may be directed by the Bank of England and its Financial Policy Committee. Any initial decision could, of course, be altered by Parliament later, and there would be a real chance of that happening if the macroprudential authorities fail to make a clear and convincing case for the actions that they take. At the EU level, the European Systemic Risk Board's powers are solely advisory, which makes it all the more critical that its analyses be convincing. The Financial Stability Oversight Council in the United States is potentially more powerful than either of these bodies, having been given a very wide grant of authority, but it appears likely to operate with a much narrower approach, except, perhaps, in financial crises.

Of course, establishing credibility by sound analyses and decisions will be harder than achieving the same result with monetary policy, because credit cycles are longer than business cycles. That means that the correctness of a macroprudential decision may not be clear for a number of years, whereas the consequences of monetary policy decisions tend to manifest themselves somewhat faster.

What Other Structural Issues Are Important for Sound Governance?

It should be said, at the risk of stating the obvious, that authorities with macroprudential powers must be structured on sound governance principles. Conflicts of interest, unmanageable organizational complexities, capture by political or commercial forces, and other such flaws must be avoided. There will be the temptation to let each of these problems creep in as a result of pressure to compromise and satisfy all parties with an interest in how the authorities are structured. For example, if every group with an interest in the outcome is given representation on a macroprudential board, the potential for crippling complexity and conflicts of interest would be great. At the same time, there must be ultimate accountability and a structure that ensures that the authorities do not operate with an excessively narrow view. There is no single right answer for how to achieve this balance, but it should be given a great deal of attention when structures and processes are designed.

What Is the Optimal Strategy for Communicating Macroprudential Actions and Their Effects?

Communication will be crucially important to macroprudential authorities. Most important, public and political support, especially critical in the early days, will depend heavily on understanding what the authorities are doing and why. Accountability also depends heavily on clarity about the intended actions and their effects. Beyond that, signaling effects should become important over time in magnifying the impact of the actions being taken. In monetary policy, the first interest rate move in a new direction tends to have a disproportionate impact because of what it signals about the direction of future changes. The effects of additional changes are still magnified somewhat by the information that the changes provide about likely future actions. Macroprudential actions may not benefit initially from the same degree of magnification, given the newness of this area, but that should change as the authorities gain credibility and the markets come to understand their actions better.

What degree of transparency should surround macroprudential decisions? If the authorities were able to reduce the process to a set of formulas, then there would be a strong argument for making those formulas public. It probably makes sense to release any formulas and their current values even if they were just a portion of the items considered by the authorities. In addition, the subjective elements of the decisionmaking processes should be disclosed as well, within reason, as with information releases from the Fed or the European Central Bank when monetary policy decisions are made.

How Can the Authorities Counteract Political Pressure Not to Puncture Bubbles?

Political pressure will doubtless be brought to bear whenever macroprudential authorities attempt to damp down the development of credit booms. Boom periods create a host of winners, some of whom are true winners, such as brokers who pocket commissions based on asset prices and volumes, and some of whom are contingent winners, because their profits are realized only if they sell while the bubble remains in place. Politicians will almost inevitably respond to the protests of these constituencies, especially as there tend to be few groups that are seen as being hurt by a boom. The arguments usually will not be in the form of naked claims of self-interest but will be wrapped in economic theories, such as the alleged productivity gains that came from the tech bubble or the benefits that purportedly arose from substantial expansion of the base of homeowners.

Central bankers already face this sort of political pressure whenever they start to raise interest rates, since doing so usually slows down the overall economy, creating many more losers than winners in the short run, even though it may be necessary for the common good in the longer run. However, they start with stronger economic theories to guide them and can point to years of experience that show why the temporary sacrifices are necessary. They also benefit from their relative political independence, gained from historical experience that has shown that lack of independence can lead to major economic problems.

Macroprudential authorities need to make the best arguments they can, but it will take courage to withstand the onslaught. Over time, a consensus should develop, as it has with monetary policy, that the overall approach is right and that political independence is necessary to gain economic benefits and minimize economic pain. On the other hand, being afraid to use the macroprudential tools available is virtually the same as not using them because of political pressure. Therefore, if they are used even partially and hesitantly, the economic results may well be significantly better than if the authority did not use them at all.

On the bright side, there is little likelihood in practice of the theoretical possibility that macroprudential authorities will overshoot by being too tough. The political pressures are almost certain to ensure that any errors are on the side of too little action.

What Are the Major Risks Facing the Macroprudential Authorities?

There are several ways in which the use of macroprudential tools could go wrong in practice, including the following:

Excessive timidity. As noted, political pressures might keep the tools from being used to any great extent. That does not appear likely to create any more problems than arise today, although it would mean that the benefits would largely fail to materialize.

Excessive aggressiveness. Again as noted, excessive aggressiveness is very unlikely to occur, given the political pressures not to act to deflate potential bubbles. A greater risk in this area would be that countercyclical buffers would be brought back down to zero too fast or too frequently. Again, however, the current system operates implicitly with buffers that are effectively at zero anyway, so while this would result in an opportunity cost that the ideal policy would not incur, it might still be better than today's situation.

Policy confusion. There is certainly a risk, especially in the early days, that policymakers might send confused signals or change their methods too frequently. That could increase the volatility of financial conditions and thereby of the overall economy. It would also likely raise the cost of capital and debt funding for financial institutions, costs that would be passed through in higher loan costs and reduced availability of credit.

Inappropriate credit allocation. If macroprudential tools are used not just to set overall credit conditions but also to make certain sectors more or less attractive, there would be a danger of getting the allocations wrong and encouraging inefficient allocation of societal resources. The misallocation could simply be due to mistakes or, more perniciously, it could result from political pressures to favor one sector or another.

Excessive interference in business decisions. Some of the potential macroprudential tools could be used to allow regulators to micromanage the financial system. For example, if countercyclical capital requirements were set on a sectoral level, authorities could be tempted to substitute their own judgment for that of the markets on exactly what kinds of loans are sensible. Some of the other tools are potentially even more heavy handed, such as the setting of total limits on credit provision by banks. Setting the limits and dividing them among the different institutions would give scope for authorities to play favorites among institutions or among uses of the credit capacity.

Excessively high average capital requirements. The addition of countercyclical capital buffers, which are always positive or zero, will raise the regulatory capital requirements, on average, over time. That is almost certain to make credit more expensive and less available, on average. If none of the intended benefits of "leaning against the wind" are achieved, then that could lead to slower economic growth. On the other hand, if capital ratios are still too low after Basel III, as some have suggested, then the buffers may have an unintended positive benefit of bringing average levels closer to the optimal ones. (Other observers, of course, believe Basel III is already too high, in which case the problem would be aggravated.)

Appendix 6A

What Macroprudential Tools Are Available?[1]

The primary purpose of countercyclical macroprudential policy is to attempt to avoid or minimize the effects of asset price bubbles supported by credit booms. Although the boom period generally increases economic growth and short-term prosperity, the inevitable bust that follows more than wipes out those benefits. As discussed in great detail in my March 2011 overview of macroprudential policy, the most severe financial crises, as well as many more modest ones, result from excessive and rapidly rising asset prices supported by high levels of financial leverage.[2] The use of credit to help fund asset purchases means that the financial system is hurt badly when such bubbles burst, with terrible knock-on effects for the wider economy, given the importance of finance to the smooth functioning of advanced economies. The most recent crisis is a perfect example, but many other financial crises have followed the same path. (By contrast, the bursting of the tech bubble early in the first decade of the 2000s, which was funded primarily by equity rather than credit, did significantly less harm to the rest of the economy.)

Macroprudential policy can assist in two ways. First, it can focus on better preparing the financial system during boom times to be able to survive busts, such as by requiring higher levels of capital as the system enters the danger zone. Second, it can attempt to keep credit busts from becoming more severe than necessary in order to minimize the damage to the real economy when credit and other financial services are withdrawn. That may well involve damping down the preceding credit boom in order to minimize the repercussions of its demise. A number of tools are available for macroprudential authorities, as discussed below.

Countercyclical Capital Requirements

This tool has received the most attention and the widest acceptance by authorities. It has been endorsed by both the Basel Committee on Banking Supervision (Basel Committee), the committee of regulators that coordinates global banking rules, and the Financial Stability Board (FSB), a multilateral body empowered by Group of Twenty (G-20) world leaders to advise on financial stability issues. The

---

1. Taken from Elliott (2011b, pp. 4–10).
2. Elliott (2011a).

G-20 itself has endorsed countercyclical capital as part of its approval of the Basel Committee and FSB recommendations.

As described earlier, the idea is to force banks (and sometimes other regulated credit providers) to hold more capital during worrisome booms. The primary purpose is to build protection against the risks that hide below the surface of overexuberant booms, so that banks will be in a better position to continue providing credit if a boom turns into a bust. A secondary purpose is to discourage excessive lending by making lending more expensive, since capital is more expensive for banks than for other funding sources.[3] This is especially important because capital tends to be too cheap during booms, due to realized and unrealized gains feeding through balance sheets and the excessive eagerness of markets to supply new capital as a result of "bubble thinking." Countercyclical capital surcharges either can be set across the board for each financial institution or type of institution or can be specific to a given credit product or sector of lending. There are pros and cons to each approach, which are detailed in appendix C.

Dynamic Loan Loss Provisioning

Dynamic loan loss provisioning is somewhat similar to countercyclical capital requirements in that banks would be forced to reserve for a higher level of loan losses during a boom than they would otherwise. It can be implemented in one of two ways. First, the rules can attempt to counteract the procyclical aspects of conventional loan loss reserving; reserves tend to fall during booms even though loans made during periods of over-optimism usually are the most dangerous. Traditional loan loss provisioning methodologies generally require or encourage banks to estimate their losses on the basis of relatively recent experience. During a boom, recent experience will show unusually low loss levels, leading to diminished provisions. Dynamic loan loss provisioning applied in this manner essentially tries to keep loan loss provisions at a level sufficient for an average downturn. Second, the rules could go beyond that to try to build quasi-capital reserves above the true best estimate of future loan losses during booms, either by focusing on losses under a stress case or by adding a margin of error in some other

---

3. Various policy analysts have pointed out that the greater expense is principally due to various policy distortions, such as preferential tax treatment for debt, and therefore society as a whole might be better off with much higher capital levels. However, as long as these distortions exist, banks will find that their private costs of capital are higher than for other funding sources, regardless of what the overall societal costs are. Therefore, having to hold more capital creates a disincentive for banks to undertake lending.

manner. The latter approach adds an element that is very similar to countercyclical capital requirements.

Spain employed dynamic loan loss provisioning for most of its banks, but not for its *cajas,* or savings banks.[4] The consensus is that this approach probably cushioned the damage to its mainstream banks, even though Spain still ended up with a major financial crisis, partly due to the *cajas* and partly to crucial underlying aspects of its economic and financial systems.

Countercyclical Liquidity Requirements

Banks are increasingly being required by regulators to hold at least minimum levels of safe, shorter-term, or highly liquid assets to cover the possibility that they will need cash quickly to stop a bank run or to handle a freeze in credit markets that makes it difficult to raise funds. The revised capital and liquidity rules recently promulgated by the Basel Committee, known as Basel III, will impose some form of liquidity requirements over time, although the details are still being worked out. Some countries already have formal liquidity requirements in place, and all regulators review liquidity issues on at least a subjective basis. Increasing liquidity requirements in a boom would have an effect somewhat similar to that of increasing capital requirements, in that it would raise both the cost to the banking system of making loans and the safety of the individual institutions and the system as a whole. (Costs go up because the whole reason that banks are tempted to fund themselves excessively with short-term debt is that it is cheaper under normal circumstances.)

Regulators generally believe that capital requirements are a more effective way to handle cyclical pressures, but there could well be room for dynamic liquidity requirements as a complement. As with countercyclical capital requirements, and indeed most of the potential macroprudential instruments, regulators will need to keep in mind the trade-off between increased systemic safety and the cost burden of higher liquidity requirements and its effects on the financial system and the larger economy. Complicating matters further, strength in one area, such as capital, can sometimes make up for relative weakness elsewhere. For example, liquidity tends not to be a serious concern when a financial institution is perceived to have plenty of capital, because bank runs and their equivalents are generally spurred by concerns about solvency, which can be alleviated by strong levels of capital.

---

4. See Jimenez and Saurina (2006) for the theoretical underpinnings of the Spanish approach.

Administrative Caps on Aggregate Lending

Regulators in some countries can limit total lending by financial institutions as a class and/or by individual financial institutions. This approach is generally used only in less advanced economies where there is more state intervention in general and banks dominate the financial sector. The tool allows quite direct control of total credit volumes but at the expense of substituting government decisions for market signals. In addition, the more complicated the financial sector and the instruments through which credit is provided, the harder it is to make the cap stick. For example, capital markets now provide much of the credit for U.S. businesses, so aggregate lending caps on banks would largely be negated by increased issuance of bonds. Trying to enforce caps in a more sophisticated environment is likely to end up involving increasingly interventionist policies that fail under the sheer weight of the required regulations.

On the other hand, a number of less financially sophisticated economies have been able to exert substantial control over credit conditions by using such administrative caps, since banks dominate the financial system and the government is in a position to directly cap bank lending.

Reserve Requirements

Banks in many countries are required to hold a certain minimum percentage of their deposits as reserves at the central bank. In the past, the United States and many other developed countries varied their reserve requirements to influence the propensity of banks to lend. That has ceased to be effective in the more advanced economies for reasons similar to those that limit the effectiveness of administrative caps on lending volumes. However, reserve requirements are still an important instrument in China and in a number of countries that are less financially developed.

Limitations on Leverage in Asset Purchases

Authorities can place limits on the amount of leverage allowed in various types of transactions as opposed to controlling the total leverage at different types of institutions. This works well only if substantial amounts of borrowing are tied to transactions, such as asset purchases, rather than to general borrowing by households or businesses. Fortunately, transactions tied to real estate and securities constitute a large portion of the credit market in most countries. Reviewed below are various types of transaction-based leverage limits. The relevance of these caps is that they could be varied over time to reduce the riskiness of loans being made during a period of overexuberance or to relax limitations during a bust.

Loan-to-Value (LTV) Ratios for Mortgages

Real estate is relatively well suited to this type of limitation because it tends to be a "big ticket" item and because it is difficult to evade restrictions by lending funds without tying in the real estate; moreover, lenders are not likely to do so because they value the collateral protection that comes with the mortgage form of the transaction. In particular, households and small businesses generally cannot obtain very much credit without using their homes or business premises as collateral.

Financial regulators often have the ability to enforce a maximum LTV ratio for mortgages, at least those made by regulated financial institutions and sometimes more broadly. At one time in the United States the common maximum LTV ratio was 80 percent for most private loans (equivalent to a 20 percent down payment), although the U.S. Federal Housing Administration would lend to qualified borrowers while requiring only a 3 percent down payment. In recent decades, the maximum LTV ratio offered by private financial institutions tended to be in the 95–97 percent range,[5] although many borrowers put down more in order to obtain a better rate. Further, most U.S. mortgages are securitized with the backing of Fannie Mae or Freddie Mac, which imposed their own LTV requirements, with the implicit penalty being a higher borrowing rate if the loan did not have the benefit of their backing.

There are limits to the degree of effectiveness of LTV ratios. Not all mortgages are securitized, some that are securitized are done outside of Fannie and Freddie, and there is a large financial sector that provides second mortgages and home equity lines that effectively allow homeowners to increase their leverage after taking the original mortgage.

One of the moves being made by the U.S. Congress and federal regulators in the wake of the housing and financial crises is to force higher LTV ratios through various mechanisms, such as placing additional regulatory burdens on mortgages that are not made with a sufficiently high down payment.

Loan-to-Income (LTI) Ratios

An alternative approach to limiting the risk of mortgages is to require borrower to have the clear ability to service the loan from their earnings, so that lenders do not rely excessively on the value of the collateral. That can clearly

---

5. There were a number of instances, however, of products for which the LTV equaled or exceeded 100 percent.

serve to mitigate the overexuberance of a real estate bubble, unless there are easy ways around the actual limits. However, the ability to protect financial institutions from loss is lessened, although not eliminated, by several factors. First, some states in the United States do not allow the mortgage lender any effective recourse to the income or other assets of borrowers if they default on their mortgage. If a borrower in one of those states chooses to default when the value of his or her home declines below the mortgage principal, then the lender has little more protection than the value of the collateral, regardless of the LTI ratio. Second, income levels can fluctuate and are correlated with overall financial and economic conditions. Borrowers with good LTI ratios at the time their mortgages are issued may still be caught in a recession and find themselves unable to pay. Regulators in Europe often have more confidence in LTI ratios than their U.S. counterparts, probably because European mortgages are generally all made on a recourse basis and income levels appear not to swing as much as they do in the United States.

Minimum Margins/Haircuts on Secured Lending

In recent years, a large proportion of financial transactions among big institutions were undertaken through various forms of secured lending, such as repurchase agreements (repos). This has been the case particularly in the so-called "shadow banking" sector, which has gained market share from banks in recent years but which has neither the same level of prudential regulation nor access to insured deposits or other stable sources of funds. The Bank of England (2009) and others have suggested that the margins and haircuts that are used might be made subject to regulatory minimums that would vary over time.[6]

The recent financial crisis was substantially worsened by large, swift increases in required margins and haircuts as providers of lending against securities responded to adverse developments such as the collapse of Lehman. Those moves forced many securities holders to sell significant amounts of their holdings regardless of the price that they could obtain, since they could no longer finance the securities at any reasonable cost under the panicked market conditions. These "fire sales" pushed securities prices down further, often leading lenders to demand even higher margins and haircuts, initiating another round of fire sales.

---

6. "Haircut" is the industry term used for the difference between the value of an asset used to secure a loan and the amount of the secured loan that will be made. The haircut covers the lenders' risk that failure by the borrower to repay the loan will force them to sell the collateral at a time when its price may have fallen.

If it were possible to avoid such strong cyclical moves by ratcheting up the minimum levels more smoothly during boom times to avoid a sudden spike in requirements during periods of panic, then there would be less need for fire sales.

In the United States, the Fed retains the ability to use margin requirements to limit the amount of borrowing against common stock, which is a special case of secured lending that is often used by individual investors and sometimes by institutions. Securities brokers in the United States may lend only a certain specified percentage of the value of a stock; if the stock declines too far in value, then they have to make a "margin call" asking for additional collateral. Apparently the Fed considered increasing the required margin during the tech bubble as a way of signaling its concern with the level of the stock market but concluded that it would have been so easy for the borrowing to occur in other ways that the move would have been toothless and seen as such. For example, much higher effective levels of leverage can also be obtained through the purchase of options or futures on stock prices without the need for direct financial leverage, undermining the effectiveness of margin requirements focused on outright purchases.

Taxation

Targeted taxes represent another way of changing the incentives for financial institutions or market participants to take certain actions. For instance, there have been various proposals to use taxes to encourage sounder liquidity management. (The U.K. bank levy exempts assets funded by deposits and capital and has a reduced rate for debt with maturities above one year, for example, in order to tilt the balance toward more stable funding sources, among other goals.)[7]

Almost any instrument that uses a minimum or maximum ratio or an absolute cap or floor could instead be arranged to tax violations of those levels rather than absolutely forbid violating them. This is discussed further below in regard to uncertainty and public policy choices. If taxation is used to influence the level of risk in the financial system rather than being imposed simply to raise revenue, then changes in tax policies could be considered to respond to booms and busts.

One key difference between taxation and the setting of safety margins, such as through capital requirements, is that taxation does not directly improve system

---

7. The financial crisis responsibility fee proposed by the Obama administration also discriminated among funding sources for similar reasons.

resilience and may lessen it by draining resources. Increased capital requirements, in contrast, provide incentive effects while also directly improving the ability of the system to withstand losses. On the flip side, taxation does produce revenues for the government that can be used for other purposes or set aside to support interventions to mitigate financial crises. The latter point, of course, also leads to questions of moral hazard if the existence of taxation leads to the assumption that government rescues would be available.

Constraints on Currency Mismatches

In many countries a considerable portion of credit activity takes place in currencies other than the country's own. That became a problem in parts of Central Europe and some other parts of the world during the recent crisis, and, in general, such exposures represent a risk factor that becomes more important during boom times. Limits could be tightened during booms and released again during busts or in more normal times.

Capital Controls

In some developing nations, capital inflows from outside the country are a major factor in credit cycles, with a strongly procyclical effect. Foreign money flows in during good times and out again in bad, exaggerating the domestic credit cycle. Some countries have begun to use capital controls in a manner that they view as macroprudential. There is a long history of economic debate on capital controls, which are too complicated to fully discuss here. There is certainly a theoretical argument for using them as a macroprudential tool; however, opponents view the possibility with deep concern. First, the existing literature shows that capital controls can have a number of adverse consequences, although it may be that the financial stability benefits would outweigh them. Second, opponents fear that governments might impose capital controls for other, less benign reasons but rationalize them by labeling them "macroprudential" in nature.

Monetary Policy

As noted earlier, there is reason to believe that overall monetary policy conditions play a significant role in helping to support or suppress financial cycles. In particular, prolonged low interest rates have been shown to encourage financial institutions and other market participants to take levels of risk that they would otherwise have shunned, levels that can become truly quite excessive in extreme cases.[8] There is an ongoing debate about whether that fact should lead monetary authorities to hold rates higher at times of overexuberance in the financial markets than they otherwise would. Opponents of this approach generally assert either that it is too hard to detect bubbles or that the damage to the wider economy from higher interest rates more than offsets the benefits of taming the financial cycle, or they maintain that both claims are true. The debate is too complicated to be adequately covered here. However, it is worth noting that the more one believes in an active monetary response to financial crises, the less likely one would be to support macroprudential tools that work by affecting the financial system widely. That does not mean, however, that such a belief would be inconsistent with more focused uses of macroprudential policy, such as dealing with bubbles confined to a single sector, like housing.

Many other potential tools exist. However, those listed above are likely to be the most relevant in the near term.

8. See Altunbas, Gambacorta, and Marques-Ibanez (2008), for example.

Appendix 6B

How Should the Various Macroprudential Tools Be Combined?[9]

The question of how to combine macroprudential tools is especially difficult. The state of understanding of macroprudential tools is still somewhat prim-
itive even when the tools are viewed one at a time. There has been little work ana-
lyzing how they might be combined most effectively, especially in combination
with countercyclical capital requirements, the favorite tool of many authorities.
In addition, the right choice may vary considerably, depending on the precise
circumstances of the country, its financial and economic system, its macroprudential governance structure, and the particulars of the systemic threat.

At this point, the most useful decisionmaking approach may be to walk
through a series of questions before choosing a set of tools to use. (The following assumes that the macroprudential authority has identified a problem.) The
difficulties in correctly identifying a need for action are discussed in considerable
detail in the chapter. The following questions should be included:

—What is the nature of the uncertainty about the systemic threat and potential responses?

—What tools are legally available and politically feasible?

—Is the systemic threat concentrated in a single sector or closely related
sectors?

—Can the activity be contained within the closely regulated financial sector?
     If so, do the authorities have sufficient control to ensure appropriate ac-
     tion without spillovers?
     If so, are the authorities in a better position than the private sector to
     make the decisions?

—Does the systemic threat or potential responses have international ramifications?

—How strong are capital and liquidity levels in the relevant financial sectors?

—How great is the systemic threat?

—What is the larger macroeconomic policy position?

What Is the Nature of the Uncertainty about the Systemic Threat and Potential Responses?

Unfortunately, policy actions must be taken despite uncertainties about their
effects. That may be an issue with macroprudential policy in particular, since it

9. Taken from Elliott (2011b), pp. 12–18.

is quite early in the systematic application of such an approach. One area that has been studied more than others in regard to policy uncertainty is the trade-off between a price-like mechanism (for example, a tax or a minimum capital or liquidity ratio that adds costs to credit provision) and a quantity limitation, such as a limit on total lending by an institution or sector. Weitzman (1974) is a seminal work establishing a set of principles that apply in many areas of regulation, such as pollution control, in which there is a choice between price and quantity mechanisms. One of the author's conclusions was that the choice of instrument depends to a significant extent on the degree of uncertainty regarding the social costs of allowing too much pollution or other negative effect relative to that regarding the cost to the private sector of obeying the rules. As with pollution control, regulation of systemic financial risk imposes costs on the private sector that must be weighed against the harm to the economy from letting risk become excessive. Weitzman shows that if the costs of regulation are relatively clear but it is uncertain whether letting systemic risk rise above a certain level would produce catastrophic results for the economy, then it is preferable to adopt quantitative limits to maximize the ability to avoid a potential catastrophe. If, on the other hand, the greater uncertainty is about the cost of imposing restrictions, then it is preferable to employ taxes or capital requirements or other actions that give the private sector flexibility to respond with the lowest-cost solution to the need to limit systemic risk. (It is difficult to put Weitzman's reasoning and conclusions into intuitive terms, so these illustrations should not be taken too literally.)

More recently, Perotti and Suarez (2009) and Jeanne and Korinek (2010) have built on Weitzman's insights with specific applications for taxes versus capital/liquidity ratios. Perotti and Suarez, for example, argue that taxation might be superior to liquidity ratios for inducing the socially appropriate behavior in regard to systemic liquidity. In general, it appears that the insights first brought to light by Weitzman argue for price-like policy tools, such as countercyclical capital requirements, as opposed to aggregate lending caps or maximum loan-to-value ratios.

Finally, each macroprudential authority will have to make its own determination of the degree of confidence that it feels in using each tool. That is, how sure is the authority of the effects, including side effects, of using the tool and how sure is it of the degree of response that it will obtain from a given movement of the instrument? One of the arguments advanced for countercyclical capital requirements is the long history that regulators have with using capital requirements in general. Many of the other tools do not come with this base of experience.

What Tools Are Legally Available and Politically Feasible?

Perhaps it goes without saying, but not every macroprudential authority will have the legal right to use every instrument. Even for those that do, there may be political constraints or costs that must be weighed in choosing which tool or tools are right for the job at hand. For example, in the United States and the United Kingdom, an increase in the capital required for a bank to hold mortgage assets would likely encounter considerably less political resistance than a decrease in the maximum LTV ratio on mortgages. This is not to say that there would be no resistance to a capital change, but it would not have strong resonance with politicians or their voters, since it seems so technical. Down payment requirements, however, are easily understood by voters, and they can translate them into their own situations and those of people that they know. A further constraint may be potential conflicts with the microprudential regulators, since most of the tools discussed here can be used for either micro- or macroprudential purposes.

The political costs and constraints may matter most in the early days of macroprudential policy, since it will not yet have had a chance to demonstrate its value. On the other hand, actions may become tougher as memory of the recent terrible crisis fades, unless other, probably smaller, crises follow before the recollection fades too much.

Is the Systemic Threat Concentrated in a Single Sector or Closely Related Sectors?

If there is a clear focus of the risk, such as a housing bubble, it would be logical to first consider applying tools aimed specifically at that sector. That has the advantage of responding directly to the specific problem and also maximizes the signaling benefit by focusing on the problematic area. However, doing so could be inappropriate or inadequate for several reasons.

There may not be a good tool available for that particular sector. There just may not be a logical tool, or perhaps that tool, such as U.S. margin requirements on equities, is too easy to work around.

The tool may be insufficient. For example, lowering the maximum allowable LTV for mortgages may reduce both the volume of risky loans and the risk inherent in each loan but still not completely eliminate a housing bubble. Lenders might even push to increase the volume of their loans, reassured by the reduced riskiness of each individual loan.

The true problem might be wider. The true problem may have just happened to manifest itself first or most strongly in one particular sector. In that case, the effect of a sector-specific action could be like that of pushing a finger into an inflated balloon—the air just moves to another part of the balloon.

Even if a sector-specific tool would not be enough to deal with the full scope of the problem, it may still make sense to apply the tool as part of a package, especially if it is a solid instrument without too many negative side effects. There could also be merit in combining it with tools of wider application if there is uncertainty about the effectiveness of what seems to be a promising sector-specific tool. Appendix C contains a more detailed discussion of the question of wide versus narrow application in the context of countercyclical capital requirements.

Can the Activity Be Contained within the Closely Regulated Financial Sector?

If the source of the systemic threat is controlled by the closely regulated financial sector and there is little potential for the activity to move outside that circle, then direct administrative controls, such as caps on lending, become feasible. An economy in which credit provision is dominated by a small set of domestic banks is a better candidate for such administrative controls, as long as there is little danger that those controls would simply create or substantially enlarge other credit providers that are less regulated. On the other hand, the more sophisticated financial systems in the advanced economies are very difficult to control in this manner, since it is much too easy for credit activity to migrate to capital markets rather than financial intermediaries or to less regulated intermediaries. For those economies, these policy options can pretty much be rejected out of hand.

If So, Do the Authorities Have Sufficient Control to Ensure Appropriate Actions without Spillovers?

Even if a less sophisticated economy is dominated by closely regulated financial institutions, whether the government has the ability to enforce its administrative controls without doing undue harm is still a question. For example, a relatively weak macroprudential or financial regulatory authority might be in a position to declare lending caps but not to enforce them effectively. Banks may be able to exert political influence to invalidate the limits in advance or to receive forgiveness after the fact for violating them. An issue that makes a high degree of control harder is that the authority must effectively divide the total cap into a series of caps on individual institutions, which can be easier to overturn by appealing to political allies than trying to overturn the entire policy. Yet the net effect of multiple political interventions could in fact negate the policy move. Further, in some economies, the accounting and auditing systems may simply not be good enough to enforce the caps. In the extreme, even the bank itself may not have sufficient controls to ensure that the total amount of all loans made by the bank do not add to more than it intended.

In addition, of course, there is the risk that cosmetic solutions will be found to continue excessive lending without violating the letter of the administrative controls, such as by providing guarantees, perhaps even implicit ones, instead of directly making loans.

If So, Are the Authorities in a Better Position than the Private Sector to Make the Decisions?

Even if administrative controls appear feasible and enforceable, a core question is whether the central authority is in a better position than the financial institutions to make the decision about lending caps or similar controls. A major risk with administrative controls is that they substitute the judgment of a government entity for the implicit judgments of the financial system. At one level, this is inherent in any macroprudential policy dealing with excessive cyclicality, since it assumes, correctly I believe, that financial markets can move to excess or make other collective mistakes. However, there is a great deal of difference between relatively nuanced regulatory actions, such as the use of countercyclical capital requirements, and direct administrative controls, which sharply limit the room for judgment by market participants.

It is likely at this point in time in some economies that the level of sophistication of the central financial authorities and the nature of the incentives that they face make the authorities more capable of arriving at the right choices than the collective decisions of those they regulate. It is critical that this be true if the macroprudential authorities are going to initiate an intrusive set of policies such as administrative controls on lending, which can lead to fairly specific intervention in the activities of financial institutions. One danger, of course, is that there is a strong tendency for people and institutions to judge their capabilities as stronger than they are and those of the people with whom they deal as weaker.

Moreno discusses a number of potential short-run benefits to emerging market economies of using many of the alternative tools besides countercyclical capital requirements. However, he adds some interesting caveats:

> Over the medium term, the use of supplementary and macroprudential tools raises issues of financial development and efficiency. On the one hand, many supplementary tools discussed here have been abandoned in advanced economies because of the heavy costs imposed on the financial system and distortions in resource allocation. On the other hand, recent experience showed clearly that market discipline is not enough to guarantee financial stability. The crisis has prompted a reassessment of how these two competing considerations should be balanced.
>
> Another concern is that the focus on supplementary tools, including capital controls, could draw attention away from the need for sound macroeconomic policies. A number of central banks take the view that there is no substitute for conservative fiscal, monetary and regulatory policies in order to prevent fluctuations in global capital flows from causing severe disruptions in [e]merging market economies.[10]

Does the Systemic Threat or Potential Responses Have International Ramifications?

Macroprudential authorities have a freer hand if they are dealing with purely domestic issues. For instance, the administrative controls discussed above could be harder or even impossible to implement effectively if the financial system is open to international financing transactions. Lending caps to hold down excessive real estate speculation, for example, could be rendered less effective because foreign lenders step in to take on the risk. That would have the advantage of transferring some of the eventual pain overseas, as the United States found (for reasons other than lending caps) after it sold large amounts of mortgage-backed securities to foreigners. However, as that example also shows, the ramifications of the resulting bust can still be quite severe for the domestic institutions. In the other direction, domestic institutions may move portions of their risky lending overseas, if the overexuberance extends across borders. That could have the advantage of slowing the local portion of the

10. Moreno (2011, p. 13).

bubble, but it exposes the domestic financial institutions to large losses on their foreign risks. That effect can be magnified by the relative ignorance of domestic institutions about their foreign lending. They have a better chance of recognizing when their lending has gone too far in a market that they are familiar with.

The international aspect does not show up only when lending caps or other administrative controls are instituted. All of the macroprudential tools that focus on the institutional level, including countercyclical capital requirements, are subject to the same international ramifications. In the case of the latter tool, there is a global consensus that if a local macroprudential authority adds countercyclical capital requirements to certain types of domestic loans, authorities in other countries will mimic that action in regard to such loans made by their banks into that country. It remains to be seen how effectively this global agreement will be followed in practice.

Macroprudential tools that focus on individual transactions rather than institutions are somewhat less affected by international issues. For instance, imposing lower maximum loan-to-value ratios on U.K. mortgages would have an effect on any mortgage made in the United Kingdom, regardless of the location of the lender. Thus, all such lending, from both domestic and foreign lenders, would be made less risky, and there would probably be some local benefit as well from dampening a housing bubble. However, the dampening effect would be reduced by the willingness of foreigners to add their lending supply. Sadly, market delusions such as housing bubbles very frequently prove attractive to foreign as well as domestic funding sources.

In sum, the international aspects of macroprudential policy are likely to reduce the effectiveness of administrative controls, giving a relative advantage to tools such as countercyclical capital requirements when authorities are willing and able to apply them in a globally coordinated manner and also providing a relative advantage to transaction-level restrictions such as loan-to-value ratios. The balance of these factors will depend significantly on a country's particular circumstances.

How Strong Are Capital and Liquidity Levels in the Relevant Financial Sectors?

The benefits of altering the minimum required levels of capital and liquidity for financial institutions will depend to some extent on their starting points. If the industry's capital levels are already high, perhaps well above the regulatory minimums, including the preferred cushions that banks hold, there might be little benefit to increasing the minimums to counter overexuberance in the markets. On the other hand, it is possible in that situation that liquidity levels are near their minimums. In fact, higher capital levels could easily lead banks to feel comfortable taking more liquidity risk and accepting it at their counterparties. Under those conditions, choosing to increase the minimum liquidity levels may do more for safety than an equivalent change in capital ratios and would also be a greater deterrent to excessive lending, since it would have more effect on the lenders' costs than an increase in a minimum capital ratio that was not currently binding.

The starting points also matter because the increase in systemic safety resulting from a given increment of additional capital or liquidity decreases the higher the initial level.[11] That is, going from an 8 percent capital ratio to a 9 percent ratio provides significantly more systemic risk reduction than raising it from 18 percent to 19 percent and certainly more than raising it from 89 percent to 90 percent. However, the marginal cost to the financial institution—and the economy—of the capital increase is fairly linear. Since the benefits decrease at higher levels while the marginal cost remains relatively constant, it makes the most sense, all else being equal, to bolster the weaker element first.

How Great Is the Systemic Threat?

The greater the perceived risk, the wider the set of tools that is likely to be optimal. First, there are limits to the effectiveness of each tool and, as noted, many of them produce less marginal benefit the more strongly they are pursued. Dealing with a big problem may, therefore, require a number of tools. Second, the bigger the problem, the more important it becomes that macroprudential policy works. A classic analysis, Brainard (1967), concludes that optimal policy in the presence of uncertainty about the effects of that policy generally argues for using all relevant tools, even if there is only one discrete target variable. This argument would push for using multiple policy tools generally, even with smaller risks, but the author believes that the offsetting disadvantages in this case suggest simpler policy choices if the systemic threat is not large. We will learn what works in the area of macroprudential policy only by making choices and seeing the effects, which will be harder the more tools that are combined. Similarly, the signaling effects on markets may be diminished if too many actions are taken at the same time. For that matter, communicating macroprudential actions to all interested parties would be easier with single policy moves.

---

11. See, for example, Miles, Yang, and Marcheggiano (2011).

What Is the Larger Macroeconomic Policy Position?

Macroprudential policy takes place in a larger macroeconomic context, necessarily influenced by policy choices in that area. Those choices affect both the level and nature of risk in the financial system, and they may make some macroprudential choices more or less attractive than they would otherwise be. For example, changes in monetary policy normally affect the difference in cost between shorter- and longer-term funding. If, as an extreme, short-term funds are actually more expensive than long-term funds for an extended period of time, then altering the minimum liquidity requirements may have less effect than usual, since banks will already have economic incentives to hold medium- to long-term funding.[12]

12. There may still be incentive effects, of course, since the inverted yield curve would point toward lower short-term rates in the future. A bank that believed the yield curve accurately predicted future short-term rates might not feel economic pressure to hold medium- and long-term funding. That said, firms that care about their stock prices, as most financial firms do, show some tendency to prefer actions that maximize near-term earnings.

Appendix 6C

How Do Traditional Monetary Mechanisms Affect Credit Volumes?[13]

In the United States, as in much of the rest of the world, the central bank conducts monetary policy primarily by taking steps to move a targeted short-term interest rate to a desired level. The interest rate level is chosen to try to balance economic growth and inflation, according to the best information and theories available to the central banks at the time. Some central banks focus almost solely on inflation rates, viewing their mission as maintaining their currency at a stable value in terms of its power to purchase goods and services. Others, such as the Federal Reserve Board in the United States, have an additional mandate related to growth; in the U.S. case it is an explicit mandate to try to minimize the unemployment rate, at least on average over the long run.

In theory, the central bank ensures that the targeted short-term interest rate moves as desired by taking a series of actions, such as buying or selling government securities on the open market in order to influence the money supply. In practice, the demonstrated ability of central banks to effectively determine the actual level of the targeted interest rates through such actions has made the signaling effect far more important than the enforcement mechanism that they would otherwise have to use. Barring exceptional circumstances, an announcement by the Fed, for example, that it wants to increase the rate at which banks lend to each other overnight (the Fed funds rate) by half a percentage point will generally lead to an almost instantaneous move of the rate to that level.

There are a number of ways in which central bank monetary policy actions are transmitted to the wider economy, many of which affect lending volumes. (For ease of presentation, the descriptions will generally focus on U.S. monetary policy, except where noted.) These monetary transmission mechanisms include the following items.

Supply and Demand of Short-Term Funds

When central banks intervene directly rather than relying on signaling effects, they most often do so by buying or selling short-term government securities. That works to influence the targeted rate, such as the Fed funds rate, because there is normally a fairly close relationship between the rate on short-term government

---

13. Taken from Elliott (2011a, pp. 12–15).

securities and the Fed funds rate, since banks generally look for a relatively stable "credit spread" on top of Treasury rates to compensate them for the credit risk that a bank might not repay the loan. (Government securities denominated in the local currency, especially short-term ones, are usually viewed as carrying no credit risk.) Higher or lower interest rates will generally be passed along to some degree to borrowers, thereby influencing the volume of new credit.

Intermediate and Longer-Term Interest Rates

Short-term rates also influence longer-term interest rates, although theoreticians argue about the extent to which a change in short-term rates induced by monetary policy actions will flow through to changes in longer-term rates. One of the reasons for the uncertainty is that many factors go into forecasting future economic conditions and therefore the future course of interest rates. For example, it is possible that an increase in short-term rates will lead to a slowing in the economy that exerts downward pressure on expectations of future interest rates.

Currency Exchange Rates

Interest rates in a country generally will also affect exchange rates for that country's currency. Higher interest rates tend to increase the demand for securities denominated in that currency, pushing up exchange rates. Working in the opposite direction, higher interest rates are generally assumed to slow economic growth, decreasing expected future demand for a country's currency. There are also other indirect effects of interest rate movements than can affect the value of the currency. As a result, interest rate movements can have a significant impact on exchange rates, but the mechanisms are complex and not always easily predictable. Exchange rates, in turn, can have many indirect effects on the overall economy and on lending volumes, although the ultimate impact can be hard to predict accurately.

Asset Prices in General

Many financial assets are of a long enough maturity that the level of interest rates can have a significant effect on their valuation. In theory and usually in practice, investors pay close attention to the value in today's dollars of the future cash flows that they expect to receive from an investment. That means that the discount rate, the interest rate used to calculate today's value of the future cash flows, is quite important. For example, a safe bond with a 5 percent coupon will be worth about its stated principal value if the discount rate is also 5 percent but will be worth somewhat less if the discount rate is 6 percent. This effect can be seen most clearly in the bond market, where an increase in general interest rates will almost always cause a decline in the price of bonds. Moreover, the same logic applies with equities and with other assets, such as real estate. Common stock prices decline when interest rates in the economy rise, all else being equal, because the future earnings of a company will be worth less in today's dollars. It is more difficult to be sure how this plays out in the stock market, unfortunately, since so many other factors affect stock prices by changing expectations of future earnings. For example, the same forces that cause interest rates to rise may also cause earnings expectations to rise, counteracting the interest rate effect.

Lending is likely to increase when monetary policy reduces the discount rates used by investors and leads to an increase in asset values. The higher asset values make borrowers more creditworthy by raising the value of their collateral and increasing the resources that they have to pay off the loan. Lower interest rates can also lower the operating costs of firms and individuals by reducing their interest expense, further increasing their creditworthiness.

Risk Aversion and Perceptions of Risk Levels

As noted earlier, banks and other credit providers tend to become willing to accept greater risk when interest rates are especially low, a practice sometimes considered due to a "search for yield." This tendency should not exist with fully rational decisionmakers operating without institutional rigidities, but it recurs frequently in the real world, leading Borio and Zhu (2008) to propose that a "risk channel" plays a significant role in monetary policy transmission. One implication is that countercyclical capital requirements or other macroprudential tools may be useful in restoring an appropriate focus on risk when markets are either too risk accepting or too risk averse.

Ioannidou, Ongena, and Peydró (2008) demonstrates that Bolivian banks took more risk and charged lower risk premiums when interest rates were lower. Altunbas, Gambacorta, and Marques-Ibanez (2008) finds a similar result in the United States and the European Union. The authors found "evidence that unusually low interest rates over an extended period of time contributed to an increase in banks' risks. This result holds for a wide range of measures of risk, as well as macroeconomic and institutional controls."

Tucker (2009) states that when bubbles are building, "important contributory factors will typically have included illusions about risk-adjusted returns; underestimating the extent to which buoyant conditions are being driven by falling liquidity premia; and a sense that, if the bubble bursts, the central bank will somehow be able to contain the spillovers. This amounts to 'risk illusion,' which should probably be as much debated as 'money illusion' is in monetary economics."

Capital Levels

As discussed in considerable detail throughout this chapter, banks generally charge more for loans and provide fewer of them when capital requirements are high. Decreases in capital requirements produce the opposite effect. Regulators, sometimes including central banks, often intervene directly to influence capital levels. In addition, some of the mechanisms described above, such as the effects on asset prices, indirectly influence capital levels. (A general increase in the value of investments will increase the market value of assets held by banks, raising the net worth of the banks. That can happen immediately for assets that are "marked to market" or occur over time as other assets are sold at a profit.)

Bank Reserves

Decades ago, one of the primary effects of a change in monetary policy was a change in bank lending due to increased or decreased reserves held at the central bank. Banks are generally required to keep a portion of the deposit moneys that they receive from customers as reserves at the central bank. In earlier times, such reserve levels were often a key constraint on the total volume of lending, especially when deposits provided the great bulk of funds available for lending. Therefore, if the Fed eased monetary policy by buying Treasuries, that would increase the capacity for lending by adding to the reserves that banks held at the Fed. Similarly, selling Treasuries would lower the reserves held at the Fed, reducing the lending capacity of banks.

This monetary transmission channel has become considerably less important as banks have developed other sources of funds besides deposits and as some types of deposits have ceased to carry reserve requirements. In addition, banks in the United States currently have very large excess reserves that they are holding at the Fed, reflecting their caution about lending in the current environment as well as a somewhat lower demand from potential borrowers. Thus, the creation of additional reserves at the banks might lead to little change in lending behavior at the moment. Despite its much-reduced importance, this reserve mechanism remains one of the key drivers in many theoretical models of monetary policy transmission, as the models have not always kept up with changes in the actual financial system.

References

Altunbas, Yener, Leonardo Gambacorta, and David Marques-Ibanez. 2008. "Does Monetary Policy Affect Bank Risk-Taking?" BIS Working Papers 298. Basel: Monetary and Economic Department, Bank for International Settlements.

Bank of England. 2009. *The Role of Macroprudential Policy* (November) (www.bankofengland.co.uk/publications/news/2009/111.htm).

Basel Committee on Banking Supervision. 2010. "Consultative Document: Countercyclical Capital Buffer Proposal" (November) (www.bis.org/publ/bcbs172.pdf).

Basel Committee on Banking Supervision and Financial Stability Board Macroeconomic Assessment Group. 2010. "Final Report: Assessing the Macroeconomic Impact of the Transition to Stronger Capital and Liquidity Requirements" (December) (http://bis.org/publ/othp12.pdf).

Bean, Charles, Matthias Paustian, Adrian Penalver, and Tim Taylor. 2010. "Monetary Policy after the Fall." Paper presented at the Federal Reserve Bank of Kansas City Annual Conference in Jackson Hole, Wyo., August.

Benigno, Pierpaolo. 2004. "Optimal Monetary Policy in a Currency Area." *Journal of International Economics* 63, no. 2: 293–320.

Borio, Claudio, and Haibin Zhu. 2008. "Capital Regulation, Risk-Taking and Monetary Policy: A Missing Link in the Transmission Mechanism." BIS Working Papers 268. Basel: Monetary and Economic Department, Bank for International Settlements.

Brainard, William. 1967. "Uncertainty and the Effectiveness of Policy." *American Economic Review* 57, no. 2 (May).

Elliott, Douglas J. 2011a. "An Overview of Macroprudential Policy and Countercyclical Capital." Brookings (March) (www.brookings.edu/research/papers/2011/03/11-capital-elliott).

———. 2011b. "Choosing among Macroprudential Tools." Brookings (June) (www.brookings.edu/research/papers/2011/06/07-macroprudential-tools-elliott).

Fatás, Antonio, Prakash Kannan, Pau Rabanal, and Alasdair Scott. 2009. "Lessons for Monetary Policy from Asset Price Fluctuations." *IMF World Economic Outlook*, Fall.

International Monetary Fund. 2009. *IMF World Economic Outlook*, Fall, chapter 3.

Ioannidou, Vasso, Steven Ongena, and José Luis Peydró. 2008. "Monetary Risk-Taking and Pricing: Evidence from a Quasi-Natural Experiment." Paper presented at the Ninth Jacques Polak Annual Conference, Washington, November.

Jeanne, Olivier, and Anton Korinek. 2010. "Managing Credit Booms and Busts: A Pigouvian Taxation Approach." CEPR Discussion Paper 8105. London: Centre for Economic Policy Research.

Jimenez, Gabriel, and Jesus Saurina. 2006. "Credit Cycles, Credit Risk, and Prudential Regulation." *International Journal of Central Banking* 2, no. 2: 65–98.

Kannan, Prakash, Pau Rabanal, and Alasdair Scott. 2009. "Monetary and Macroprudential Policy Rules in a Model with House Price Booms." Working Paper. International Monetary Fund (November).

Lafrance, Robert, and Pierre St-Amant. 1999. "Optimal Currency Areas: A Review of the Recent Literature." Bank of Canada Working Paper 99-16 (October).

Miles, David, Jing Yang, and Gilberto Marcheggiano. 2011. "Optimal Bank Capital." Discussion Paper 31. London: External MPC Unit for the Bank of England (January).

Moreno, R. 2011. *Policymaking from a "Macroprudential" Perspective in Emerging Market Economies*. BIS Working Papers 336. Basel: Monetary and Economic Department, Bank for International Settlements (www.bis.org/publ/work336.pdf).

Perotti, E., and J. Suarez. 2009. *Liquidity Risk Charges as a Macroprudential Tool*. Policy Insight 40. London: Centre for European Policy Research.

Tucker, Paul. 2009. "The Debate on Financial System Resilience: Macroprudential Instruments." Lecture at the Barclays Annual Lecture. London (October) (www.bis.org/review/r091029e.pdf).

Weitzman, Martin. 1974. "Prices vs. Quantities." *Review of Economic Studies* 41, no. 4: 477–91.

Contributors

Gavin Bingham
Systemic Policy Partnership, London

Charles W. Calomiris
Columbia Business School

Douglas J. Elliott
Brookings Institution

Yasuyuki Fuchita
Nomura Institute of Capital Markets Research, Tokyo

Richard J. Herring
The Wharton School, University of Pennsylvania

Kei Kodachi
Nomura Institute of Capital Markets Research, Tokyo

Robert E. Litan
Bloomberg Government

Morgan Ricks
Vanderbilt Law School

Index

Brookings Institution

The Brookings Institution is a private nonprofit organization devoted to research, education, and publication on important issues of domestic and foreign policy. Its principal purpose is to bring the highest quality independent research and analysis to bear on current and emerging policy problems. The Institution was founded on December 8, 1927, to merge the activities of the Institute for Government Research, founded in 1916, the Institute of Economics, founded in 1922, and the Robert Brookings Graduate School of Economics and Government, founded in 1924. Interpretations or conclusions in Brookings publications should be understood to be solely those of the authors.

Nomura Foundation

Nomura Foundation is a nonprofit public interest incorporated foundation which aims to address social and economic issues involving Japan and the rest of the world by devoting private sector resources to promote international exchanges and the interchange between social science theory and practice. The foundation also provides grants and scholarships to support the social sciences, arts and culture, and up-and-coming international artistic talent. In the area of World Economy Research Activities it sponsors research, symposiums, and publications on current trends in capital markets of advanced and emerging economies as well as on topical issues in global macroeconomic stability and growth. It relies on a network of institutions from Europe, the United States, and Asia to assist in organizing specific research programs and identifying appropriate expertise.

Nomura Institute of Capital Markets Research

Established in April 2004 as a subsidiary of Nomura Holdings, Nomura Institute of Capital Markets Research (NICMR) offers original, neutral studies of Japanese and Western financial markets and policy proposals aimed at establishing a market-structured financial system in Japan and contributing to the healthy development of capital markets in China and other emerging markets. NICMR disseminates its research among Nomura Group companies and to a wider audience through regular publications in English and Japanese.

Wharton Financial Institutions Center, University of Pennsylvania

The Wharton Financial Institutions Center is one of twenty-five research centers at the Wharton School of the University of Pennsylvania. The Center sponsors and directs primary research on financial institutions and their interface with financial markets. The Center was established in 1992 with funds provided by the Sloan Foundation and was designated as the Sloan Industry Center for Financial Institutions, the first such center designated for a service-sector industry. It is now supported by private research partners, corporate sponsors, and various foundations and nonprofit organizations. The Center has hundreds of affiliated scholars at leading institutions worldwide, and it continues to define the research frontier, hosting an influential working paper series and a variety of academic, industry, and "crossover" conferences.

Trexler Library
Muhlenberg College
2400 Chew St.
Allentown, PA 18104